Privacy versus Security
in the Age of Global Terror

Library and Archives Canada Cataloguing in Publication

Silva, Mario, 1966-, author
    Privacy versus security in the age of global terror / Mario Silva.

Includes bibliographical references and index.
Issued in print and electronic formats.
ISBN 978-1-77161-260-9 (softcover).--ISBN 978-1-77161-261-6
(HTML).-- ISBN 978-1-77161-262-3 (PDF).--ISBN 978-1-77161-263-0
(Kindle)

1. Privacy, Right of. 2. Electronic surveillance. 3. Electronic
surveillance--Social aspects. 4. Terrorism--Prevention. 5. Computer
crimes--Prevention. 6. National security. 7. National security--Data processing. 8. Data protection. 9. Computer security. I. Title.

JC596.S55 2017   323.44'8   C2017-901271-1
                                          C2017-901272-X

Published by Mosaic Press

Copyright © 2017 Mario Silva

Printed and Bound in Canada

Interior Design by Courtney Blok

Cover Design by Joanne Howard / Small Dog Design

ONTARIO ARTS COUNCIL
CONSEIL DES ARTS DE L'ONTARIO
an Ontario government agency
un organisme du gouvernement de l'Ontario

We acknowledge the Ontario Arts Council
for their support of our publishing program
We acknowledge the Ontario Media Development Corporation
for their support of our publishing program

Funded by the   Financé par le
Government   gouvernement   Canada
of Canada   du Canada

MOSAIC PRESS
1252 Speers Road, Units 1 & 2
Oakville, Ontario L6L 5N9
phone: (905) 825-2130
info@mosaic-press.com

Privacy versus Security
in the Age of Global Terror

DR. MARIO SILVA

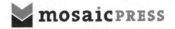

CONTENTS

INTRODUCTION

In today's technological world, everything is possible. Through the pervasiveness of computers, efficiency is at an all-time high in both personal and professional realms. This tech-savvy generation has spurred an exponential rise in globalization and human progress. While technology has been used to facilitate unprecedented advances for the betterment of society, in the wrong hands it can also be used to society's detriment. Cyber security has become a worldwide issue and involves a balancing act between attacker and defender, with technological advances affecting both sides. When security is insufficient in the technological realm, a sense of vulnerability develops in society as a result.

The internet-age has challenged the implications and execution of both personal and national protection and security, and has also stirred issues about the concept of privacy. The privacy of an individual in any country is a prime duty of both governmental and non-governmental agencies. Due to rapid transformations in technology, it has become a difficult task for governments to give assurances of privacy to their individual citizens. Digital intelligence can be collected when any individual decides to access content on the internet, mainly through cookies and beacons that are traced by companies through the user's IP address. The arrival of smart phones in the market created another avenue through which the activity of an individual can be monitored and their privacy thus compromised.

Data security is a matter of concern for the corporate world as well. A security breach is an unauthorized access of data achieved by bypassing underlying security mechanisms. Through technological advancement, hackers—with the help of hooks and spooks—steal consumer data and misuse it for their own profit. Precaution is the only real prevention available in such cases.

As technology becomes increasingly more pervasive, issues of privacy must be addressed. Privacy is a fundamental—though not absolute—human right which is recognized by the Universal Declaration of Human Rights and by many other international treaties. Privacy hinges upon human dignity and other key mores, such as freedom of expression or speech. Privacy has become one of the greatest concerns with respect to human rights in the modern age because privacy of the individual in this era is, for the most part, unavailable and effectively non-existent. Trading in compromised privacy is becoming a business for the corporate world, an opportunity to earn increased profits through data manipulation.

The rise of terrorism and lethal terrorist attacks by extremist groups has created a number of problems for the management of digital privacy and security. Governments must monitor the digital world and utilize technology in an effort to prevent such attacks, but they must do so without violating the human rights of their citizens. In response to the terrorist attacks of September 11, 2001, the United States Congress swiftly passed a series of counter-terrorism laws, such as the United States of America Patriot Act. The European Union, following the terrorist attacks in Madrid on March 11, 2004, also adopted counter-terrorism measures.

Within this context of fear and in order to address the threat of terrorism, new surveillance technologies were created to track and collect information on a broad population of potentially threatening individuals. Many questions have been raised, however, as to whether this intrudes on the fundamental right of privacy. Balancing security and privacy is a seemingly impossible—but nonetheless achievable— task in the age of global terrorism.

Recently, Glenn Greenwald's book on whistleblower Edward Snowden and the National Security Agency thrusted the issue of state surveillance back into the public consciousness. As a result of the revelations of whistle-blower Edward Snowden, the world is now explicitly aware of the virtually unconstrained mass electronic shadowing that the US government and certain associates, most notably Britain, are directing. Questions have seldom been asked about the government's targeted surveillance for national security on evidentiary showing. The US government's mass surveillance, without such restrictions, has largely eliminated the right to privacy in a world that virtually relies upon electronic communication. The current level of surveillance occurring in contemporary society is inconsistent with human rights.

Protection of privacy has become one of the critical issues of discussion in this technological world. As internet democracy is one of the largest emerging agendas, reformed practices are required to ensure protection against the surveillance of individuals.

PART I: PRIVACY

Conception and Defining Privacy

The term "privacy" has broad historical roots in discussions of philosophy, sociology, and in political and legal debates. Privacy is a concept that has existed since ancient times. The Aristotelian classification of the polis, the public sphere of politics and political activity, and the oikos, the private or domestic sphere of the family, as two distinct spheres of life clearly differentiates the public and private domains. Aristotle argued that there was an antithesis between the political activities of the polis and the economic activities of the oikos, and this can be termed as the separation of private activity from public life. [1] Debate over this distinction can be seen in political discussion today in Western society with regards to the role of religion in a secular society.

As political theory developed and the functions of the state expanded, the public/private distinction was taken to refer to the appropriate realm of governmental authority, as opposed to the realm reserved for self-regulation. John Stuart Mill, in his 1859 essay *On Liberty*, argued that there was a need for a clear distinction between where individual liberty

---

1 McKeon, Michael *The Secret History of Domesticity: Public, Private, and the Division of Knowledge, 2006, JHU Press:* pgs 7-8.

takes precedence and where society has the right to inter-vene. Mill posited that governments should protect individ-ual rights in order for individuals to realize their wants, and restrain individual action only as necessary to prevent undue infringement. [2] John Locke, in his *Two Treatises of Govern-ment*, contends that personal liberty is the key component of a society that works toward the individual's and the com-monwealth's best interest. [3]

The concept of privacy was further developed with the legal conceptualization of the term, often said to have be-gun with the famous essay by Samuel Warren and Louis Brandeis, titled *The Right to Privacy* (1890). Brandeis and Warren defined protection of the private realm as the foun-dation of individual freedom in the modern age. Given the increasing capacity of government, the press, and other agencies and institutions to invade previously inaccessible aspects of personal activity, they argued that the law must evolve in response to technological change. Traditional pro-hibitions against trespass, assault, libel, and other invasive acts had afforded sufficient safeguards in previous eras, but these established principles could not, in their view, protect individuals from the "too enterprising press, the photogra-pher, or the possessor of any other modern device for re-wording or reproducing scenes or sounds." [4] Consequently, in order to uphold the "right to one's personality" [5] in the face of modern business practices and invasive inventions, they concluded that legal remedies had to be developed to enforce definite boundaries between public and private life. [6]

---

2 Shamir, Hila. "The Public/Private Distinction Now: The Challenges of Privatization and of the Regulatory State", *Theoretical Enquiries in Law*, 15(1) (2014), URL: http://www7.tau.ac.il/ojs/index.php/til/article/viewFile/527/491.

3 Guardster .com, *The Right To Privacy*, 2015, URL: http://www.guardster.com/?Tutori-als-The_Right_to_Privacy.

4 Samuel D. Warren and Louis D. Brandeis, *The Right to Privacy: On The Right To Be Let Alone*, Quid Pro Books, 2014.

5 Ibid.

6 Warren, Samuel D and Brandies Louis D, "The Right to Piracy", *Harvard Law Review*, December 1890, URL: http://faculty.uml.edu/sgallagher/Brandeisprivacy.htm.

Another seminal work that conceptualizes privacy in the legal dimension is that of William Prosser. In his article "Privacy" (1960), Prosser described the four "rather definite" privacy rights violations as follows: 1) Intrusion upon a person's seclusion or solitude, or into his private affairs; 2) Public disclosure of embarrassing private facts about an individual; 3) Publicity placing one in a false light in the public eye; and 4) Appropriation of one's likeness for the advantage of another. [7]

Another advocate of the concept of privacy, Charles Fried, contended in 1968 that strong normative justifications of privacy conventions were to be articulated in terms of functional explanations. He wrote that:

> Privacy is not just one possible means among others to insure some other value, but... it is necessarily related to ends and relations of the most fundamental sort: respect, love, friendship and trust. Privacy is not merely a good technique for furthering these fundamental relations; rather without privacy they are simply inconceivable... Privacy is the necessary atmosphere for these attitudes and actions, as oxygen is for combustion. [8]

Since the rise of technology and digitization, scholars have had a new impetus to further define the nuances that govern the concept of privacy.

William Parent argued that "privacy is the condition of not having undocumented personal knowledge about one possessed by others," [9] while Julie Inness defined privacy as "the state of possessing control over a realm of intimate decisions, which include decisions about intimate access, in-

7 Prosser, William L, "Privacy", *California Law Review*, 1960, URL: http://scholarship.law.berkeley.edu/cgi/viewcontent.cgi?article=3157&context=californialawreview

8 Fried, Charles, "Privacy, *Yale Law Journal*, Vol. 77, No 3, 1968: pgs 475- 493.

9 Parent, W.A, "Privacy, Morality, and the Law", Philosophy and Public Affairs 12(4):269-288.

timate information, and intimate actions." [10]

According to Ernest Van Den Haag, "Privacy is the exclusive access of a person (or other legal entity) to a realm of his own. The right to privacy entitles one to exclude others from (a) watching, (b) utilizing, (c) invading (intruding upon, or in other ways affecting) his private realm." Anita Allen asserts that "a degree of inaccessibility is an important necessary condition for the apt application of privacy." [11]

One of the most comprehensive classifications of privacy has been delineated by Roger Clarke. He identifies four major types of privacy: i) privacy of the person, ii) privacy of personal behaviour, iii) privacy of social communications, and iv) privacy of personal data. The first type of privacy makes reference to what is also known as bodily privacy, and aims at protecting the physical space and the body of a person. The second type of privacy aims at safeguarding the personal behaviour of individuals, such as religious practices and sexual activities. The third type of privacy covers the set of relationships and social ties in which any individual builds and operates. Finally, the privacy of personal data refers to the integrity and protection of all the sensitive data possessed by an individual. [12]

If there are advocates for the concept of privacy, then there are also skeptics who view privacy as a selective chimera to cover up society's ills. Judith Thompson has argued that privacy as a concept serves no useful function, for what we call privacy really amounts to a set of other more primary interests. The meaning and value accorded to privacy claims are irreducibly heterogeneous since privacy is merely a composite of unrelated elements, such as property rights and interests in self-ownership. [13]

---

10 Mills, Jon. L, *Privacy: The Lost Right* , Oxford University Press.

11 Solove, Daniel, " Conceptualizing Privacy", *California Law Review*, 90(4), 2002: 1088- 1155

12 Clarke, Roger, *What is Piracy*, August 7 2006, URL: http://www.rogerclarke.com/DV/Privacy.html

13 Thompson, Judith Jarvis, "The Right to Privacy", *Philosophy and Public Affairs*, 4(4), 1975: pgs 295-314.

According to Richard Posner, privacy is protected in ways that are economically inefficient. Posner argues that concealment or selective disclosure of information is usually to mislead or manipulate others, or for private economic gain, and thus protection of individual privacy is less defensible than others have thought because it does not maximize wealth. Posner writes: "The trend has been toward expanding the privacy protections of the individual while contracting those of organizations, including business firms. This trend is the opposite of what one would expect if efficiency considerations were motivating privacy legislation." [14]

The major criticisms leveled against the concept of privacy can be summarized below:

1) Privacy is a form of individualism that neglects the common good.

2) The privacy concept separates public from private life, which can result in problems; for example, privacy as a patriarchal value that legitimates violence in families.

3) Privacy can shield the planning and carrying out of illegal or antisocial activities and can be deceptive by concealing information in order to mislead others or misrepresent the character of an individual.

4) The privacy concept advances a liberal notion of democracy that can be opposed by the idea of participatory democracy.

5) The notion of privacy is bound up with the idea of private property and can shield the rich and powerful from public accountability, and wealth and power structures from transparency. [15]

---

14 Posner, Richard, "The Right to Privacy", *Georgia Law Review*, 12 (1977): pgs 393- 422.

15 Centre for Science, Society & Citizenship, "Discussion Paper about the Theoretical Foundations of PACT", September 2012 URL: http://www.projectpact.eu/privacy-security-research-paper-series/privacy-security-research-paper-series/%232_Privacy_and_Security_Research_Paper_Series.pdf

There are some who argue that there is no fundamental right to privacy and that a right to personal privacy is not adequately grounded in any legal doctrine. This was the view of the late United States Supreme Court Justice Robert Bork. Nevertheless, most legal scholars would agree that privacy is a meaningful and valuable concept in today's society. Privacy as a legal right is cherished by society as a means to be free from interference by governments and other potentially abusive entities. However, it can also been viewed negatively as a cloak under which to hide immoral or illegal activities.

The right to privacy is firmly anchored in international law and is included in the Universal Declaration of Human Rights and the International Covenant on Civil and Political Rights (ICCPR), to date ratified by 167 states around the world. Under its article 17, the ICCPR provides that "No one shall be subjected to arbitrary or unlawful interference with his privacy, family, home or correspondence, nor to unlawful attacks on his honour and reputation." It further states that "Everyone has the right to the protection of the law against such interference or attacks." [16]

The term "unlawful" has been interpreted by the Human Rights Committee in its General Comment 16 to mean that no interference can take place "except in cases envisaged by the law. Interference authorized by states can only take place on the basis of law, which itself must comply with the provisions, aims and objectives of the Covenant." [17] The committee noted that article 17 must be guaranteed against all such interferences and attacks whether they emanate from state authorities or from natural or legal persons. Furthermore, the law is intended to guarantee that "even interference provided for by law should be in accordance with the provisions, aims and objectives of the Covenant and should be, in any event, reasonable in the particular circumstances." [18]

---

16 International Covenant on Civil and Political Rights (ICCPR)
17 http://hrlibrary.umn.edu/gencomm/hrcom16.htm
18 Ibid.

Integrating Privacy into Law – An Introduction

The internet is at once a new communications medium and a new locus for social organization on a global basis. Due to its decentralized and interactive nature, is the first electronic medium to allow every user to "publish" and engage in commerce. Users can reach and create communities of interest despite geographic, social, and political barriers. The internet is an unprecedented mechanism for delivering governmental and social services, from education and healthcare to public information. As the World Wide Web grows to fully support voice, data, and video, it will become in many respects a virtual "face-to-face" social, political, and individual milieu. [19] No issue highlights this better than privacy, always a fluid and context-situated concept, even more so now as the boundary between private and public activity is shifting.

While technology has improved our lives and fosters greater participation in the global public sphere, it has also exposed human rights abuses. We have become vulnerable to more surveillance, interference, and damage, and our rights to privacy have been greatly diminished. Current surveillance threatens individual rights and "inhibits the free functioning of a vibrant civil society." [20]

Online digital communications are now part of the fabric of our everyday lives. The information that users enter into digital space cannot be obliterated completely, especially given the pace with which technology is improving; for hackers, invading one's private space is not very difficult. There have been many cases evidently proving that the privacy of any individual is just a click away from becoming public.

The increasing sophistication of information technology, with its capacity to collect, analyze, and disseminate infor-

---

19 Berman. J and Mulligan. M, (1999). *Privacy in the Digital Age*, Volume 23, Number.

20 http://www.ohchr.org/EN/Issues/DigitalAge/Pages/DigitalAgeIndex.aspx

mation on individuals, has introduced a sense of urgency to the demand for legislation. Furthermore, new developments in medical research and care, telecommunications, advanced transportation systems, and financial transfers have dramatically increased the level of information generated by each individual.

According to opinion polls, concern over privacy violations is now greater than at any time in recent history. Uniformly, populations throughout the world are expressing fears about encroachment on privacy, prompting an unprecedented number of nations to pass laws which specifically protect the privacy of their citizens. Human rights groups are concerned that advancing technology is being exported to developing countries which lack adequate protections. Developed nations are moving towards achieving maximum privacy control over their citizens' data, but are the countries not yet able to achieve developmental stability ready to face the task?

There is no doubt that governments have a legitimate right to gather, restrict, and protect certain sensitive information, but in doing so they must also guarantee that they are not abusing this right and are acting within the context of international human rights law. The increasing use of "data mining" by intelligence agencies "blurs the boundary between permissible targeted surveillance and problematic mass surveillance which potentially amounts to arbitrary or unlawful interference with privacy." [21]

The United Nations Special Rapporteur on the promotion and protection of human rights and fundamental freedoms, Ben Emmerson, noted that while agencies counter terrorism, "there should be a debate on the extent to which the public... is prepared to tolerate official access to metadata." [22]

In the United States, concerns over individual privacy only came to attention in 1965 during a court ruling for

---

21 http://www.ohchr.org/EN/NewsEvents/Pages/DisplayNews.aspx?NewsID=13758&LangID=E
22 http://www.ohchr.org/EN/NewsEvents/Pages/DisplayNews.aspx?NewsID=13758&LangID=E

amendments in the Bill of Rights. [23] It was only in the early 1970s that countries began adopting broad laws intended to protect individual privacy. Throughout the world, there was a general movement towards the adoption of comprehensive privacy laws that set a framework for protection. Most of these laws are based on the models introduced by the Organization for Economic Cooperation and Development and the Council of Europe.

The European Union has always been highly concerned about privacy rights and promoting their set of de facto standards that companies should imbibe, thereby allowing citizens of its member countries to significantly control the amount of personal data collected by companies' websites.

In 1995, conscious both of the shortcomings of law and the many differences in the levels of protection in each of its states, the European Union passed a Europe-wide directive which provided citizens with a wider range of protections over abuses of their data. The directive on the "Protection of Individuals with regard to the processing of personal data and on the free movement of such data" [24] set a benchmark for national law.

This directive also imposes an obligation on member states to ensure that personal information relating to European citizens is covered by law when it is exported to, and processed in, countries outside of Europe. This requirement has resulted in growing pressure outside of Europe for the passage of privacy laws. More than forty countries now have data protection or information privacy laws and more are currently in the process of being enacted.

The 2014 UN General Assembly resolution on the right to privacy in the digital age called on all states to "review their procedures, practices and legislation regarding the surveillance of communications [...] with a view to upholding

---

23 Roland Jon, (2004); Constitution Society, Retrieved March 2015 from http://www.constitution.org/col/intent_14th.htm

24 PRIVACY AND HUMAN RIGHTS; An International Survey of Privacy Laws and Practice. Retrieved in March 2015 from http://gilc.org/privacy/survey/intro.html

the right to privacy by ensuring the full and effective implementation of all their obligations under international human rights law." [25] Notwithstanding the 2014 UN resolution, many states have been adopting laws that increase their intrusive powers of surveillance in ways that fall short of applicable international human rights standards.

The United Nations has increasingly expressed concerns with modern forms of communications surveillance and its effects on human rights. In the 2015 resolution on the right to privacy in the digital age, the Human Rights Council expressed deep concerns about the negative impact that surveillance may have on the exercise and enjoyment of human rights, most notably the right to privacy. [26] During the Universal Periodic Review in 2015, many states noted that they had already witnessed increased attention to issues of digital privacy, and the Human Rights Committee has also expressed serious concerns about surveillance powers in various states.

Since then, the United Nations and the European Union have been looking forward to enacting changes in the framework which are designed to maximize the safeguarding of the privacy of their people. A United Nations resolution was adopted last year specifying that unlawful or arbitrary surveillance, interception of communications, and collection of personal data, including metadata, are "highly intrusive acts." [27] As the universal guardian of human rights, the United Nations plays a key role in defending the right to privacy, as well as freedom of opinion and expression in our digital world.

Many new measures will hopefully be implemented in the European Union's new rule book. For example, requiring that companies request explicit consent from consumers before using their personal data. Another measure they

---

25 UN doc. A/RES/69/166, 10 February 2015.

26 UN doc. A/HRC/RES/28/16, 1 April 2015.

27 http://www.reuters.com/article/us-spying-un-idUSKBN0IQ28320141106

hope to achieve is the "right to be forgotten," a rule that would allow individuals to ask for web pages to be removed. With all of this, the European Union hopes to create a single standard for online privacy, copyright, and consumer rights, which may not sit well with America, who claims that a certain amount of privacy invasion is necessary to protect their country.

Canada has its own laws in place regarding the issue of privacy. In 2011, Defense Minister Peter MacKay reinstated a surveillance program in which the metadata attached to every phone call and every internet-based communication carried out by a Canadian is subject to collection and analysis by Communications Security Establishment Canada (CSEC) in the Department of National Defense. Supporters of this program defend it by pointing out that phone conversations are not recorded; rather, CSEC keeps a log of every call made and draws connections to possible threats to national security.

There are many challenges with respect to the right to privacy being guaranteed by legislative, administrative, or judicial authorities around the world. Although robust national legal frameworks are essential to ensuring effective protection against unlawful or arbitrary interference, most national legislations have not adopted such measures. They have few, if any, independent oversight to review surveillance measures and lack effective enforcement as a safeguard against abuse.

Digital Privacy – Why is it Important?

Humans, as social animals, need company but still require autonomy for the sake of maintaining a personal sanctuary. At times, human beings want to withdraw themselves from society and thereby create a conscious breach between individual and society.

The constitutional right to privacy gives individuals the

liberty to make decisions and lead their lives of their own accord, without any governmental intimidation, intrusion, or interference. People's moral choices, religious beliefs, personal relationships, and controversial opinions are not governed by governmental constitution. Under Common law, an individual has the right to protect himself from public scrutiny, be it from a neighbor's prying eyes; from an investigator's eavesdropping ears; a news photographer's intrusive camera; and even from electronic surveillance.

Every entity, whether person or corporation, now has its own virtual presence; the private lives of people are more transparent to the public than ever before. Private lives have become a matter of gossip; digital media acts as a stimulus to cater to consumer desire for fresh news about celebrities and their private lives. The headlines of the news are so provocative that everyone is seduced into taking an interest in peeping into the private sphere of public figures. The magnetic magic of the internet is fast-spreading and even ordinary people disclose their personal information and images over social media.

Nearly every activity in a person's life today has a connection with the web. The infusion of technology into people's everyday lives has made them more dependent upon it and the world has been accepting this merge with the digital realm. Any activities performed through an internet-connected computer are open to several possible methods of external tracking. Whenever a user accesses sensitive personal information on the internet, they trust that their privacy will not be leaked. What they may not realize is that cookies and beacons are being used by companies to track information, using their IP address to gather personal information for an organization's use. When one opens any website of interest, there are often many links and floating ads which clutter the page. In order to avoid these ads, one deliberately clicks to close the links. However, the moment one tries to close these ads, their information is tracked through cookies, which are small pieces of data that are saved by websites through the web browser. Smart phones are vulnerable to the same tracking.

In *End of Privacy*, Charles J. Sykes analyzes the challenges to privacy posed by technological change, media aggressiveness, governmental and business intrusion, and even our own propensity to share information about ourselves. We are logged in to an online shopping center and click an option that allows cookies; even before logging off, we are being traced or mapped. [28] Every time we apply to a job, book tickets, use credit and debit cards, pay taxes, enter a relationship, etc., we unknowingly or perhaps knowingly become part of a data web. The private sectors develop new techniques for tracking us and thereby create a seamless data web that blurs the lines between government surveillance and commercial marketing. We are living in a surveillance society. [29]

Amitai Etzioni, a professor at George Washington University and leader of the Communitarian Movement, says that the threat to privacy is by "electronic surveillance." He adds: "I fear Microsoft more than the Mafia or the Federal Bureau of Investigation, because Microsoft put a secret window into our computers that allow them to see how you think." [30]

The bits and bytes left behind from citizens' electronic interactions can be put together to draw conclusions about their habits, friendships, and preferences using data-mining formulas and increasingly powerful computers. Data mining is the computational process of discovering patterns in large 'data sets' involving methods at the intersection of artificial intelligence, machine learning, statistics, and database systems. This involves the analysis of "big data," a term for data sets that are so large or complex that traditional data pro-

---

28 Charels Sykes, *The End of Privacy*, The Attack on Personal Rights at Home, at Work, On-Line, and in Court, St. Martin's Press, 1999

29 Ibid.

30 http://privacyinternational.org/node/52

cessing applications are inadequate to deal with them. With the help of some very powerful computers and algorithms, analysts detect trends and create digital files about people. This process is perfectly legal and is used widely by the corporate world. According to research agencies, United States of America companies and other organizations now spend more than $2 billion each year to obtain third-party data about individuals. Research has revealed that these methods can increase profits in the retail sector by a staggering 60%. Another study discovered that personal data could help companies achieve greater business efficiencies and customize new products. For instance, Walmart bought a predictive analytics start-up called Inkiru. The company makes software that crunches data to help retailers develop marketing campaigns that target shoppers when they are most likely to buy certain products.

There are organizations that sell such data, called data-brokers. For example, a small Arkansas company called Axciom Corp. maintains extensive files about the online and offline activities of more than 500 million consumers worldwide. [31] Acxiom maintains its own database on about 190 million individuals and 126 million households in the United States. Separately, it manages customer databases for, or works with, 47 of the Fortune 100 companies. Another example a company called Retention Science. This Santa Monica-based data analytics firm uses predictive algorithms and data, such as aggregated household income, purchasing histories, and credit scores to help companies predict a customer's purchase probability and build retention-marketing campaigns. In addition to the data supplied by a client, Retention Science relies on the data it licenses from third-party providers to target the right consumers at the right time. It aims to create targeted campaigns while keeping in mind the consumer's privacy. Retention Science has established hard-

31 Singer.Natasha., "The Government's Consumer Data Watchdog", *The New York Times*. (May, 2015) http://www.nytimes.com/2015/05/24/technology/the-governments-consumer-data-watchdog.html?_r=1

and-fast rules governing its use of consumer data; it refuses to share data across clients and insists that all of its data scientists, many of whom are professors and researchers, sign confidentiality agreements.

Companies like Google, Facebook, and Yahoo are learning from search engine requests. Web surfing activity, as well as location tracking on mobile devices, is used to find patterns and determine user interests. All of these factors are combined in order to show ads tailored to each individual about products that are likely to catch their eye and pique their interest. Video subscription services use data to further improve the browsing experience for the user by recommending shows based on the user's viewing history. E-retailer Amazon also does something similar when it highlights or recommends specific products to shoppers visiting its site.

A study showed that if the healthcare industry in the United States used big data effectively and creatively to drive quality and efficiency, the healthcare sector could create over $300 million every year in value. Nearly two-thirds of this value creation would come from reduction of healthcare expenditure by nearly 8% in the US. Similarly, the European developed economies could save more than $149 million in improvements in operational efficiency by the use of Big Data. This would also help them in reducing errors and frauds, while boosting tax revenue collections.

The digital age is creating new opportunities for the private sector that end up making life for the average person much easier with each passing day. As a result, quality of life has increased for the average person. However, this also comes with new threats to personal privacy and companies who collect personal user data should ensure that the information collected is safe from intrusion and is manipulated in an ethical fashion. There is also another type of information that is not of a personal nature, but is clearly vital for a company. For example, almost all companies store valuable information—such as patents, marketing campaigns, and strategic plans—that, if accessed by rivalling companies, could cause them to lose their competitive advantage, potentially driving them out of business. This could have catastrophic consequences for the economy. Companies are migrating from manual to automated processes, which make such companies depend totally or partially on computers for their correct functioning. Everyday individuals are almost forced to share some of their sensitive personal information with the company through the use of computers or the internet. It is in a company's best interest to protect data as securely as they can; in the end, their customers' loyalty is their best ally. This is very good news for the customers who have learnt to trust major companies with their personal information. Generally, the larger and more reputed the company, the more they have invested in their customers' privacy protection and, as a result, the more trustworthy they are. These companies will not trade the fortune they are making honestly for a potential money-making opportunity that exploits their users' privacy. Customers should pay attention to a company's history and reputation before providing private information. Care should be taken to avoid disclosing personal information to little-known companies, whose intentions are not yet known.

Privacy needs to be protected because information about an individual might be used by someone who wishes to do harm. Simple facts like home or school locations can be accessed by anyone, making it easy to trace someone's whereabouts. All attributes of the individual can become known, even their whereabouts and interactions with others can be plotted. Technologically, many new methods of surveillance have been developed, including cameras, satellites, wiretaps, email tracing orders, and heat sensors. Information revealed about a person may belittle his/her reputation or may create prejudice against them. Privacy is thereby a key to the maintenance of human dignity and liberty. In the same fashion, almost any detail of personal information can be used against an individual. The divulgence of information about someone's personal activities can cause embarrassment and further problems for them, such as the loss of their job. Privacy also has a psychological importance. It is necessary for human beings to control access to their locations and information in order to avoid mental suffering. Individuals have a psychological need for privacy.

On a global scale, there is a national security issue. Privacy of a country's valuable information needs to be protected from its enemies, since it can felicitate terrorist activities, invasion, and general wrongdoings, which would affect a large number of people. Invasion of a nation's privacy can have serious consequences. The government of every nation in the world has also adopted the digitalization of their policies in the form of e-commerce, which is being supported on a large scale as well. The success of online transactions, which have a relatively high degree of privacy insecurity, is an important element to consider when establishing an e-governance. The use of electronically gathered information can be beneficial for both planning and delivering services, and efficiently allocating resources.

The business growth that has resulted from the help of computers and the global village means that the policies that are being formulated are actually leading to more privacy concerns for everyone. For example, all types of organizations are taking advantage of cloud computing, which is an invaluable time-saving but potentially vulnerable resource.

Privacy has both moral and intrinsic values and should be protected by individuals as well as by any private or public entity. The government thus has a responsibility for protecting privacy, since it is the only entity capable of passing laws for such purposes.

Since the government has the potential to both invade and protect privacy, it should establish real checks and balances in order to avoid passing a law that enables the exploitation of individual privacy. It is also necessary to have a legislature that is technically savvy in order to keep up with technologies that invade privacy. Governments should learn from the innovative private sectors. Privacy protection laws tend to lag behind privacy invasion technologies. It seems that more attention should be paid to this gap and update legal frameworks to account for problems that have arisen from new technologies. Legislatures should fix gaps which were unforeseen by the original framers. Having a void in the law is dangerous, since there is always going to be someone taking advantage of such holes in order to harm others.

In the United States, the right to privacy is not mentioned once in the Constitution, but the United States Supreme Court has said that several of the amendments create this right: the First Amendment gives the right to assemble privately and peacefully; the Third Amendment forbids the government from sectioning soldiers in a private house without the owner's consent; and the Fourth amendment bars the police and other government agents from searching individuals without a probable cause. The Fourteenth Amendment prevents states from denying its citizens certain fundamental rights that are considered indispensable to the concepts of equality or liberty, including the right to sovereignty, dignity, and self-determination. Privacy is protected by international human rights rules and laws where privacy is regarded as a fundamental right.

The United States Congress passed a privacy law known as the Cyber Intelligence Sharing and Protection Act (CISPA). [32] The act was amended to the National Security Act of 1947 in order to safeguard the information of citizens from any threat. [33] However, the government itself seems to have taken advantage of the private information of the citizens; CISPA permits private companies like Gmail, Facebook, Pinterest, and Youtube to possibly pass along the account

---

32 http://gizmodo.com/, CISPA: The Awful Anti-Privacy Law That Won't Prevent Another Sony Hack.

33 http://gizmodo.com/ , What Is CISPA?.

information of individuals to governmental agencies for official purposes. [34] There are also many cyber laws which allow governmental and non-governmental organizations to access personal information for advertising and marketing purposes.

In order to safeguard their national economies, governments must take measures to stop threat-increasing activities. The information that is collected by organizations could present a threat to the country and potentially also be an invitation to terrorism. The economies need to determine the circumstances that could potentially be damaging to the nation. Since all the information of the world is now accessible through the internet, a firm set of policies with restrictions would only work to increase safety but not make it absolute. If no action is taken, however, the extensity of the virtual giant could engulf the world in the hands of threat, the later consequences of which are not easy to digest.

The government has a great responsibility when it comes to the protection of privacy. It is absolutely critical that any group handling personal data understands the importance of protecting it, and the consequences of misuse. In response to the growing need to safeguard the privacy of a nation, there are sets of privacy laws which are being followed by every governmental and non-governmental organization in the world. Managing privacy is not an easy task today. With rapid transformations continuing to occur in technological trends, the measures necessary to maintain secrecy have expanded beyond the imagination. The confusion created by this ever-shifting expanse makes it difficult for lawmakers and organizations to keep pace. Unable to hold particular individuals responsible, the policymakers seem not to have noticed the complications arising as both security and invasive technology continue to shift.

---

34 http://gizmodo.com/, ...that would let websites you use hand over your personal data and read your email...

PART II: PRIVACY LAWS

E very nation has its own privacy laws. The basis of privacy law is personal data—"Privacy law refers to the laws that deal with the regulation of personal information about individuals, which can be collected by governments and other public as well as private organizations and its storage and use." [35] A country's privacy laws can be classified into two categories: 1) general privacy laws which regulate or operate on the broader sphere. These affect the policies designed by the government to govern various different areas of information, and 2) specific privacy laws which regulate, operate, or govern specific fields of information, including: communications, finance, health, information, online privacy, and privacy in one's home.

Privacy Laws in Canada

In Canada, there are a number of legislations that relate to privacy rights, and there are various government organizations and agencies responsible for overseeing compliance with these laws. The purpose behind devising privacy laws in Canada is twofold:

---

35 Wikipedia, https://en.wikipedia.org/wiki/Privacy_law

1) To govern how organizations are allowed to collect, use, and disclose your personal information and;

2)Enable individuals to access and manage personal information collected by organizations. [36]

Canada has two federal privacy laws, the Privacy Act, which covers the personal information-handling practices of federal government departments and agencies, and the Personal Information Protection and Electronic Documents Act (PIPEDA), the federal private-sector privacy law.

The Privacy Act

In 1977, the federal government of Canada decided that privacy should be the responsibility of a member of the new Canadian Human Rights Commission. The human rights commissioner responsible for privacy was Inger Hansen, who was appointed for a four-year term in 1977 and reappointed in 1981. Meanwhile, officials of the Organisation for Economic Co-operation and Development (OECD) had been actively working on developing a broad set of fundamental principles to protect personal data that could be adopted by member countries and other nations, and thus avoid restrictions on trans-border data flow.

In September of 1980, the Organisation for Economic Co-operation and Development Council adopted a set of eight fair information principles which were brief, technology-neutral, and written in accessible language. These qualities made them remarkably adaptable to the changing social and technological environment and have also contributed to their enduring influence and importance. [37]

Canada's Privacy Act, then being drafted, reflected the Organisation for Economic Co-operation and Development

---

36 Privacysense (2015) How Privacy Law in Canada Works; URL: http://www.privacysense. net/how-privacy-law-canada-works/

37 Stoddart, Jenifer (2013), The Necessary Rebirth of the Privacy Act, Remarks at the Library of Parliament November 29, 2013 Ottawa, Ontario, URL: https://www.priv.gc.ca/media/sp-d/2013/ sp-d_20131129_02_e.asp.

fair information principles. It also modeled the role of a new Privacy Commissioner on that of an ombudsman.

Main Features of the Privacy Act

The Privacy Act came into force, along with the Access to Information Act, on July 1, 1983. The purpose of this Act was to extend the present laws of Canada that protect the privacy of individuals with respect to personal information held by a government institution, and that provide individuals with a right of access to that information. The Act also gives individuals the right to see and correct personal information held by the Government of Canada and prevents unauthorized use and disclosure of that information. Some important provisions under the Privacy Act include the following:

1) Personal information should not be collected unless it directly relates to the institution's activity or program. Individuals should be aware of the purpose for which personal information is being collected. The institution should take reasonable steps for ensuring that the personal information is as complete, accurate, and up-to-date as possible.

2) Personal information should be retained by the institution for an adequate period of time, in order to ensure that the individual in question has an opportunity to access that information. Institutions should dispose of personal information appropriately.

3) Personal information should be used for the purpose it was collected. It should not be disclosed without the consent of the individual in question, unless provided for in the Act.

4) Individuals have the right to access their personal information held by a government institution, as long as the individual can provide adequate information to locate it. Individuals can also request correction or attach notations to their personal information held by institutions. [38]

The Privacy Act was enacted by the Canadian Parliament to regulate the collection, use, and disclosure of personal information by federal government institutions, thereby respecting the privacy rights of individuals. It imposes restrictions on 150 federal

---

38 CIPP Guide (2015), Canadian Privacy Act, URL: https://www.cippguide.org/2010/05/18/canadian-privacy-act/

government departments and agencies.

The Privacy law imposes fair information obligations on the federal government in terms of how it collects, maintains, uses, and discloses personal information under its control; and it puts in place an independent ombudsman, the Privacy Commissioner, to resolve problems and oversee compliance with the legislation. In addition to investigating complaints about the operation of the Privacy Act, the Privacy Commissioner can conduct audits of the fair information practices of government institutions and carry out special studies referred to the Commissioner by the Minister of Justice.

Evaluating the Privacy Act

In a world marked by new forms of threat that emanated both nationally as well as globally, it was felt that the new security challenges of the 21st century called for a review of Canadian privacy laws. Since the adoption of the Privacy Act, the focus of privacy concerns has shifted. According to the Canadian Media Awareness Network, "With the development of new information and communication technologies, the ability of the state and the private sector to collect, record and 'mine' personal information has grown exponentially." [39] As early as 1996, Bruce Phillips, then Privacy Commissioner of Canada, warned, "We are in fact buying and selling large elements of our human personae. The traffic in human information now is immense. There is almost nothing the commercial and governmental world is not anxious to find out about us as individuals." [40]

In 2006, the Office of the Privacy Commission (OCP) initiated the review of the Privacy Act, as the concerned legislation had not been updated since its inception in 1982. [41] The following major recommendations were made:

1) The Act needed to be modernized to address trans-border data flows;

---

39 https://www.scribd.com/document/14180737/Information-Technology-Ethics-Reader-By-Marielle-Obillo

40 Cited in Law Reform Commission of Saskatchewan (2012), Renewing the Privacy Act: Final Report, March, URL: http://lawreformcommission.sk.ca/Renewing_the_Privacy_Act_Final_Report.pdf.

41 https://www.priv.gc.ca/parl/pa_r_e.asp

2) There was a need to ensure greater transparency, accountability, and oversight over the activities of national security agencies, including more stringent reporting requirements to Parliament;

3) The scope of the act needed to be expanded in the following recommended ways: a) all bodies or offices through which public funds are expended should be subject to the Privacy Act unless Parliament specifically excludes them; b) Expansion of the definition of the Personal application to include both recorded and unrecorded information about an identifiable individual; c) the powers of the Federal Court needed to be expanded. The Federal Court should be able to review not just claims of denial of access to personal information held by government, but also improper collection, use, and disclosure of personal information. The Court should also be empowered to assess damages against offending institutions; and d) Extension of the rights of access, correction, and notation with respect to personal information held by a government should be made to every person, and not exclusively to those in Canada. [42]

The push for a review of the Act continued well into 2008, demanding a need for reform of the Act. The following ten basic recommendations were suggested:

1) Before government institutions collect personal information, they should be legally required to conduct a "necessity test," to prove the need for collecting the information.

2) All privacy rights and protections made under the Privacy Act should be able to be brought to Court for review. The Federal Court should also have the authority to award damages against offending institutions.

3)Leaders of government institutions should be required to assess privacy programs or systems before implementation. Assessment results should be reported publicly.

4)The Privacy Act should include a clear public education goal for the OPC.

5)The OPC should have greater authority to report on privacy policies and practices of government institutions.

6) The Privacy Commissioner should have greater authority to

---

42 Office of the Privacy Commissioner of Canada (2014), Privacy Act Reform, URL: https://www.priv.gc.ca/information/pub/pa_reform_060605_e.asp.

refuse or discontinue investigating complaints that are not in line with the public interest.

7) The Privacy Act should more closely align with the Personal Information Protection and Electronic Documents Act (PIPEDA).

8) Government departments and agencies should be required to more rigorously report their privacy activities to Parliament.

9) The Privacy Act should be subject to an ongoing five-year Parliamentary review.

10) The Privacy Act should more explicitly protect the disclosure of personal information by the Canadian government to foreign states. [43]

The emergence of powerful information and communication technologies, the challenge of managing electronic information, and the social and political demands of engaged citizens are compelling reasons to modernize the Privacy Act. The need of the hour is to expand the concept of accountability in privacy protection, emphasizing the need for organizations to demonstrate that they have mature, functioning privacy programs.

The Personal Information Protection and Electronic Documents Act (PIPEDA)

Established in 2000, PIPEDA, also known as the Personal Information Protection and Electronic Documents Act, is Canada's federal privacy law. It applies to personal information collected during the course of commercial activities, and to personal information about employees of federal works, undertakings, and businesses, whereas personal information collected, used, and disclosed by the federal government and many crown corporations is governed by the Privacy Act. Commercial activities are defined as any transaction, act, or conduct that is commercial in nature, such as selling, buying, or leasing. PIPEDA applies to organizations that are federally regulated and fall under the legislative authority of the Parliament of Canada, such as the telecom-

---

43 CIPP Guide (2015), Canadian Privacy Act, URL: https://www.cippguide.org/2010/05/18/ canadian-privacy-act/.

munications and broadcasting industry, and all local businesses in Yukon, Nunavut, and the Northwest Territories. The intended purpose of the legislation was to promote consumer trust in electronic commerce, and to support and promote electronic commerce by protecting personal information that is collected, used, or disclosed in certain circumstances, by providing for the use of electronic means to communicate or record information or transactions, and by amending the Canada Evidence Act, the Statutory Instruments Act, and the Statute Revision Act.

PIPEDA also applies to the private sector of each province unless a province has enacted its own privacy law that is substantially similar to PIPEDA.

PIPEDA is based on the following ten Privacy Principles:

1) Accountability: An organization shall designate someone to be accountable for the management of personal information. This includes the collection, usage, disclosure, retention, and transfer of personal information to third parties for processing. [44]

2) Identifying Purposes: An organization must clearly identify the purposes for which personal information is collected, either before or at the time of collection. This also helps organizations comply with the Openness and Individual Access principles. [45]

3) Consent: The knowledge and consent of individuals are required when an organization collects, uses, or discloses personal information, and it must be in such a way that the individual clearly understands. [46]

4) Limiting Collection: The personal information an organization collects should only be limited to that which is necessary for the purposes identified. [47]

5) Limiting Use, Disclosure, and Retention: An organization shall limit the ways it uses, discloses, and retains personal information. This means that an organization should not use or

---

44 Privacysense (2015), The 10 Privacy Principles of PIPEDA – Accountability, URL: http://www.privacysense.net/10-privacy-principles-of-pipeda-accountability/.

45 Ibid.

46 Ibid.

47 Ibid.

disclose personal information for purposes other than those for which it has identified and received consent. The organization should only retain personal information for as long as is necessary to fulfill its purposes. [48]

6) Accuracy: An organization should ensure that the personal information it collects is accurate, complete, and up-to-date for the purposes for which it is being used. [49]

7) Safeguards: An organization should protect personal information with security safeguards that are appropriate for the sensitivity of the personal information held. Personal information should be protected against loss or theft, unauthorized access, disclosure, copying, use, or modification, regardless of storage format (paper, electronic, etc). [50]

8) Openness: An organization should make its policies and procedures about management of personal information readily available and should not provide barriers to access. [51]

9) Individual Access: Upon an individual's request, an organization shall make known to the individual the existence, use, and disclosure of personal information and give access to it. If an individual challenges the accuracy or completeness of his or her personal information, the organization shall amend the information where appropriate. This can involve correcting, deleting, or adding personal information. [52]

10) Challenging Compliance: Individuals shall be able to challenge an organization's compliance on any of the privacy principles of PIPEDA. This means that an organization must have procedures in place in order to receive and respond to complaints and inquiries. The procedures should be simple and easy to navigate. [53]

There remains some debate about whether there exists a common law tort for breach of privacy. There have been a number of cases identifying a common law right to privacy but the requirements have not been articulated.

---

48 Ibid.

49 Ibid.

50 Ibid.

51 Ibid.

52 Ibid.

53 Ibid.

In Eastmond v. Canadian Pacific Railway & Privacy Commissioner of Canada, Canada's Supreme Court found that CPR could collect Eastmond's personal information without his knowledge or consent because it benefited from the exemption in paragraph 7(1)(b) of PIPEDA, which provides that personal information can be collected without consent if "it is reasonable to expect that the collection with the knowledge or consent of the individual would compromise the availability or the accuracy of the information and the collection is reasonable for purposes related to investigating a breach of an agreement." [54]

Provincial and Territorial Privacy Legislation

Canada has ten provinces and three territories, each with different sets of privacy legislation. They are briefly enumerated below:

Alberta has specific privacy legislation for organizations operating in the private and public sector, as well as health specific legislation for health service providers. Alberta's public sector privacy legislation is the Freedom of Information and Protection of Privacy Act, while private sector privacy legislation is the Personal Information Protection Act (PIPA), and has been deemed to be substantially similar to Canada's federal privacy legislation, the Personal Information Protection and Electronic Documents Act (PIPEDA). [55]

British Columbia's public sector privacy legislation is the Freedom of Information and Protection of Privacy Act (FIPPA), while private sector privacy legislation is the Personal Information Protection Act (PIPA). [56]

Manitoba's public sector privacy legislation is the Freedom of Information and Protection of Privacy Act (FIPPA), while the

54 http://laws-lois.justice.gc.ca/eng/acts/P-8.6/section-7-20150618.html

55 Privacysense (2015), Alberta's Privacy Legislation, URL: http://www.privacysense.net/privacy-legislation-alberta/.

56 Privacysense (2015) British Columbia's Privacy Legislation, URL: http://www.privacysense.net/privacy-legislation-british-columbia/

health specific privacy legislation is the Personal Health Information Act (PHIA). [57]

New Brunswick's public sector privacy legislation is the Right to Information and Protection of Privacy Act (RTIPPA) and the Personal Health Information Privacy and Access Act. [58]

Newfoundland and Labrador's public sector privacy legislation is the Access to Information and Protection of Privacy Act (ATIPPA). PIPEDA applies to the private sector. [59]

Nova Scotia's public sector privacy legislation is the Freedom of Information and Protection of Privacy Act (FOIPOP). PIPEDA applies to the private sector. [60]

Ontario has two statutes for public sector privacy legislation: the Freedom of Information and Protection of Privacy Act (FIPPA) and the Municipal Freedom of Information and Protection of Privacy Act (MFIPPA). Ontario's health specific privacy legislation is the Personal Health Information Protection Act (PHIPA). Prince Edward Island's public sector privacy legislation is the Freedom of Information and Protection of Privacy Act, while the Personal Information Protection and Electronic Documents Act (PIPEDA) applies to the private sector. [61]

Quebec's public sector privacy legislations are the Act Respecting Access to Documents Held by Public Bodies and the Protection of Personal Information and the Act Respecting the Protection of Personal Information in the Private Sector are deemed

57 Privacysense (2015), Manitoba's Privacy Legislation, URL: http://www.privacysense.net/privacy-legislation-manitoba/

58 Privacysense (2015), New Brunswick's Privacy Legislation, URL: http://www.privacysense.net/privacy-legislation-new-brunswick/.

59 Privacysense (2015), New Foundland's Privacy Legislation, URL: http://www.privacysense.net/privacy-legislation-newfoundland-and-labrador/.

60 Privacysense (2015), Nova Scotia's Privacy Legislation, URL: http://www.privacysense.net/privacy-legislation-nova-scotia/

61 Privacysense (2015), Ontario's Privacy Legislation, URL: http://www.privacysense.net/privacy-legislation-ontario/

similar to PIPEDA. [62]

Saskatchewan has two statutes for public sector privacy legislation: The Freedom of Information and Protection of Privacy Act (FOIP) and the Local Authority Freedom of Information and Protection of Privacy Act. The Protection and Electronic Documents Act (PIPEDA) applies to the private sector. [63]

The Northwest Territories' public sector privacy legislation is the Access to Information and Protection of Privacy Act (ATIPP). PIPEDA applies to the private sector. [64]

Nunavut's public sector privacy legislation is the Access to Information and Protection of Privacy Act (ATIPP), which is borrowed from Northwest Territories' privacy legislation. PIPEDA applies to the private sector. [65]

The Yukon's public sector privacy legislation is the Access to Information and Protection of Privacy Act (ATIPP) while PIPEDA applies to the private sector. [66]

Issues in Canadian Privacy Law: Selected Cases

This section examines selected case laws relating to privacy law jurisprudence and then assesses the major trends in the jurisprudence.

1) Randall v. Nubody's Fitness Centre—Nubody's Fitness Centre disclosed the applicant's frequency of gym use to his employer, without consent. Even though the Federal Court found a breach of PIPEDA, it saw it as "an unfortunate misun-

62 Privacysense (2015), Prince Edward Island's Privacy Legislation, URL: http://www.privacysense.net/privacy-legislation-prince-edward-island/

63 Privacysense (2015), Quebec's Privacy Legislation, URL: http://www.privacysense.net/privacy-legislation-quebec/

64 Privacysense (2015), Saskatchewan's Privacy Legislation, URL: http://www.privacysense.net/privacy-legislation-saskatchewan/

65 Privacysense (2015), Nunavut's Privacy Legislation, URL: http://www.privacysense.net/privacy-legislation-nunavut/.

66 Privacysense (2015), Yukon's Privacy Legislation, URL: http://www.privacysense.net/privacy-legislation-yukon/.

derstanding" and found no injury to the applicant that could justify damages. The judge was of the view that the breach of PIPEDA was the result of a misunderstanding with respect to the question of consent by subscribers to its corporate membership program, and that the breach was not the result of any sort of malicious behavior that would justify the award of damages. [67]

2) Nammo v. Transunion—A credit reporting agency mistakenly disclosed inaccurate information about the applicant to a bank, resulting in the applicant being turned down for a loan. Applying its earlier reasoning in Nubody's, the Court found that this did constitute an egregious situation. The judge was of the view that one of the central objects of PIPEDA is to encourage those who collect, use, and disclose personal information to do so with an appropriate degree of accuracy. The circumstances warranted an award of damages based on the considerations of vindication and deterrence. Ultimately, the court awarded the applicant $5,000.00, inclusive of the humiliation he suffered as a result of the breaches of PIPEDA by Transunion. [68]

3) Chitrakar v. Bell TV—Chitrakar applied for relief against Bell TV under s. 14(1) of the Personal Information Protection and Electronic Documents Act (PIPEDA), because Bell TV ordered a credit report without his consent. The Federal Court allowed the Federal Court allowed the application and awarded damages of $10,000 plus exemplary damages of $10,000. The court remarked: "Privacy rights are being more broadly recognized as important rights in an era where information on an individual is so readily available even without consent. It is important that violations of those rights be recognized as properly compensable." [69]

The following three cases constitute an example whereby there is increased judicial recognition of non-pecuniary privacy harms:

4) Jones v. Tsige—Jones and Tsige both worked at the same bank, and Tsige had formed a common-law relationship with Jones' ex-husband. An action for damages was brought when Jones found that Tsige had accessed her banking information

---

67 Office of the Privacy Commissioner of Canada (2010), Randall v. Nubody's Fitness Centres, URL: https://www.priv.gc.ca/leg_c/court_p_09_e.asp

68 Office of the Privacy Commissioner of Canada (2010), Nammo v. TransUnion of Canada Inc. URL: https://www.priv.gc.ca/leg_c/court_p_12_e.asp.

69 Privatech (2013), PIPEDA Damage Award for Unauthorized Credit Check, October 13, URL: https://privatech.ca/2013/12/03/pipeda-damage-award-for-unauthorized-credit-check/.

174 times over a period of four years. The issue in this case was whether Ontario Law recognizes a right to bring a civil action for damages for the invasion of personal privacy. The court ruled that there was, and the summary dismissal in trial court of Jones' action for damages was reversed. Three key features were used in finding liability for the defendant's conduct: it was intentional; it was an invasion of private affairs without lawful justification; and a reasonable person would regard the conduct as highly offensive/a cause for distress. The court also ruled that such an action must be deliberate and significant (it was both), and gave examples of categories for what could be considered "highly offensive" to invade: financial or health records; sexual practices. [70]

5) Alberta (Information and Privacy Commissioner) v. United Food and Commercial Workers—This case involved a constitutional challenge to Alberta's private sector privacy legislation on the grounds that it unjustifiably prohibited unions' expressive activity in the context of lawful picketing. The judgment stated that Alberta's privacy law imposes restrictions on a union's ability to communicate and persuade the public of its cause, impairing its ability to use one of its most effective bargaining strategies in the course of a lawful strike. This infringement of the right to freedom of expression is disproportionate to the government's objective of providing individuals with control over personal information that they expose by crossing a picket-line. [71]

6) R v. Vu, the SCC—In R v Vu, [2013] 3 SCR 657 [Vu], a landmark decision regarding section 8 of the Canadian Charter of Rights and Freedoms, the Supreme Court of Canada unanimously ruled that specific prior authorization is needed to search individuals' computers and similar devices. Following suspicions that the appellant Thanh Long Vu was stealing electricity, Constable Carter of the RCMP filed an Information to Obtain a Search Warrant (ITO) for the purpose of locating evidence to support such charges. The warrant indicated that officers wanted to locate evidence regarding the diversion of electricity, the identity of the owner of the property, and "computer generated notes," but it did not include specific information about the search of computers.

In recognizing the heightened privacy interests in computers, the SCC held: 1) "It is difficult to imagine a more intrusive invasion of privacy than the search of a personal or home com-

---

70 Canclliconnects (2014), Summary of Jones v Tsige, November 20, URL: http://canliiconnects.org/en/summaries/31442.

71 Mccarthy Tetrault (2013), SCC Strikes Down Alberta Privacy Legislation on Speech Grounds, November 15, URL: http://www.mccarthy.ca/article_detail.aspx?id=6553.

puter;" 2) home computers "store immense amounts of information, some of which, in the case of personal computers, will touch the 'biographical core of personal information;'" 3) they "contain information that is automatically generated, often unbeknownst to the user;" 4) "Computers... create information without the users' knowledge and retain information that users have tried to erase. These features make computers fundamentally different from (other) receptacles." In a nutshell, the ruling stated that the particular privacy interests in computers or other similar devices require specific judicial pre-authorization before being searched in accordance with section 8 of the Charter. [72]

The next two cases highlight how the privacy jurisprudence in Canada entails a greater understanding of the potential impacts of information technology on privacy issues:

7) Telus Communications Company v. the Queen: This involved a case where the SCC grappled with whether the police's prospective daily acquisition of text messages stored on Telus' servers was lawful under the general warrant power, or whether the more onerous threshold of wiretap authorization was required. The majority found that collecting text messages constituted an interception within the meaning of s. 183 of the Criminal Code. It was ruled that text messaging is, in essence, an electronic conversation that bears several hallmarks of traditional voice communication: transmission is generally instantaneous and there is an expectation of privacy in the communication. [73]

8) R. v. Tse, 2012 SCC 16—This case concerned the constitutionality of the relevant section of the Criminal Code which allows police wiretapping without prior judicial warrant in narrow exigent circumstances. The Supreme Court of Canada held that section 184.4 of the Criminal Code, which deals with emergency wiretaps, was unconstitutional. Although section 184.4 is the only wiretapping provision that does not require either consent of a party or prior authorization, the court noted that each interception undertaken under this section "is lim-

72 The Court (2014), R vs U: The SCC Rules that Computers Require Distinctive Treatment Under Section 8 of the Chater, February 6, URL: http://www.thecourt.ca/2014/02/06/r-v-vu-the-scc-rules-that-computers-require-distinctive-treatment-under-section-8-of-the-charter/.

73 The Court (2012), Appel Watch: Telus Communications Company v. Her Majesty- the queen, URL: http://www.thecourt.ca/2012/10/19/appeal-watch-telus-communications-company-v-her-majesty-the-queen/.

ited to urgent situations where there is an immediate necessity to prevent serious harm and judicial pre-authorization is not available with reasonable diligence." However, "In its present form, s. 184.4 contains no accountability measures to permit oversight of the police use of the power. It does not require that 'after the fact' notice be given to persons whose private communications have been intercepted. Unless a criminal prosecution results, the targets of the wiretapping may never learn of the interceptions and will be unable to challenge police use of this power. There is no other measure in the Code to ensure specific oversight of the use of s. 184.4." [74]

The cases highlighted in this section point to the fact that, while privacy rights must give way to justifiable infringements in the name of security and law enforcement, there must be transparency and accountability for the collection, use, and disclosure of citizens' personal information.

European Privacy Laws

The European Union is a federation of 27 member states, governed by a European Parliament and advised by a European Commission. The European Commission articulates a directive, which is then passed by the Parliament. Each member country must then take that directive and enact it into their own national law; the law is then enforced on a country to country basis.

Comparatively, the European Union has taken quite a different approach to privacy; Europe's privacy laws are different from those of the US and many other countries. Privacy is considered a fundamental human right, enshrined in the constitution. There are comprehensive federal privacy laws implemented in each European Union country's national law. Each of the European Union member states has their own data protection law and their own data protection officers.

There are guiding rules in the European Union for "sensitive" personal information, such as political opinions, racial or ethnic origin, religious or philosophical beliefs, trade union membership, health, information about sex life, etc., in addition to the normal protections that are required for all personal information. The Eu-

---

74 Court House Libraries (2013), Response to the Supreme Court of Canada Decision in R. v. Tse Act, August 6. http://www.courthouselibrary.ca/training/stream/13-08-06/Response_to_the_Supreme_Court_of_Canada_Decision_in_R_v_Tse_Act.aspx.

ropean laws also include limitations on cross-border transfers. In the European Union, there are two primary laws that directly impact marketers: the 2009 Cookie Directive and the Data Protection Directive. The 2009 Cookie Directive, which covers only online communication technologies and requires that the user's consent is obtained before marketers can access or store cookies on their computers or other devices. This directive was not very effective and new revisions came into force on May 26, 2012, as the European Union Privacy and Electronic Communications Directive. This requires all websites which use cookies to obtain consent from the site's visitors before storing or using their information. This revision was necessary because website visitors rarely read the privacy policies of different websites, and are often not aware that their personal information is being tracked. If the websites fail to comply with this new law, they will be fined up to €500,000.

Data Protection Laws in Europe—from 1995 to 2016

The Data Protection Directive governs the transfer and processing of all personal data whether it is online or offline. In 1995, the European Union Data Protection Directive established the first-ever legal framework for personal data protection across multiple countries. The Directive has shaped how the European Union member states—and countries across the world—look at individuals' privacy rights in their personal data. The Directive 95/46 of the European Parliament and the Council of 24 October 1995 on the protection of individuals with regard to the processing of personal data and on the free movement of such data (Data Protection Directive 95/46/EC) was established to provide a regulatory framework to guarantee secure and free movement of personal data across the national borders of the European Union member countries, in addition to setting a baseline of security for personal information wherever it is stored, transmitted, or processed. [75] There are thirty-three articles and

---

75 . Gordon, Adam, Guide to the CISSP CBK, Fourth Edition, 2015, (online) https://books.google.co.in/
books?id=ONcgCAAAQBAJ&pg=PA39&dpg=PA39&dq=%22+Directive+95/46+of+the+European+Par-
liament+and+the+Council%22&source=bl&ots=KH5_EQAqCz&sig=1209yoVbhFTbv0dGkeeqI5UZ-
8m4&hl=en&sa=X&ved=0ahUKEwioj5eqjaLKAhUPkY4KHX94ChsQ6AEIKjAC#v=onepage&q=%22%20
Directive%2095%2F46%20of%20the%20European%20Parliament%20and%20the%20Council%22&f=false

eight chapters in that directive. It came into force in 1998.

The European Union data protection directive is an example of what is called a Safe Harbour Law. It is a comparatively strict privacy protection for European Union citizens and it prohibits European firms from transferring personal data to other countries or overseas countries which do not meet the standards of European Union privacy laws. It does create exceptions for some foreign companies who have agreed to meet the European Union standards under the directives of Safe Harbour principles. Some American companies like Google, Amazon, and others, are operating within the European Union, subject to the Safe Harbour Laws. Safe Harbour privacy principles allow United States companies to register their certification if they meet the following requirements:

1. Notice—Individuals must be informed that their data has been collected and how it will be used;

2. Choice—Individuals must have the option to opt out of the collection and forward transfer of data to third parties;

3. Onward Transfer—Third parties who receive the transferred data must follow the same data collection principles;

4. Security—Reasonable efforts must be made to prevent the loss of collected information;

5. Data Integrity—Only relevant and reliable data may be collected;

6. Access—Individuals must be able to access information held about them, and correct or delete it if it is inaccurate;

7. Enforcement—There must be effective means of enforcing these rules. Enforcement of these rules by US companies doing business in Europe is the responsibility of the US federal trade commission. [76]

The 1995 directive is not directly applicable to the European Union member states. It requires each member state to adopt a law that has the minimum requirements that are in the directive,

---

76 European Court of Justice 2000/520/EC: Commission Decision of 26 July 2000 pursuant to Directive 95/46/EC of the European Parliament and of the Council on the adequacy of the protection provided by the safe harbour privacy principles and related frequently asked questions issued by the US Department of Commerce (notified under document number C(2000) 2441) (Text with EEA relevance.) 25 August 2000, retrieved 30 October 2015

which means that there are 27 separate laws. The 1995 directive prescribes a "framework for privacy laws based on the Organisation for Economic Co-operation and Development (OECD) principles. This framework also prohibits data transfer to countries lacking 'adequate' privacy protections. Each European Union member country was required to adopt laws consistent with the Directive within three years of its passage." [77]

In 2016, we will witness what may be the most important event to date in the short history of personal data protection law. The European Union will adopt the General Data Protection Regulation (GDPR), resetting the pace of reform and raising the bar for data protection in the European Union and across the world. When it takes effect, the EU General Data Protection Regulation will replace the 1995 Directive.

When data protection law was introduced to Europe in 1995, less than 1% of the European Union population used the internet. Since then, the IT industry has undergone vast changes; at present, the European Parliament is discussing how to update current rules to make it easier for people to access and control their own data and simplify administrative requirements for companies. The main aim behind the updating of the 1995 directive is "to establish a single, pan-European law to replace the current inconsistent patchwork of national laws and also to modernize the principles enshrined in the 1995 Data Protection Directive." [78] Another goal for updating the directive is also to see the potential cost-savings for companies that do business in Europe, which will also benefit a larger group of people. The particular benefits that this new regulation provides companies include:

1. One uniform coherent law across Europe;

2. Only one authority will supervise the performance of companies and whether they are abiding by the Laws of the EU;

---

77 http://fra.europa.eu/sites/default/files/fra-2014-handbook-data-protection-law-2nd-ed_en.pdf

78 Crano, Lorrie, Web Privacy with P3P, 2002, (online) https://books.google.co.in/books?id=KVEV7c-7gghEC&pg=PA25&dq=The+1995+directive+prescribes+a+framework+for+privacy+laws+based+on+the&hl=en&sa=X&ved=0ahUKEwj0rrPJjqLKAhUC1xoKHdW7C5cQ6A-EIJDAA#v=onepage&q=The%201995%20directive%20prescribes%20a%20framework%20for%20privacy%20laws%20based%20on%20the&f=false

3.There will be no partiality—all companies will abide by the same rules prescribed by the European Government. [79]

The benefits for the European Union citizens are:

1.Improved, revised, and more secure Data Protection Laws;

2. People are authorised to control, change, or delete their personal information. [80]

The new regulation covers many aspects of data, from data creation to the disposal of data upon completion of the task for which it was required. The primary concern of the law can be understood from the following 3 key articles:

1."Security of Processing (Article – 30) –
a) Prevent any unauthorized access to personal data
b)Prevent any unauthorized disclosure, reading, copying, modification, erasure or removal of personal data.

2.Notification of a personal data breach to the supervisory authority (Article 31)

3.Communication of a personal data breach to the data subject (Article 32) [81]

According to these new regulations, a company or an organization has to abide by three important rules:

1.They should implement appropriate security measures to protect personal data.

2.They should have a clear data protection policy

3.They should have a named data protection officer (except SMEs). [82]

---

79 http://europa.eu/rapid/press-release_MEMO-15-6385_en.htm

80 Anthony Merry, The proposed EU Data Regulation and what this means for you, (online) https://www.sophos.com/zh-cn/medialibrary/PDFs/partners/williams-event/pro-posed-eu-data-regulations-wembly.pdf

81 https://www.sophos.com/zh-cn/medialibrary/PDFs/partners/williams-event/pro-posed-eu-data-regulations.pdf

82 Anthony Merry, The proposed EU Data Regulation and what this means for you, (online)https://www.sophos.com/zh-cn/medialibrary/PDFs/partners/williams-event/pro-posed-eu-data-regulations-wembly.pdf

For the sake of the proper implementation of these rules, the European Parliament is, at present, debating on attaching fines as part of this law. Fines for unprotected data breaches will range up to €100 million or 5% of annual global turnover. On the other hand, on the part of individuals, if one suffers a breach and can show that the personal data cannot be accessed by unauthorized people (e.g. it was encrypted), then the likelihood of being fined would be very greatly reduced, and the individual person would not need to notify affected data subjects of the breach.

Europe needs strict data protection laws because at present, in Europe, "Nearly 65% of people are worried about the security of their corporate data and their personal data; 49% of people are not clear or doubt the organization's data security policy; only 51% of company laptops are encrypted; and, only 23% of them secure both customer and employee data." [83] Because of the striking statistics, significant action is required immediately to secure personal data on the part of the government, and on the part of multinational companies and individual organizations. In order to comply with the upcoming regulations in Europe, they will be required to:

1. Implement 'appropriate security measures' to protect personal data (Encryption is widely agreed to be the best data security measure available);

2. Notify affected parties in the event of a personal data breach;

3. Pay fines in the event of a personal data breach. [84]

Historically, Europe has strict laws enshrined in its constitution, but when it comes to implementation, enforcement has been fairly minimal. A significant question arises with regards to whether "liberal Europe–traditionally friendly towards refugees, promoter of human rights and defender of modern liberal values, often giving unsolicited advice to Asian and African states on the need to respect religious diversity and human rights–[will] survive the shocking recognition that 'security comes first, the rest can fol-

---

83 http://www.computerweekly.com/news/4500270456/EU-data-protection-rules-affect-everyone-say-legal-experts

84 https://www.sophos.com/zh-cn/medialibrary/PDFs/partners/williams-event/proposed-eu-data-regulations.pdf

low'?" [85] However, the revision of the previous 1995 directive and the drafting of a new regulation by the European Parliament is a positive step towards the formation and implementation of stricter laws.

Some of the recent trends observed in the case of European Privacy Laws are:

1. Increased enforcement and enquiries in certain states, for example, in Germany, Netherlands, and France, where we can see the data protection authorities being much more active and affective.

2. Actions by competitors and consumer groups. Companies are being sued by their competitors for using information in ways that are inconsistent with the promises that they have made to the consumers.

3. There is a new draft regulation that has been proposed by the European Union which, if it comes into force, would be directly applicable to member states, and will have a direct effect on company upbraiding in Europe.

4. There will be breach notification in the regulation and more countries will be seen adopting breach notification obligations.

5. An interesting feature of the new regulation is that it does have an extra-territorial effect, meaning companies outside of the European Union, that target EU citizens, will be covered by the new regulation if adopted. [86]

New Concepts to be Introduced in the General Data Protection Regulation (GDPR)

• The GDPR broadly maintains the definition of personal data provided by the Data Protection Directive (i.e. any information relating to an identified or identifiable natural person or 'data subject'), but added to that definition are examples of identifiers, such as location data or online identifiers (Article 4 (1)). It further specifies that online identifiers, provided by devices, applications, tools, and protocols, including Internet Protocol (IP) addresses, cookie identifiers, as well as other identifiers, such as Radio Frequency Identification tags (RFID),

---

85 http://www.thehindu.com/todays-paper/tp-opinion/straws-in-the-paris-wind/article7920972.ece

86 http://europa.eu/rapid/press-release_IP-15-6321_en.htm

could be used to identify individuals, in particular when combined with unique identifiers.

• The GDPR introduces a new concept that does not exist under the Data Protection Directive, namely, pseudonymization. Pseudonymization is the "processing of personal data in such a way that the data can no longer be attributed to a specific data subject without the use of additional information, as long as such information is kept separately and subject to technical and organizational measures to ensure non-attribution to an identified or identifiable person" (Article 4 (3b)). In practice, pseudonymization refers to privacy-enhancing measures that aim to reduce the risk of singling out one individual in a data pool. It is also a tool for compliance, helping data controllers and processors meet their data protection obligations (Recital 23a)

• The GDPR introduces definitions for specific categories of sensitive data, namely genetic data and biometric data. Genetic data are defined as "all personal data relating to the genetic characteristics of an individual that have been inherited or acquired, which give unique information about the physiology or the health of that individual, resulting in particular from an analysis of a biological sample from the individual in question" (Article 4 (10)). The GDPR clarifies that genetic data uniquely identifying an individual is considered to be sensitive data. The GDPR also introduces the concept of biometric data, meaning "any personal data resulting from specific technical processing relating to the physical, physiological, or behavioral characteristics of an individual which allows or confirms the unique identi identification of that individual, such as facial images, or dactyloscopic data" (Article 4 (11)).

• The GDPR has extraterritorial effect by extending its scope of application to non-European Union controllers or processors, where the processing activities are related to: (a) the offering of goods or services to individuals located in the European Union; or (b) the monitoring of their behavior (Article 3). Non-European Union controllers and processors that are subject to European Union data protection law must appoint in writing a representative in the European Union (Article 25). The GDPR clarifies that the concept of 'offering goods or services' is not limited to offerings that require a payment from the individuals.

• The GDPR generally strengthens individuals' rights (i.e., notice obligation, rights of access, rectification, erasure, right to object, and right not to be subject to automated decision making, including profiling) and includes a number of new rights (i.e. restrictions of processing, data portability).

• Under the GDPR, individuals have a right to obtain from controllers the erasure of their personal data without undue delay where: (1) the data are no longer necessary in relation to the purposes for which they were collected or otherwise processed; (2) individuals withdraw their consent for the data processing; (3) individuals object to the processing of their personal data; (4) the data were unlawfully processed; (5) a law requires the controller to erase the data; or (6) the data have been collected in relation to the offering of information society services to children (Article 17 (1).

• As concerns data that has been made public by the controller, the Council provides that the controller should take reasonable steps to notify the request for erasure to the controller who received the data (Article 17 (2a) and Recital 54). What constitutes "reasonable" steps will depend on the available technology and the cost of implementation.

Finally, the GDPR provides a number of situations in which the right to be forgotten does not apply, namely when the processing of personal data is necessary for the right of freedom of expression, compliance with a legal obligation, reasons of public interest in the area of public health, archiving purposes or for the establishment, exercise or defense of legal claims (Article 17 (3) and Recital 53).

• The GDPR creates a new right to data portability. This right further strengthens the individuals' control over their own personal data by allowing them to export personal data from one controller to another, without hindrance from the first controller.

Controllers must make the data available in a structured, commonly used, machine-readable and interoperable format that allows the individual to transfer the data to another controller (Article 18 (1) and Recital 55). This right applies even where the data processing is based on consent or the performance of a contract and carried out by automated means (Article 18 (2) (a) and (b)).

• The GDPR will contain new obligations to implement privacy-enhancing measures at the earliest stage of the conception of products and services that involve the processing of personal data (privacy by design) and to, by default, select the techniques that are the most protective of individuals' privacy and data protection (privacy by default) (Article 23 (1) and (2), Recital 61).

These two principles will be important for companies when building new products and services.

• Finally, controllers need to document any personal data breach. The GDPR provides much more detailed requirements for processing agreements than the Data Protection Directive.
Perhaps the most significant change is that all European Union national data protection acts will either be repealed or severely reduced in scope (for example, to be limited to points that the GDPR does not cover). In some Member States this may lead to federalism issues (e.g., in Germany).

The GDPR provides much more detailed requirements for processing agreements than the Data Protection Directive.

Perhaps the most significant change is that all European Union national data protection acts will either be repealed or severely reduced in scope (for example, to be limited to points that the GDPR does not cover). In some Member States this may lead to federalism issues (e.g., in Germany).

Penalties and Enforcement

Under Article 79, violations of certain provisions will carry a penalty of "up to 2% of total worldwide annual turnover of the preceding financial year." Violations of other provisions will carry a penalty of "up to 4% of total worldwide annual turnover of the preceding financial year." The 4% penalty applies to "basic principles for processing, including conditionals for consent," as well as "data subjects' rights" and "transfers of personal data to a recipient in a third country or an international organization."

Businesses face sanctions of up to 4 per cent of global turnover under the agreement, meaning that big internet firms could be hit with fines totalling billions for major breaches of the law.

Under the agreed rules, companies will have to employ a data protection officer if they handle significant amounts of data, along with a host of other measures aimed at giving consumers more say over what businesses can do with personal information. There is a significant challenge for organizations that hold sensitive data to achieve and maintain compliance with so many regulations that have relevance to information privacy.

The European Commission has also set up the "Working party on the Protection of Individuals with regard to the Processing of Personal Data," commonly known as the "Article 29 Working Party." The Working Party gives advice about the level of protection in the European Union and third countries. The Working Party negotiated with United States representatives about the protection of personal data, and the Safe Harbor Principles were the result. The Safe Harbor was approved as providing adequate protection for personal data by the European Commission on July 26, 2000.

Erasure—"The Right to be Forgotten"

The term "right to be forgotten" is a relatively new idea and is linked to the right to privacy. Also referred to as the right to erasure, this is an emerging concept born from the rise of the digital age. The European Union and many other countries have been struggling with legislation that deals with the issue of erasure. The debate centres on the desire of citizens to determine and advance their lives without being eternally stigmatized by information online relating to past behaviour. The legal protection of the right to privacy in general—and of data privacy in particular—varies greatly around the world.

The notion of "the right to be forgotten" is derived from numerous pre-existing European ideals and has been seen surfacing in cases across the globe:

Canada
On February 18, 2016, the Supreme Court of Canada (SCC) granted Google Inc. leave to appeal a decision of the British Columbia Court of Appeal (BCCA) that upheld an interim injunction restraining Google.

Germany
In a 2009 case, the court ruled to remove information from Wikipedia concerning a convicted murderer. Wikipedia is based in the United States, where the First Amendment protects freedom of speech and freedom of the press, under which the articles on Wikipedia fall. In Germany, the law seeks to protect the name and likenesses of private persons from unwanted publicity.

Argentina
Argentina has seen law suits by celebrities against Google and Yahoo! in which the plaintiffs demanded the removal of certain search results, and required the removal of links to photographs.

United Kingdom
In the United Kingdom, there is a longstanding belief, specifically under the Rehabilitation of Offenders Act 1974, that after a certain period of time, many criminal convictions are "spent," meaning that information regarding said person should not be regarded when obtaining insurance or seeking employment.
The United Kingdom Parliament enables some criminal convictions to be ignored after a rehabilitation period. Its purpose is that people do not have a lifelong blot on their records because of a relatively minor offence in their past.

France
In 2010, France passed Chartes du droit à l'oubli numérique (the right to be forgotten).

European Court of Justice ruling on Google—Google Spain vs. Mario Costeja Gonzalez

In 2014, the European Court of Justice (ECJ) issued a landmark judgment stating that individuals have a right to ask search engines to remove links containing personal data about them, if the information about the individual is "inadequate, irrelevant or no longer relevant." [87] The case was brought by a Spanish man, Mario Costeja Gonzalez, who complained that an auction notice of his repossessed home on Google's search results infringed on his privacy because the proceedings concerning him had been fully resolved for a number of years and hence the reference to these was entirely irrelevant. He requested, first, that the newspaper be required either to remove or alter the pages in question so that the personal data relating to him no longer appeared; and second, that Google Spain or Google Inc. be required to remove the personal data relating to him, so that it no longer appeared in the search result.

The Spanish court referred the case to the Court of Justice of the European Union asking (a) whether the European Union's 1995 Data Protection Directive applied to search engines such as Google; (b) whether European Union law (the Directive) applied to Google Spain, given that the company's data processing server was in the United States; (c) whether an individual has the right to request that his or her personal data be removed from accessibility via a search engine.

The European Court of Justice (ECJ) ruling stated that, regarding the territorial scope, Google was subject to EU data protection laws for its search engine business. Although the Google search engine was operated by Google Inc. outside of the European Union, its Spanish subsidiary was promoting and selling advertising space for the search service, which generates profit for Google Inc. This was sufficient for the processing by Google Inc. to be treated as occurring "in the context of the establishment" of the Spanish company, and so be subject to European

---

87 European Commission (2014), Factsheet on the "Right to be forgotten" ruling, (C-131/12); URL: http://ec.europa.eu/justice/data-rotection/files/factsheets/factsheet_data_protection_en.pdf

Union data protection laws. According to the European Court of Justice, each of Google's activities of collecting, retrieving, recording, organizing, storing, and disclosing personal data in the form of search results must be classified as "processing." As regards the extent of the responsibility of the operator of the search engine, the Court held that the operator is, in certain circumstances, obliged to remove links to web pages that are published by third parties and contain information relating to a person from the list of results displayed following a search made on the basis of that person's name. In response to the question of whether the directive enables the data subject to request that links to web pages be removed from such a list of results on the grounds that he wishes the information appearing on those pages relating to him personally to be 'forgotten' after a certain time, the Court holds that, if it is found, following a request by the data subject, that the inclusion of those links in the list is, at this point in time, incompatible with the directive, then the links and information in the list of results must be erased.

It may be mentioned here that the concerned Directive is Directive 95/46/EC of the European Parliament and of the Council of 24 October 1995 on the protection of individuals with regard to the processing of personal data and on the free movement of such data, which has the objective of protecting the fundamental rights and freedoms of natural persons (in particular the right to privacy) when personal data are processed, while removing obstacles to the free flow of such data. [88] Under the European Convention on Human Rights, a European citizen has an explicit right to "private and family life, his home and his correspondence" under Article 8. This needs to be balanced with Article 10 on the Freedom of Expression, which includes the right to receive information.

The decision has already polarized opinion. Some view it as an important step toward recognizing an individual's right to pri-

88 *Official Journal of the European Communities* (1995), Directive 95/46/EC of the European Parliament and of the Council of 24 October 1995 on the protection of individuals with regard to the processing of personal data and on the free movement of such data.; No L 281/31;URL: http://ec.europa.eu/justice/policies/privacy/docs/95-46-ce/dir1995-46_part1_en.pdf.

vacy on the Internet. [89] Others have argued that it is an attack on freedom of expression and the right to know. The case certainly raises practical issues, as search engine operators will need to make difficult decisions as to what amounts to "inadequate, irrelevant or no longer relevant" [90] information. This decision may also result in additional costs for businesses not only managing the requests but also dealing with challenges brought by individuals. [91]

In the wake of this ruling, Google has received more than 220,000 requests to remove information, showing significant demand. [92] As of June 2014, Google has established a form where individuals can request removal. This form allows an individual or someone representing an individual to enter a request by submitting photo ID of the individual for whom the request is being submitted. The form then allows the submitter to list one or more URLs they want removed, and requires them to provide an explanation to justify their request. [93]

In order to fully understand the modalities of how the leading research engines should comply with the privacy ruling in the 28 member European Union block, Google set up an eight member advisory committee. As regards the limitations of powers, the committee can only provide recommendations to Google and does not have the binding power to force the company to change its operations. It also has no legal powers in Europe, where individual countries' data protection authorities have the final say in decisions relating to enforcements of the privacy rul-

---

89 James Vincent (2014), "We should be thankful the ECJ is sticking up for our 'right to forget'", The Guardian, May 13, URL: http://www.independent.co.uk/voices/comment/weshould-be-thankful-the-ecj-is-sticking-up-for-our-right-to-forget-9365072.html.

90 Ibid.

91 Eleni Frantizou (2014), Further Developments in the Right to be Forgotten: The European Court of Justice's Judgment in Case C-131/12, Google Spain, SL, Google Inc v Agencia Espanola de Proteccion de Datos, Human Rights Law Review 14 (4): 761-777.

92 European Commission (2014), Factsheet on Right to be Forgotten Ruling (C-131/12), URL: http://ec.europa.eu/justice/data-protection/files/factsheets/factsheet_data_protection_en.pdf. Powles, Julia (2015), February 19, The Guardian, URL: http://www.theguardian.com/technology/2015/feb/19/google-acknowledges-some people-want-right-to-be-forgotten.

93 O' Kane Olivera (2015), The Right to Be Forgotten or Is It? No. It Is the Right to Erasure of Certain Data, March 27, Carson Mcdowll, URL: http://www.carson-mcdowell.com/news-an-devents/insights/the-right-to-be-forgotten-or-is-it-no-it-is-the-right-to-erasure-of-certain-data.

ing. [94] In February 2015, the report was released and outlined five elements that Google should take into account while making decisions on requests for the removal of search results. The first issue is identifying the role of the individual in public life. The second aspect pertains to the nature of information. The third aspect pertains to the source of the information.

The advisory committee stated that information published by "recognized bloggers or individual authors of good reputation with substantial credibility and/or readership will weigh in favor of public interest." [95] With regards to the personal information on social networking sites, the committee was of the opinion that the individual delete it of their own initiative. The fourth and fifth issue is concerned with the timing and accuracy of the information, as well as generally recommending more transparency and specifying that individuals should not be easily identified. The Advisory Council also recommended that the search engine should make the removal request form easily accessible and intelligible to data subjects. The advisory committee was also of the view that Google should make it a point to inform webmasters when information from their site is being delinked and, in certain specific cases, Google should talk to content publishers before making a delisting decision. Publishers should also be able to challenge decisions, which individuals can already do if their request is turned down. [96]

Peter Barron, Google's European communications director, has remarked that Google's internal procedures were close to the guidance issued by European regulators. He further said that Google was considering the recent report compiled by members of its independent advisory council. However, IT watchdogs have been critical of the advisory committee's inference of the ECJ judgment that versions of Google aimed at people in the

94 Lawson, Robert (2014), Google sets up advisory committee to deal with 'right to be forgotten' requests, July 11, Tech Times, URL: http://www.techtimes.com/articles/10265/20140711/google-sets-advisory-committee-deal-withright-forgotten-requests.htm

95 http://barnoldlaw.blogspot.ca/2015_02_15_archive.html

96 Meyer, David (2014), Google advisory council: Right to delist should only apply in EU, February 6, gigaom.com, URL: https://gigaom.com/2015/02/06/google-advisory-council-rightto-delist-should-only-apply-in-eu/.

European Union should conform to this right, but that versions aimed at people outside the European Union should not need to. Critics argue that information is subject to the laws not of where it was generated, written, uploaded or processed, but to the laws of where it was viewed. [97]

Meanwhile, the issue of Google and right to forgotten has also triggered a debate across the Atlantic. Proponents say the "right to be forgotten" strikes a fair balance between personal privacy and free speech and gives individuals the ability to control their own lives in a world where more and more personal data is collected, bought, and sold by third parties. Critics argue that this right amounts to censorship that cannot be justified in free and democratic societies. The removal of such material in search results, they argue, allows for the suppression of information that the public has a right to know.

The Right to be Forgotten raises several questions relating to corporate responsibility, the right to privacy, and the right of access to information. One of the major concerns is the impact this new right will have on the right to freedom of expression and whether creating this right would be tantamount to rewriting history.

Concerns have been raised that the Proposed Data Protection Regulation, as pertaining to erasure, is written broadly and that it is a form of censorship, requiring companies to go to great lengths to identify third parties with the information and remove it, this might compromise the integrity of Internet-based information.

Multinationals that do business around the world will have to make their personal information protection policies conform to this enhanced standard, which will improve customer relations.

"Wikipedia founder Jimmy Wales has described the European Union's Right to be Forgotten as 'deeply immoral,' as the organisation that operates the online encyclopedia warned the ruling will result in an internet 'riddled with memory holes.'" [98]

---

97 Op Cit No 2. .... 2nd reference ... Worstall, Tim (2015), Google Advisory Group Has Completely Misunderstood Territoriality In The Right To Be Forgotten, February 6, Forbes, URL: http://www.forbes.com/sites/timworstall/2015/02/06/google-advisory-group-has-completelymisunderstood-territoriality-in-the-right-to-be-forgotten/.

98 http://www.telegraph.co.uk/technology/wikipedia/11015901/EU-ruling-on-link-removal-deeply-immoral-says-Wikipedia-founder.html

Finally, a concern has been raised that "Privacy by default" will encourage politicians, celebrities, and other public figures to put their lawyers on track when they find inconvenient information online. [99]

The ability to control the information one reveals about oneself over the Internet, and who can access that information, has become a growing concern. These concerns include whether email can be stored or read by third parties without consent, or whether third parties can continue to track the web sites someone has visited.

The advent of various search engines and the use of data mining created a capability for data about individuals to be collected and combined from a wide variety of sources very easily but is more challenging for those who are concerned with privacy. Time will tell if the new Data Regulation will be an effective tool for enhancing privacy or an unreasonable burden on government and business.

Privacy laws in the United States of America

The noise over individual privacy has seen manifold increase with the advent and proliferation of internet access all over the world. With the United States leading the world in a gamut of services and activities, maintaining the privacy of its citizens has become a top priority for the United States government.

Today, privacy concerns have become ubiquitous but what it means differs from person to person. The classic definition of privacy was provided by United States Supreme Court Judge Louis Brandeis in 1890 as a "right to be let alone." [100] In general, privacy refers to the right to autonomy, to be free from interference in one's life from state and corporate organizations.

With privacy protection being considered synonymous to the protection of liberty in the United States, unprecedented focus is being put on individual autonomy. Also, with Americans preferring that the government refrain from creating government

---

99 http://ieet.org/index.php/IEET/more/9519

100 The Importance of Privacy. http://library.royalroads.ca/copyright-office/privacy-information-basics-students-and-researchers/importance-privacy. March 2008 - More about the importance of privacy in a democratic society.

watchdogs in order to "warrant privacy" to citizens, newer laws are being passed in the country to ensure that citizens are left alone and their privacy is protected from the government.

Although there is no direct legal framework provided for privacy in the United States Constitution, the Constitution imposes certain limitations on the government for intrusion into people's lives. From trespassing or eavesdropping as forms of privacy invasion morphing into newer technological manifestations, it is only recently that privacy as a separate legal concept has started gaining recognition.

The privacy laws of the United States have been framed in consonance with the Universal Declaration of Human Rights article on privacy, stating that "No one shall be subjected to arbitrary interference with his privacy, family, home or correspondence, nor to attacks upon his honour and reputation. Everyone has the right to protection of the law against such interference or attacks." [101]

Initially, the legal framework in America for privacy offered protection only in the cases of physical interference, which went on to gradually include the intellect and feelings of a person into the ambit of privacy. With the growth of media enterprises and their invasion into the precincts of personal lives, interest in privacy grew and privacy laws also started garnering attention once the scope of privacy rights broadened to include both the tangible and intangible possessions of an individual.

Privacy and Torts

An act of privacy invasion usually comprises one of four distinct torts: appropriation of name or likeness (using a person's name or identity for any purpose without consent); intrusion upon seclusion (a physical or electronic intrusion into an individual's private space); publicity placing a person in false light (publication of false or offensive information about a person); or publicity given to private life (publication of non-newsworthy, defamatory private facts

---

101 The Universal Declaration of Human Rights. http://www.un.org/en/universal-declaration-human-rights/ - More about the milestone document on Human Rights

about a person which offends the public's sense of decency). [102]

Appropriation of name or likeness as a violation of privacy occurs when the name, likeness, or identity of an individual is abused by another for benefit. The act of appropriation is done for advertising or trade purposes without the consent of the individual. It is the longest-recognized of all privacy torts. While it helps protect against commercial exploitation of an individual's personality, it cannot be applied in the cases of movies or works of fiction.

More than twenty states in the United States recognize appropriation as a tort that is characteristically diverse in cases of individuals and celebrities. The individual's right to privacy is a personal right to be left alone, the violation of which causes mental harm to the person. The celebrity's right to publicity, on the other hand, is a property right—a right to profit—the violation of which may lead to monetary loss for the celebrity in question.

Although an individual's privacy rights provides them an exclusive control over the commercial value of their name, it has no provision for claiming loss of money, as normally such people do not profit financially from their image. While celebrities can claim money in these matters, they cannot—as can a private person—assert infamy of their image.

Intrusion upon seclusion is an information-gathering and not a publication tort, whereby a person intentionally infringes upon the private affairs of another person. It is a physical, mechanical, or electronic intrusion into the seclusion of an individual and is deemed greatly offensive to a well-reasoned person. For example, hacking someone's computer or placing cameras in their bedroom.

An individual is entitled to privacy without any intrusion in reasonable circumstances, but in public places one cannot expect non-interference from others. As the common law of the United States holds, one can eavesdrop in public, or record anything they see, and must also assume they themselves could be filmed

---

102 Common Law Privacy Torts. https://web.archive.org/web/20130424122836/http://www.cas.okstate.edu/jb/faculty/senat/jb3163/privacytorts.html - More about the four types of privacy torts described here.

or photographed when in public. Also, as per previous court rulings, a person cannot be subjected to intrusion simply because she/he is suspected of having committed a crime.

Publicity placing a person in false light [103] is another type of privacy tort whereby such publicity is given to a person that it places her/him in a false light before the public; for example, a newspaper publishing the picture of an innocent person in a story about drug-addicts. It may also include stating someone's views in a false way to place them in a negative light or in a way which is highly offensive to any reasonable individual. A person's date of birth and military record are both matters of public record that may be disclosed without invading privacy.

Publicity given to private life [104] becomes a privacy tort when affairs concerning an individual's private life are publicized in such manner as to attract liability for privacy invasion. A matter which attracts such liability is one whose publication is either highly offensive to a reasonable individual or is not of justifiable concern to the populace; for example, publicizing the fact that one's teacher is a bisexual.

The public disclosure of private facts results in invasion of privacy when the facts are so intimate or embarrassing that their publication is an indignation to the public sense of decency. Mostly, it is the media which behaves recklessly in such cases by blurring the lines between information useful to public and sensational information gained by prying into private lives.

Common law also prevents business competitors from stealing trade secrets by forbidding engaging in a deceptive way to obtain confidential commercial information.

Privacy in the Constitution and Other Laws

The basis for right to privacy exists in the constitutional limits on the government's intrusion into citizens' personal matters, even during

---

103 http://injury.findlaw.com/torts-and-personal-injuries/invasion-of-privacy--false-light.html

104 Ibid.

passing of legislations or exercising of powers. However, the United States Constitution provides protection of privacy to citizens only against state offenders, and it is the previous court orders which extend relief in matters of privacy invasion by private individuals.

While the Constitution provides no explicit privacy right, various amendments made to it have broadened the scope of privacy laws in the United States. These amendments include the First Amendment, protecting privacy of beliefs; the Fourth Amendment, protecting privacy of persons and possessions; and the Fourteenth Amendment, protecting the right to due process of citizens, among other amendments.

The **First Amendment** (Privacy of Beliefs) in the Bill of Rights of the United States Constitution states that "Congress shall make no law respecting an establishment of religion, or prohibiting the free exercise thereof; or abridging the freedom of speech, or of the press; or the right of the people peaceably to assemble, and to petition the Government for a redress of grievances." [105]

The **Fourth Amendment** (Privacy of the Person and Possession) states "The right of the people to be secure in their persons, houses, papers, and effects, against unreasonable searches and seizures, shall not be violated, and no Warrants shall issue, but upon probable cause, supported by Oath or affirmation, and particularly describing the place to be searched, and the persons or things to be seized." [106]

The **Third Amendment** (Privacy of Home) provides that "No soldier shall, in time of peace be quartered in any house, without the consent of the Owner, nor in time of war, but in a manner to be prescribed by law." [107]

The **Ninth Amendment** states that "The enumeration in the Constitution, of certain rights, shall not be construed to deny or disparage others retained by the people." [108]

The "Liberty Clause" of the **Fourteenth Amendment** provides that no state shall "deprive any person of life, liberty or property,

---

105 The Right of Privacy. http://law2.umkc.edu/faculty/projects/ftrials/conlaw/rightofprivacy.html - More about US Supreme Court decisions and amendments to US Constitution w.r.t. Privacy laws.

106 Ibid.

107 Ibid.

108 Ibid.

without due process of law." [109]

The Privacy Act [110]

Apart from the amendments provided in the Bill of Rights, the United States government also introduced a Privacy Act in 1974 to afford citizens with safeguards against privacy invasion through the misuse of records by agencies of the Federal government. It is a "records management act" which provides safeguards in data processing only against the federal government and against state governments or the private sector.

"The act establishes a code of fair information practices that governs the collection, maintenance, use and dissemination of information about individuals that is maintained in systems of records by federal agencies." [111] The act mandates agencies to publically notify, through publishing in the Federal Register, their system of records, and bans the disclosure of personal information of an individual without their consent, thus protecting them against unwarranted privacy invasion.

Electronic Communications Privacy Act

The Electronic Communications Privacy Act (ECPA) of 1986 addresses the interception of wire, electronic, or oral communications, "while those communications are being made, are in transit, and when they are stored on computers." [112] It requires that government officials "seek and receive permission from a federal judge" before intercepting telephone conversations, emails, and data stored electronically.

The Electronic Communications Privacy Act thus prohibits attempted or actual interception, procurement, (e, or disclosure of oral, wire, or electronic communication, and use of information obtained through such measures, as evidence. It requires autho-

---

109 Constitution of United States. Amendments 11-27. http://www.archives.gov/exhibits/charters/constitution_amendments_11-27.html

110 https://www.aclu.org/united-states-bill-rights-first-10-amendments-constitution

111 Privacy Act of 1974. http://www.justice.gov/opcl/privacy-act-1974- Privacy Act of USA

112 Electronic Communications Privacy Act of 1986 https://it.ojp.gov/PrivacyLiberty/authorities/statutes/1285- More about the provisions of the act.

rization through a court order before setting a trace on a call, and also provides protection to the contents stored by service providers. The act is regularly updated to match pace with new technological advancements.

Right to Financial Privacy Act

The Right to Financial Privacy Act of 1978 protects the confidentiality of the financial records of an individual from the government. This act works in consonance with the Fourth Amendment in the Bill of Rights to protect personal bank records and to restrain financial institutions from obtaining "comprehensive" consent from their customers for release of records as barter in business transactions. It also provides customers full access to any disclosure of their information made by the institution, thus regulating their privacy. [113]

Fair Credit Reporting Act

The Fair Credit Reporting Act "governs access to consumer credit report records and promotes accuracy, fairness, and the privacy of personal information assembled by Credit Reporting Agencies (CRAs)." [114] It is the CRA through which municipal, state, or federal law enforcement agencies gain the basic identifying information of any consumer. Instituted in 1970, and amended in 1996 and 2003, this act ensures credit reporting in an accurate manner in the private sector.

Identity Theft and Assumption Deterrence Act

The Identity Theft and Assumption Deterrence Act was introduced to prevent the unauthorized use of another person's identity. Enacted in 1998, the act criminalizes the misuse of another

---

113 Levin, Avner & Nicholson, Mary Jo. "Privacy Law in the United States, the EU and Canada: The Allure of the Middle Ground." http://uoltj.ca/articles/vol2.2/2005.2.2.uoltj. Levin.357-395.pdf - More about US legislations protecting privacy of citizens from government as well as private sector. Refer to study all unreferenced privacy acts in the article.

114 Gramm Leach Bliley Act. https://www.ftc.gov/tips-advice/business-center/privacy-and-security/gramm-leach-bliley-act

individual's identity for a "felonious purpose," [115] sanctioning a penalty of imprisonment of up to fifteen years and a maximum fine of $250,000. It does not offer protection of one's privacy, but rather imposes criminal sanctions for privacy invasion. Establishing the person whose identity is stolen as a victim, the act also holds a provision for seeking restitution.

Financial Modernization Act

The Financial Modernization Act, commonly referred as the Gramm-Leach-Bliley Act (GLBA), was enacted in 1999 and is the first act which attempts regulation of privacy in the financial sector. It "requires financial institutions—companies that offer consumers financial products or services like loans, financial or investment advice, or insurance—to explain their information-sharing practices to their customers and to safeguard sensitive data." [116]

The Act takes a proactive stance by attempting active privacy regulation rather than capping government access to financial information. It directs financial institutions to form a privacy policy which is required to be brought to their customers' attention. This act provides customers the option to regulate the privacy of their information by sharing institutions' practices with them as well as by allowing them to opt out of information sharing with other businesses.

Children's Online Privacy Protection Act

The Children's Online Privacy Protection Act "imposes certain requirements on operators of websites or online services directed to children less than 13 years of age, and on operators of other websites or online services that have actual knowledge that they are collecting personal information online from a child under thirteen years of age." [117] Enforced in 1998, the Act aims to pro-

---

115 http://www.cap-press.com/pdf/Saltzburg%20Crim%20Law%20supplement%202016%20 WM.pdf

116 Children's Online Privacy Protection Rule. https://www.ftc.gov/enforcement/rules/ rulemaking-regulatory-reform-proceedings/childrens-online-privacy-protection-rule

117 https://www.ftc.gov/enforcement/rules/rulemaking-regulatory-reform-proceedings/chil- drens-online-privacy-protection-rule

tect the personal information of children from being collected and misused by commercial websites.

This Act mandates such commercial websites to furnish notice of their information-collection practices to the parents and to obtain their consent prior to any collection of personal information of children. It also requires such websites to allow parents to review and correct any information about their children which has been collected using these services.

Cable Communications Policy Act

The Cable Communications Policy Act incorporates several privacy measures to regulate the United States cable industry, [118] including not allowing companies to collect personal information without prior consent and restraining them from disclosing it to third parties. Likewise, the Videotape Privacy Protection Act also prohibits video stores from divulging the records of their customers without prior consent.

The above-mentioned acts are the examples of the piecemeal approach of the United States government towards maintaining and ensuring the privacy of its citizens in the absence of an explicit right to privacy in the Constitution. Beginning as early as the 20th century, the Supreme Court has endeavoured through its decisions, and the government through introduction of privacy-specific acts, to guarantee Americans a fairly expansive right to privacy.

The concept of privacy has received much consideration at various levels, with courts taking help from the Fourteenth Amendment's liberty clause to prohibit private institutions, as well as the State, from interfering in the private decisions of citizens. The court orders have, over the years, moved to encompass decisions regarding procreation, child rearing, marriage, etc., into the ambit of privacy.

It is argued by judges that the liberty clause of the Fourteenth Amendment forbids the state or any of its agencies from engaging in such conduct which is conflicting to the idea of a state formed on the "concept of ordered liberty." [119] Keeping this in mind, the court decisions pertaining to privacy gain a positive

---

118 https://www.fcc.gov/media/engineering/cable-television

119 https://supreme.justia.com/cases/federal/us/364/206/case.html

light, thus providing a new dimension to the privacy doctrine.

It is this concept of ordered liberty which led the United States Supreme Court in 1969 to conclude unanimously that an individual has the right to possess and view pornography under the right to privacy. Justice Marshall wrote in this regard: "Whatever may be the justifications for other statutes regulating obscenity, we do not think they reach into the privacy of one's own home. If the First Amendment means anything, it means that a State has no business telling a man, sitting alone in his own house, what books he may read or what films he may watch." [120]

Drawing support from the first, fourth, ninth, and fourteenth Amendments of the Bill of Rights, judges since the 1970s have pushed the sector of privacy into unchartered frontiers by extending the right to privacy to include women's rights to undergo abortion (Roe vs. Wade, 1972) or engaging in homosexual sodomy (Lawrence vs. Texas, 2003). The government and courts view upholding the personal choices of individuals as central to their autonomy and dignity and to the liberty protected by the Fourteenth Amendment.

The country is treading a path of privacy laws leading to citizens having full rights to engage in reasonably appropriate conduct without any intervention from outside influences; the State cannot demean their existence or control their conduct in any way. The right to liberty under the provision of the Due Process Clause acts as a promise on the behalf of the Constitution that "there is no realm of personal liberty which the government can enter." [121]

However, the future of privacy protection remains dangling on a loose string, partly because the Acts for privacy protection seem to occasionally clash with well-established constitutional provisions, creating gaps in privacy laws. Another reason is the increasing technological advancement, leading to novel ideas for invading the privacy of individuals.

Americans are becoming increasingly concerned about DNA

---

120 http://law2.umkc.edu/faculty/projects/ftrials/conlaw/rightofprivacy.html
121 https://www.law.cornell.edu/wex/due_process

[122]databases and video surveillance providing their personal information to the government, or if already in the hands of government, then about the abuse of that information. Although such protection from government is warranted, protecting one's privacy from falling into the hands of potential abusers in the private sector also deserves equal, if not more, attention.

What terrifies Americans is not the existence of databases of their personal information in public or private organizations but the government's access to such databases, indicating that their conception of privacy is largely based on the protection of their liberty, rather than their dignity. In light of this view of Americans about their privacy, most privacy laws and acts are instituted keeping in mind the protection of citizens from harm, and not with the protection of their privacy as the main objective.

The American privacy-law scenario needs to formally extend the protection of privacy to the private sector. Such renewed emphasis on the concept of privacy is needed, not only to protect Americans from the prying eyes of the government, but also to ensure their safety in an ever-increasing perilous milieu, where a small leak of information may become a big gain for nefarious elements or organizations.

The most frequently quoted statement in this regard says that "The makers of our Constitution understood the need to secure conditions favourable to the pursuit of happiness, and the protections guaranteed by this are much broader in scope." [123] The laws pertaining to protection against invasion of privacy must not only uphold the sanctity of an individual and of his intellect and feelings, but also work to protect the misuse of related information by any agencies, public or private.

122 Deoxyribonucleic acid (DNA) is a molecule that carries the genetic instructions used in the growth, development, functioning and reproduction of all known living organisms and many viruses.

123 Justice Brandeis's dissent in Olmstead vs US (1928). http://law2.umkc.edu/faculty/projects/ftrials/conlaw/rightofprivacy.html

PART III: SECURITY IN THE AGE OF TERRORISM

Conceptualizing Security

Security has been conceptualized as a continuing process—a quasi-central virtue acting as a vehicle for political actions. Maria Julia Trombetta defines securitization as the very political act of defining what counts as a threat. Through the label "security," problems are turned into existential threats that require emergency measures, which may include breaking otherwise binding rules or governing by decrees rather than by democratic decisions. [124] French scholar Thierry Balzacq, who specializing in International Relations Theory, conceptualizes security as a sustained strategic practice aimed at convincing a target audience to accept the claim that a specific development is threatening enough to deserve an immediate policy to alleviate it. [125] Scott Watson conceptualizes security "not as an objective condition but rather as a process marked by the intersubjective establishment of an existential threat with sufficient saliency to have political effects." [126]

Security is a double-edged sword. Organizations implement

---

124 Trombetta, Maria Julia, "Environmental security and climate change: analysing the discourse," *Cambridge Review of International Affairs*, 21:4, 2008: 585-602.

125 Balzacq, Thierry, "The Three Faces of Securitization: Political Agency, Audience and Context," *European Journal of International Relations*, 11 , 2005: 171- 201

126 Watson, Scott "The 'human' as referent object? Humanitarianism as securitization," *Security Dialogue* 42:1, 2011: 3-20.

security measures to protect digitally stored and transmitted information. In fact, the government mandates protection of personal information in the health care and financial services industries. On the other hand, the government compromises privacy and demands access to protected information in the name of preserving national security. [127]

Privacy and security are part of the legal frameworks for Human Rights. According to Article 12 (85) of the Universal Declaration of Human Rights (UDHR), "No one shall be subjected to arbitrary interference with his privacy, family, home or correspondence, or to attacks upon his honour and reputation. Everyone has the right to the protection of the law against such interference or attacks." [128] Similarly, Article 29 of UDHR states that "in the exercise of his rights and freedoms, everyone shall be subject only to such limitations as are determined by law solely for the purpose of securing due recognition and respect for the rights and freedoms of others and of meeting the just requirements of morality, public order and the general welfare in a democratic society."

For Derek Bambauer, security is the interface between privacy and information, or rather a mediator between information and privacy selections. Security defines which privacy choices can be implemented. Security and privacy interact on two levels. First, different security architectures make privacy regimes more or less tenable, thereby influencing their development and adoption. The second interaction occurs with the selection of the security precautions to be taken. For Bambauer, "Privacy determines who ought to be able to access, use, and alter information. It justifies these choices with reference to larger values— values that compete for priority and attention. Security implements that set off choice." [129] Bambauer finally argues that security failings should be penalized more readily, and more heavily, than

---

127 Konstantaras, Andrews, "Understanding the balance between privacy and security," Techtarget.com, 2003, URL: http://searchsecurity.techtarget.com/Understanding-the-balance-between-privacy-and-security.

128 United Nations, *Universal Declaration of Human Rights*, URL: http://www.un.org/en/universal-declaration-human-rights/.

129 Bambauer, Derek E, "Privacy Versus Security," *Journal of Criminal Law & Criminology*, 103:3, 2013: 667-684. http://scholarlycommons.law.northwestern.edu/jclc/vol103/iss3/2.

privacy ones, "because there are no competing moral claims to resolve and because security flaws make all parties worse off." [130]

Analysts suggest ways in which a balance between privacy and security can be achieved. Andrews Konstantaras suggests that it is fallacious to treat the two concepts as mutually exclusive domains and even more erroneous to regard them as inherently contradictory. The author opines that a public-private sector partnership is the key to achieving the balance between privacy issues and security measures, and remarks that:

> [The] best way to resolve [the conflict] is with more collaboration and, yes, compromise between security and privacy. Many conflicts can be avoided if the public and private sectors work together to ensure that security and privacy considerations are addressed and adequately represented at all stages in the development of computer systems, corporate policies and government regulations. [131]

Peter Roff suggests that the creation of a meaningful balance between privacy and security is a major prerequisite in the information age and suggests that in order to achieve this balance, governments should oversee the activities of those who are empowered by law to invade our privacy or monitor our electronic communication. [132] According to Amnesty International, any measures to interfere with privacy must always be proportionate to a legitimate aim being pursued, and justifications for doing so must be subject to judicial oversight and parliamentary scrutiny that are transparent,

---

130 Ibid.

131 Konstantaras, Andrews, "Understanding the balance between privacy and security," Techtarget.com, 2003, URL: http://searchsecurity.techtarget.com/Understanding-the-balance-between-privacy-and-security.

132 Roff, Peter, "A Better Way to Balance Privacy and Security," *U.S News & World Report*, August 27 2013, URL: http://www.usnews.com/opinion/blogs/peter-roff/2013/08/27/young-americans-on-the-nsa-and-the-balance-of-privacy

robust, and independent. [133]

National Security—Understanding the Stakes and Addressing the Threat

The parameters of privacy and security have changed with the rapid growth of technology, and today every organization is welcoming new security measures to maintain its confidentiality. Some of the challenges organizations face involves failure to maintain to maintain surveillance due to inability to properly care for the physical technological equipment, and the growing popularity of wireless internet. Wireless internet connection has become increasingly popular around the world, and provides more comfortable use of internet with regards to physical mobility and avoiding entanglement with wires; however, these networks are also more susceptible to digital break-ins.

The omnipresence of technology and the growing branches of the internet are fostering a world where every real entity is being operated side by side with a virtual counterpart. The internet is considered a virtual global village, bolstering globalization. The adoption of the standards of the internet age and infusion of it into the organizational structures of businesses has been far-reaching. Today every organization, irrespective of the industry, has a virtual infrastructure on the internet. Today, everyone is just a click away from their destinations. Networking sites do not neglect any opportunity to gather the data of people around the world. Some of the dominating giants of the digital world are Facebook and Twitter, which have shaken the world from their inception and have opened the doors for full access to the private lives of individuals. Privacy techniques of organizations have moved beyond their own physical premises with the adoption of cloud computing. Security measures of organizations are now being operated through an interconnected virtual

---

133 Bochenek, Michael (2013), UN response to surveillance must strike balance between privacy and security, amnesty.org, 25 October 2013, https://www.amnesty.org/en/latest/news/2013/10/un-response-surveillance-must-strike-balance-between-privacy-and-security/.

web of security systems. This advancement has been helping the world to manage the systems judiciously and is proving to be a timesaving investment for organizations.

The emergence of smart phones has also contributed to managing the privacy and security of data. Smart phones use operating systems, much like a compact computer but with some limitations. Irrespective of the operating system, all phones have an option provided in them to link a web account to the phone data. All of an individual's information is then synchronized within the virtual world. Should a phone be lost or damaged, then private information that has been linked with the account can be recovered through the virtual backup.

With this rapid technological revolution, cyber-crime has advanced in tandem, and the possibility looms that the privacy and security of an individual or organization will be breached to the detriment of individuals, companies, or even nations. Cyber policies in every nation should be strengthened with more advanced technological solutions; otherwise, the world of the virtual giant may eventually be the only world that is left.

Our dependency on the virtual world has made the human race more susceptible to the risk of intervention from unknown sources, causing unimaginable menace. Technology has enabled us to store huge amounts of data in minimal storage space in the virtual world, locked behind passwords and usernames, which assure the safety of the identity of every individual user. These security precautions, however, are becoming less effective, making the security of users vulnerable to exposure. Password protected accounts in the past have been hacked and caused breaking news situations across the world.

A security breach is any incident that results in an unauthorized access of data, applications, services, networks, and/or devices by bypassing their underlying security mechanisms. A security breach occurs when an individual or an application illegitimately enters a private, confidential, or unauthorized logical IT perimeter. A security breach is also known as a security violation. A security breach happens when data or records containing personal information, such as social security numbers, credit card or bank account numbers, or driver's license numbers are lost, stolen, or accessed improperly. This kind of information can be used by criminals to commit identity theft. [134]

Hackers may breach secure accounts with utilitarian motives, causing financial damage, or they may simply aim to shame security agencies and flaunt their own capabilities. There have been many such incidents where high security risks were detected, including hacks into intelligence service sites. The threats scale from harming an individual to spying on confidential national documents.

Security was put at risk at the national level when a certain group of hackers hacked into the security accounts of the investigation agencies of the countries like the United States and North Korea. Cyber-security, which involves protecting both data and people, is facing multiple threats, notably cybercrime and online industrial espionage, both of which are growing rapidly. A recent estimate by the Centre for Strategic and International Studies (CSIS), a think-tank, puts the annual global cost of digital crime and intellectual-property theft at $445 billion—a sum roughly equivalent to the Gross Domestic Product (GDP) of a small, wealthy European country, such as Austria. [135]

Terrorists or agents of hostile powers could mount attacks on companies and systems that control vital parts of an economy, including power stations, electrical grids, and communications networks. Such attacks are hard to achieve, but are not impossible. One precedent is the destruction in 2010 of centrifuges at a nuclear facility in Iran by a computer program known as Stuxnet, the handiwork of American and Israeli software experts.

An attack on JP Morgan compromised the personal information of 76 million households; it was considered an invasion of the United States financial system and a threat

---

134 Janssen, Cory, Security Breach; Techopedia; http://www.techopedia.com/definition/29060/security-breach

135 http://www.europarl.europa.eu/RegData/etudes/STUD/2015/536470/IPOL_STU(2015)536470_EN.pdf

to American national security. [136] This act of hacking was a financial setback for the nation. Hacking into accounts of industrialists and businessmen has created a wave of undesirable scenarios. PF Chang's, White Lodging, and Goodwill industries are some of the companies who have been victims of such an ordeal. To add to the list, even the computers in the White House were hacked, exposing the vulnerability of the supposedly best-protected people in the country. Apart from financial loss, the hackers also aim at creating subsequent incidents, causing terror amongst users.

There have been media hacks where the digital intruders exposed personal information and pictures of famous people. The iCloud hack was one such incident, and the hacked Gmail accounts of 4.93 million users by Russian hackers was also an embarrassing incident. Another recent one involved Sony Pictures, whose account was hacked prior to the movie release of "The Interview." A message circulated to theatres in the United States threatening a terror attack as consequence to screenings of the film. Such incidents are a slap in the face of the developed world and reveal that no one is safe; the digital claws of hackers are not so far away from your throat.

The biggest day-to-day threats faced by companies and governmental agencies come from crooks and spooks hoping to steal financial data and trade secrets. Smarter, better-organized hackers are making life tougher for the cyber-defenders but, even so, a number of things can be done to keep everyone safer than they are now. One idea is to encourage internet-service providers (ISPs), or the companies that manage internet connections, to shoulder more responsibility for identifying and helping to clean up computers infected with malicious software (malware). Another is to find ways to ensure that software developers produce code with fewer flaws so that hackers have fewer security holes to exploit.

Prevention is only possible in these cases through pre-

---

136 Security Breach, North Carolina Department of Justice. Retrieved April 1, 2015 from http://www.ncdoj.gov/ Help-for-Victims/ID-Theft-Victims/Security-Breach.aspx (footnotes 5,6,7and 8); Giles, Martin. (2014). Defending the Digital Frontier, the Economist. Retrieved from http://www.economist.com; ibid for 6 & 7 ; Sanchez, Raf. (2014, October 3). Senator: JP Morgan data breach is threat to US national security. The Telegraph.

cautions, on both the users and the site creator's side. Security can be maintained through vigilance and following simple protocols that every website provides while creating accounts on any social medium. Policies to ensure safety in the digital world are being continually incorporated in developed nations. Sanctions are being posed by United States President Barack Obama on hackers to ensure national security in the country. The European Union has been more vigilant in this respect and has already formulated policies to keep their citizens safe.

National Security Laws

Following the misfortune and pandemonium caused by the Paris attacks in November of 2015, the attention of the international community has once again been drawn to the geopolitical dynamics of the world. The resulting implications were gigantic, with the United States leading a coalition to launch airstrikes against Daesh, and France declaring a war against the terrorist outfit. With nations fearing for the safety of their citizens, massive security checks and measures are being introduced at several levels.

While the attacks by Daesh have reawakened the world to a terror of wars over ethnic or religious identity, the expanding economy has stitched various nations together and been of greater use to the militant groups than to their target nations. The growing global economy has intensified nuclear dangers across the world, imperiling peace and pushing nations to seek stronger and more durable approaches to national security. With threats to political independence and territorial integrity and security, several nations have supported efforts to secure a peaceful and co-operative international environment, indicating a growing universal ambition and commitment to sovereignty.

As nations move forward to face the challenges set by terrorists, they must recognize the importance of their security laws as a path not only to contain such threats but also to forge cooperative approaches with other nations. Security laws play an unprecedented role in any nation in preparing for the future. Security laws must address intelligence and military assistance to form a forward-moving integrated strategy.

On paper, the notion of national security seems straight-forward—the government should protect the nation and its citizens by any means against any kind of national emergency. Initially focussed on military strength, the ambit of the national security of a nation has broadened into a complex amalgamation of diplomacy, economic power, political power, and all such values which sponsor national security.

The International Encyclopaedia of the Social Sciences defines the concept of national security as "the ability of a nation to protect its internal values from external threats." [137] Delineating further, Amos Jordon and William Taylor said that "National security has a more extensive meaning than protection from physical harm; it also implies protection, through a variety of means, of vital economic and political interest, the loss of which could threaten fundamental values and the vitality of the state." [138]

"A nation has security when it does not have to sacrifice its legitimate interest to avoid war, and is able, if challenged, to maintain them by war," [139] wrote Walter Lippmann in 1943. In consonance to this definition, several nations hold the view of national security as a condition "where the most cherished values and beliefs, democratic way of life, institutions of governance and unity, welfare and well-being as a nation and people are permanently protected and continuously enhanced." [140]

The security laws of various nations prescribe security regulations to integrate the intelligence community and to help maintain the privacy and strengthen the liberties of citizens. In 1986, United States President Ronald Reagan, in a

---

137 Prabhakaran Paleri, National Security: Imperatives and Challenges, Tata McGraw-Hill Education, 2008 at 45.

138 Romm, Joseph J. Defining National Security: The Nonmilitary Aspects. Page-5. https://books.google.co.in/books?id=shxDOnuVcyYC&q=National+Security+Policy&source=gbs_word_cloud_r&cad=5#v=snippet&q=National%20Security%20Policy&f=false

139 Ibid.

140 Threat to National Security. http://www.dlsu.edu.ph/offices/sps/rotc/pdf/ms1/threat-NatlSecurity.pdf

top secret directive, wrote: "The primary objective of United States security policy is to protect the integrity of our democratic institutions and promote a peaceful global environment in which they can thrive." [141]

In United Kingdom or European law, the term national security is not specifically defined, which allows governments to retain the flexibility necessary to ensure adaptation to changing circumstances. However, in matters pertaining to government policies of the United Kingdom, this term is taken to refer to "the security and well-being of the United Kingdom as a whole." [142] The concept involves not just investigating and containing active threats, but also identifying possible future threats. The European Security Strategy (ESS), adopted in 2003 by the European Council, provides the conceptual framework for the Common Foreign and Security Policy (CFSP), including what would later become the Common Security and Defense Policy (CSDP). For the first time, this document, titled "A Secure Europe in a Better World," [143] presents a brief but comprehensive and analytical discussion about the European Union's security environment, the key security challenges, and the subsequent political implications. The European Security Strategy picks out five key threats against National Security: terrorism, regional conflicts, state failure, organized crime, and explosion of weapons of mass destruction.

The Russian Federation defines national security as "a system of views on how to secure the individual, society and the state against external and internal threats in every sphere of national life." [144] National security is interpreted as "the security of its multinational people as the bearer of sovereignty." [145]

---

141 The Purpose of National Security Policy, Declassified. http://fas.org/blogs/secrecy/2012/10/nsdd_238/

142 What is national security? https://www.mi5.gov.uk/home/about-us/what-we-do/protecting-national-security.html

143 https://www.consilium.europa.eu/uedocs/cmsUpload/78367.pdf

144 National Security Concept of the Russian Federation. http://archive.mid.ru//bdomp/ns-osndoc.nsf/1e5f0de28fe77fdcc32575d900298676/36aba64ac09f737fc32575d9002bb-f31!OpenDocument

145 Ibid.

With the expansive range of threats increasing with the involvement of militant outfits and drug cartels, amongst other traditional inter-country rivalries, measures to secure national security have also turned over a new leaf world-wide. Common measures in this regard involve use the use of diplomacy to isolate threats, exploiting economic power to facilitate cooperation, implementing measures and legislations for emergencies, and maintaining advanced armed forces.

The laws concerning the national security of any nation aim to establish integrated procedures and policies for all governmental departments and agencies to set in place a comprehensive agenda for national security. This helps the nation to stand prepared in the face of an adversity or a potential threat to its security and to take requisite actions for safety.

Issuing the National Security Strategy in 2010, United States President Barack Obama talked about national security as including "military security, energy security, environment integrity, and economic competitiveness" [146] and complementing the efforts of the United States "to integrate homeland security with national security, including the seamless coordination among Federal, state, and governments to prevent, protect against, and respond to threats and natural disasters." [147]

The laws relating to national security do not just make available military might to provide for national security requirements, but also to analyze the potential ramifications of national emergencies on the availability of resources and production capability, and recommend development of preparedness measures for the same, so as to meet the needs of national security.

Another factor to be kept in mind with regard to security laws is that today the foremost threat to any country is posed by terrorist outfits, whose members are ready to face their own deaths in the name of achieving their objectives. War-

---

146 https://www.whitehouse.gov/sites/default/files/docs/2015_national_security_strategy.pdf

147 National Security Strategy https://www.whitehouse.gov/sites/default/files/rss_viewer/national_security_strategy.pdf

ring with such an entity, not specific to a physical place or country, makes it an onerous task for any nation to ensure its security. Attempts made to date by nations to defend against terrorist activity have not been on par with expectations and have failed to mollify people's fears about their safety. The unfortunate truth remains that security measures are only preventive in nature and thus are effective only to a certain point, failing to underwrite complete security protection.

If terrorist groups are bent on attacking a nation and dying in the process of supporting their staunch beliefs, it is the intelligence and security legislation which come to the aid of the nation—not much otherwise can be done. With relaxed immigration and citizenship rules, terrorists can easily enter any country, study or work there, and attack the same land with weapons of mass destruction when they find a suitable time.

Focusing on renewed action plans for ensuring security, the national security laws of most developed nations have done more to remove liberties from citizens than to directly minimize or eliminate the threats. It is the citizens with no intention of causing harm to others who suffer, and increasingly will, at the hands of such security laws, rather than those who endeavour to cause harm. Such myopia in security laws, with focus only on issues like nuclear weapons of mass destruction, military defense, cyber security threats, etc., serves a regressive purpose which could be exploited. Although vital in addressing the concept of national security, these concerns must be integrated along the lines of such issues as economic sustainability and infrastructure to ensure a durable approach. If internal threats and concerns remain ineffective, the tools meant to enable the country could be used against it.

The present geopolitical scenario remains murkier than ever, especially in the context of the Daesh and Syrian refugee predicament. Every nation is striving for stronger tactics to defend their homeland and commit to a resilient front, but a united approach of various nations to the same problem has yet to be formally and effectively recognized in order to ensure a solution to the current crisis.

No nation, no matter how powerful, can stand up to these global threats alone and win. An integrated strategy composed of sturdy alliances among nations must form a key component of the security laws of those nations as a path to successfully forming strong and dynamic independence and sovereignty. Forging cooperative coalitions among countries is the way forward for effective national security laws.

National security laws must be amended to incorporate current world expectations for the government, and military assistance and intelligence must also be addressed accordingly. Renewed advances in the leadership and interests concerning national security, if addressed effectively, can prove to be the primary defining force in fighting the global war against terrorism. Keeping in mind that the concept of national security entails protecting the interest of one's land and citizens, it also must avoid infringing upon the national security of other nations. The provisions should thus clearly delineate both what the government is expected to do and what it is expected not to do.

Focus should be concentrated on the influence of soft power (an approach which attracts and co-opts) and hard power (use of force or coercion) over security roles in order to do away with the debate over their trade-offs. While it is common fallacy to assume that the two powers are interchangeable, the truth remains that each power holds its own unprecedented importance in the security dynamics of any country and it is inaccurate to suggest that soldiers could take the place of diplomats and vice-versa. [148]

The concept of national security becomes redundant if safeguarding the interests of one's country means assault on another country without any reasonable provocation. Protecting the integrity of the systems and domestic institutions of one's nation does not by any means indicate that such acts should be allowed to bear a negative impact on foreign nations. Nations are free to exert power to influence others so long it does not interfere with the sovereignty of any other

---

148 Holmes, Kim R. What is National Security? http://index.heritage.org/military/2015/important-essays-analysis/national-security/ - More about the importance of "hard power" in maintaining security of a nation under the head "Focusing the Idea of National Security."

country.

The objective of security must be carried out by maintaining a balance of power between one's security and one's interests in connection with friends and allies. This act of balancing provides a guarantee of freedom to all nations from being negatively impacted by a developed or powerful nation, and ensures support of allies in maintenance of national security.

National security does not need to, and no longer can, be confined only to the breadth of one's country. In a world which is characterised by interconnection, events in one part of the world are inextricably influencing other parts of the world to such an extent that a development on the other side of the world can easily call a country's national security into question. In the recent past, time and again, it was reaffirmed that the fundamental connection between national security and international cooperation is crucial for world peace. There is a need to fabricate national laws for security which shape the international order for fighting the undercurrent of global challenges.

Incorporating national security as an international issue has several advantages, the most crucial being that it appeals to all nations by reason of common elements in security policy. While providing a convenient frame for reference, it opens up possibilities for discussion and comparison of security laws, and the possible amendments that could be introduced. It makes room for contemplation on common problems and threats faced by countries and the potential steps to contain such threats.

Adding a dimension of conflict resolution to discussions over international threats automatically augments cooperation among nations. Likewise, consideration of common international concerns will result in gradual increase of security for all nations involved. Constructing an international frame for security concerns will help the nations involved to understand the magnitude and composite role of internal as well as external factors that form the national security quandary.

By viewing national security in continuum with international security, the nations involved can begin to envisage the same set of values, which ultimately will help maintain not just national but international security. The application of varied techniques to tackle security issues will forge better bonds between nations and stimulate feelings of cooperation, support, and peace.

Initiatives to form international cooperation for protection and prevention against threats must be met with seamless coordination amongst agencies at various levels. Also, the cultivation of any international/national order for maintenance of security must be integrated with an uncompromising commitment to the upholding of human rights, rule of law, and democracy, the absence of which simply fails to meet the purpose of national security.

The trajectory of action in the case of any national security breach must be guided by a commitment to justice and rejection of human rights abuses, including torture and inhumane treatment of suspects. Building a foundation based on human rights will help nations garner increasingly consistent support from each other and aid in outlining a steady support system.

Above all, the commitment of a nation to extend the promise of national security to all citizens and to build a strong foundation for support in cases of emergency can only materialize when the nation is aware of its own strengths and shortcomings. It is only through this awareness that an international architecture of security can be made effective by complementing the strengths and weaknesses of each nation.

For the maintenance of peace, advancing of prosperity and in dealing with the challenges thwarting these goals, renewed efforts and legislations are required, not in isolation by each nation, but as a collective whole. It is these collaborative actions which will help serve such universal interests as preventing nuclear war, securing nuclear resources and supplies, and combating extremism and armed conflicts.

In today's interconnected world, expanding the outreach to several nations provides an opportunity to seal support and cooperation from them, along with gaining a wider perspective on matters of security. The cornerstone of allied international efforts lies in the shared interests and motives of the nations to serve the common purpose of national security through maintaining international security. Effective partnerships with influential nations increase their cooperation with each other not only in bilateral matters but also in issues of global concern.

When nations engage in their defense and security arrangements, it is imperative that they take suitable account of the implications their policies and legislations will bear on the security of other nations. It is fundamental to the efforts of promotion of a just world that each nation's efforts for security facilitate cooperation, and not competition, with other nations so as to address the existing problems without holding back.

Mobilization of international coalitions is becoming increasingly important to security laws of any nation, as it not only provides a constructive and divergent approach to security issues, but also underpins the commitment of a nation to an international order based on unity and peace. Constructive national steps are being pursued by nations in order to generate effective results on their territory and on international land.

While the allied efforts for international security require active participation and commitment from all nations involved, the paramount thrust lies on extensive adoption of security measures designed by countries in coherence with one another. Rather than the pursuance of unilateral benefits, it is the co-operative approach for promoting international security which will prove beneficial in the long run.

As a report by the United Nations Department for Disarmament Affairs suggests:

> Only by recognizing that security is not divisible, either in its military, economic, social and political dimensions or as between its national and international aspects, can nations evolve the co-operative measures necessary to achieve security in an interdependent age. This requires a comprehensive and co-operative

approach to international security. [149]

Adding further, the report asserts:

The unrestrained pursuit of national security interests at the expense of others is not conducive to international security and may even lead to disaster. With the existence of nuclear weapons such policies constitute a potential threat to the survival of mankind. It is imperative that nations reconcile the contradictions between individual national security interest and the overall interest of the international security and peace. [150]

Addressing Security in Canada

Canada has, over the years, gained popularity as a "middle power" in international politics. Popular for its propensity to pursue multilateral solutions, the country's security and foreign policies are characterised by mutual aid and peace-keeping. The North American nation also plays a crucial role in the dynamics of international cooperation.

Emphasising international security and peacekeeping through international organizations and coalitions, Canada continues to reinforce the mediation role which it has maintained throughout the 20th century to present day. On the international stage, Canada has been a long-term constructive player in the promotion of international peace and justice by refraining from a unilateralist approach.

Canada has been instrumental in key events, such as endorsing peace during the Cold War, the formation of the United Nations peacekeeping force, opposing the system of apartheid in South Africa, and refusing to join the American war under Bush against Iraq. Active involvement in the resolution of these disputes outside of its own province has put Canada in a pivotal position, despite not being a superpower.

---

149 Paragraph 60, Concepts of Security, Report by UN Department for Disarmament Affairs http://www.un.org/disarmament/HomePage/ODAPublications/DisarmamentStudySeries/ PDF/SS-14.pdf

150 Ibid.

151

Canada has a reputation for working actively for the representation of smaller nations in the United Nations Organization and for the prevention of their dominance and exploitation by various superpowers. This country's involvement in numerous humanitarian missions and peacekeeping efforts has led to its being elected to the United Nations Security Council several times; Canada has played a crucial role in the peacekeeping programs of the United Nations since 1945.

It was by successfully deescalating the Suez Crisis that Canada's formerly insignificant global image gained credibility. [152] This put it on the global front as a nation endeavouring for the "common good" of every nation. John Kirton, director of the G8 Research Group at the University of Toronto, asserts that GlobalScan surveys show that the affection people feel for Canada is especially directed towards the "demographic openness and multicultural tolerance." [153]

A founding member of the United Nations, Canada is a member of the G20, the World Trade Organization, the Organization for Economic Cooperation and Development, and various other forums and international organizations for political, economic, or cultural matters. The country also has historic associations with the United Kingdom, United States of America, France, and member countries of the Commonwealth of Nations.

Canada has cooperated with many of its allies to address the threats to Canada's security from violent extremists. More often than not, the threats to Canadian security have been linked with terrorism-related developments abroad. The emergence of violent extremist groups in Canada is also attributed to international developments. Such home-grown

151 Joshee, Reva & Johnson, Lauri. "Multicultural Educational Policies in Canada and the United States." https://books.google.co.in/books?id=I8jr_pE3YPwC&pg=PA23&redir_esc=y#v=onepage&q&f=false – more about Canadian society.

152 Tattrie, Jon. "Suez Crisis," July 2, 2006. http://www.thecanadianencyclopedia.ca/en/article/suez-crisis/ - More about the Suez Crisis.

153 Westhead, Rick. "Canada's Interntaionl Reputation Rising: Survey," May 23, 2013. http://www.thestar.com/news/world/2013/05/23/canadas_international_reputation_rising_survey.html - More about Canada's international reputation and GlobalScan survey.

groups are heavily involved in recruitment of supporters, raising of funds, and acquiring support by any means possible for the propagation of their agendas.

Canada, like any other country, is not immune to terrorism and is home to various domestic and international terrorist groups which continue to challenge Canadian authorities over a variety of issues. The past few decades have witnessed killings of several hundred Canadian civilians on domestic lands as well as international, from Kenya, to Bali, to New York. To tackle the issue, the Government of Canada needs to undertake supplementary measures for the protection of its citizens.

The violent extremism by radical Islamist groups spearheads the threat Canada faces against such forces, with several radical Islamist groups marking the country as an acknowledged target for their sectarian pursuits. Domestic and international extremist pose a threat to Canadian security, either by a direct attack against the country or by use of Canadian territory to support global missions. [154]

With the heightened trepidation of terrorism and the undercurrent of anxiety about personal safety rippling through individuals all over the world, it is high time that the international community severed its old habits of mistrust in favour of building a common ground in order to ensure not just the security of any one prominent nation, but security worldwide. Though security measures are integral, they need to be framed in a transparent way so that an individual's right to privacy is not invaded.

Defining Terrorism

"Terrorism has become the systematic weapon of a war that knows no borders or seldom has a face." – Jacques Chirac

The root word "terror" (from the Latin "terrere"—"to frighten") entered the Western European lexicon through French in the fourteenth century and was first used in En-

---

154 Building Resilience against Terrorism: Canada's Counter-Terrorism Strategy. http://www.publicsafety.gc.ca/cnt/rsrcs/pblctns/rslnc-gnst-trrrsm/index-eng.aspx - More about terrorism threat in Canada.

glish in 1528. [155] "Terrorism" gained its political connotations from its use during the French Revolution during the regime de la terreur of Robespierre that saw the execution of more than 17,000 people. [156] Terrorism, initially associated with state-perpetrated violence, was used for describing non-state actors following its application to the French and Russian anarchists of the 1880s and 1890s.

In the 20th century, terrorism came to be associated with acts of violence that caused destruction of life and property. In 1930, during the League of Nations period, a definition of the term was proposed at the Third Conference for the Unification of Penal Law at Brussels, which read: "The intentional use of means capable of producing a common danger that represents an act of terrorism on the part of anyone making use of crimes against life, liberty or physical integrity of persons or directed against private or state property with the purpose of expressing or executing political or social ideas." [157] The most significant early modern attempt to define terrorism as an international crime was undertaken by the League of Nations in 1937 with the Convention for the Prevention and Punishment of Terrorism. Article 1(2) of the convention cumulatively defined "acts of terrorism" as "criminal acts directed against a State and intended or calculated to create a state of terror in the minds of particular persons, or a group of persons or the general public." [158]

The United States Department of Defense has defined terrorism as "the calculated use of unlawful violence or threat of unlawful violence to inculcate fear; intended to coerce or to intimidate governments or societies in the pursuit of goals that are generally political, religious, or ideological."

---

155 Schmidt, Alex (1988) The Problems of Defining Terrorism, in Martha Crenshaw & John Pimlott eds., *Encyclopaedia of World Terrorism*, New York: ME Sharpe.

156 Higonet, Patrick (2012), Robespierre's Rules for Radicals, Foreign Affairs, July, /August, URL https://www.foreignaffairs.com/reviews/2012-07-01/robespierre-s-rules-radicals.

157 Saul Ben (2005), Attempts to Define Terrorism in International Law, Netherlands International Law Review, LII, 57: 83, URL: http://www.cicte.oas.org/olat/documents/Defining%20TERRORISM%20in%20International%20Law.pdf.

158 Saul Ben (2005), Attempts to Define Terrorism in International Law, Netherlands International Law Review, LII, 57: 83, URL: http://www.cicte.oas.org/olat/documents/Defining%20TERRORISM%20in%20International%20Law.pdf.

[159] Violence, intimidation and fear form key components of this definition, and each of these elements produces terror among the victims.

The Federal Bureau of Investigation defines terrorism as "the lawful use of force and violence against persons or property to intimidate or coerce a government, the civilian population, or any segment thereof, in furtherance of political or social objectives." [160] On a similar note, the British Government defined terrorism in 1974 as "the use of violence for political end, and includes any use of violence for the purpose of putting the public, or any section of the public, in fear." [161]

In 1992, the United Nations defined terrorism as "an anxiety-inspiring method of repeated violent action, employed by (semi-) clandestine individual, group or state actors, for idiosyncratic, criminal or political reasons, whereby – in contrast to assassination – the direct targets of violence are not the main targets." [162]

In the United States Code (USC) of the United States of America, terrorism has been defined as "violent acts or acts dangerous to human life that violate federal or state law and appear to be intended to intimidate or coerce a civilian population, or to influence the policy of a government by intimidation or coercion or to affect the conduct of a government by mass destruction, assassination or kidnapping." [163]

The United Kingdom Terrorism Act (2000) defines terrorism as:

The use of threat of action designed to influence the government or an international governmental organization or to intimidate the public, or a section of the

---

159 What is Terrorism? http://www.terrorism-research.com/ - Definitions of terrorism as provided by various agencies

160 https://www.fbi.gov/stats-services/publications/terrorism-2002-2005

161 http://www.esrc.ac.uk/public-engagement/social-science-for-schools/resources/what-is-terrorism/

162 What is terrorism? http://www.terrorism-research.com/

163 Definitions of Terrorism in the U.S. Code. https://www.fbi.gov/about-us/investigate/terrorism/terrorism-definition.

public; made for the purpose of advancing a political, religious, racial or ideological cause; and it involves or causes serious violence against a person or serious damage to a property or a threat to a person's life or a serious risk to the health and safety of the public or serious interference with or disruption to an electronic system. [164]

The approach of international law towards defining terrorism varies greatly, with differences emerging in conceptual and political understanding among nation states. Still, consensus is maintained over the understanding of terrorism as conceptualized by the Convention on Suppression of Financing of Terrorism (1999), which was the first attempt at defining international terrorism.

Article 2 of the convention refers to:

Any... act intended to cause death or serious bodily injury to a civilian, or to any other person not taking an active part in the hostilities in a situation of armed conflict, when the purpose of such act, by its nature or context, is to intimidate a population, or to compel a government or an international organization to do or to abstain from doing any act. [165]

Terrorism is a violent act with political intentions, which aims at a particular audience apart from the direct victims of the act. Being coercive in nature, terrorism resorts to violent and destructive acts as a means to a radical end. The use of such actions is justified by terrorists as an imperative to bring about change in the status quo. [166]

There remains no country today which is not the victim of terrorism, be it directly or indirectly. This method of con-

---

164 https://www.mi5.gov.uk/home/the-threats/terrorism.html - Description of terrorism as understood by UK government

165 International Convention for the Suppression of the Financing of Terrorism. http://www.un.org/law/cod/finterr.htm - Read more about the instrument which attempted to define international terrorism for the first time.

166 Terrorist Behavior. http://www.terrorism-research.com/behavior/

flict has survived and evolved through centuries to assume the front it wields today. Flourishing in the modern age, terrorism has adapted in order to exploit the advancements enjoyed by society, and increasingly complex counter-terrorism methods are developed in response.

With multiple countries in conflict over their controversial actions in pursuance of their own vested interests, the damaging force of terrorism has propelled them to reckon with unchartered territories of cooperation. Terrorism is no longer contained in the boundaries of Muslim-populated areas and has become the harsh reality of the modern world. [167]

Terrorism remains an asymmetric form of violent conflict in which zealot groups attack innocent civilians. The nuisance that terrorism creates has shifted from playing a subsidiary role in a nation-state, to a full-fledged, prominent one affecting international dynamics. The integration of a militant organization with various small sub-state entities, like drug cartels or other criminal organizations, helps terrorists assume unprecedented control in their region of influence.

The scope of terrorism moves beyond national borders and affects an audience beyond the primary victims. Attacks are intended to draw the attention not only of the local people and the government, but also that of the international community. In this pursuit of attention to their cause, terrorists intend to launch attacks at such targets who oppose their agenda.

The ultimate goal of terrorists is to instil fear into a population, so that they can be played in the hands of terrorists for the fulfilling of their objectives. The induction of fear into these people is a measure of success for the terrorists which can be attained by physical harm, or its threat, negative financial impact on the economy, or cyber-attacks on crucial technological infrastructures. The uproar caused by terrorist attacks, the fear induced in civilians' hearts, and the reaction of government, all determine the effectiveness of such an act, influencing the future paths and methods to be

---

167 Hoffman, Bruce. "Inside Terrorism." https://www.nytimes.com/books/first/h/hoffman-terrorism.html - About history of terrorism and differences in defining the term.

employed by the terrorists.

Although there is no internationally agreed upon definition of terrorism supplied by the United Nations, they nonetheless describe terrorism as "any action that is intended to cause death or serious bodily harm to civilians or non-combatants, when the purpose of such an act, by its nature or context, is to intimidate a population, or to compel a Government or an international organization to do or abstain from doing any act." [168] Recognizing that terrorism attacks the values of rule of law, respect for human rights, tolerance among individuals, and peaceful conflict resolution, the United Nations also recognizes that terrorist organizations thrive in the framework of political oppression, poverty, regional conflict, extremism, and human rights abuse.

Even though countries are still struggling to both conceptualize and reach a consensus on the legal definition of terrorism, several aspects of these definitions stand supported by all. The foremost element remains the use of violence by terrorists. In contrast to some definitions of terrorism, a lethal course of action against public facilities is not sufficient; rather, terrorism also involves danger to human life or major economic loss as a result of violence. [169]

Another traditional element crucial in defining terrorism is the creation of a climate of fear or terror in the population to serve one's objectives. The action of causing insecurity or intimidation among people serves the intentions of the terrorists to coerce government or any organization into caving in to the terrorists' motives, which may or may not be political in nature. The intentions of terrorists do not just always influence, but also at times coerce organizations as well as individuals to do or refrain from doing an act. [170]

Governments find it arduous to deal with an entity with no defined legal or territorial boundaries. Exploiting media

168 http://www.un.org/News/dh/infocus/terrorism/sg%20high-level%20panel%20report-terrorism.htm – More about terrorism as understood by the United Nations Organization.

169 Various Definitions of Terrorism. http://www.azdema.gov/museum/famousbattles/pdf/Terrorism%20Definitions%20072809.pdf

170 Walter, Christian. "Defining Terrorism in National and International Law." https://www.unodc.org/tldb/bibliography/Biblio_Int_humanitarian_law_Walter_2003.pdf - More about the elements of the definition of terrorism in national and international law.

exposure and social media outreach to its own gain, terrorism has emerged as a pervasive evil in a society which relies on violence to induce any political, social, or religious change. [171]

With terrorism boasting a history older than modern nation states, it remains a quandary to analyze the legitimacy of actors who pursue terror for the fulfilment of their objectives. [172] The issue of "moral equivalency" and emphasis on the outcome of an act, rather than on intent, can further blurs the task of defining terrorism.

Notwithstanding the dilemma over the definition of terrorism, the existence of terrorists has emerged as a scourge for the whole international community. While the most commonly perceived notion holds that terrorism is an "outside" phenomenon, it still remains to be recognized that terrorism actually begins with the people who are perched on the radical fringe of the causes they support, to the extent that they advocate violence to be morally justifiable for their causes. Such groups often view efforts at modernization or at secularism as a threat to their own religious beliefs and formulate newer tactics to achieve their objectives.

Understanding terrorism requires three different perspectives: of the terrorist, of the victim and of the general populace. The phrase "one man's terrorist is another man's freedom fighter" fits perfectly with the terrorists who view themselves as carrying the burden of reforming society and ridding it of evil. Like the so called "Islamic State" of Iraq and Syria does, terrorist organizations believe their fight to be a legitimate rebellion against overbearing modern society.

While all terrorists view their actions as legitimate, whatever the cost may be, the victims of any terrorist activity beg to differ; for them, a terrorist is a criminal who has no regard for human life. The general public's view of terrorism remains unstable, with numerous people supporting the cause of terrorists as a desired change they wish to see brought into the world, whatever be the cost. The same reason holds true

---

171 Terrorism: A Modern Scourge. http://www.terrorism-research.com/goals/scourge.php

172 History of Terrorism. http://www.terrorism-research.com/history/

when increasing number of people are enticed to join terrorist organizations in the name of "jihad." [173]

In recent years, there have been an inordinate number of causes as well as social contexts where terrorism has been employed as a means to an end. Committing exceptionally violent acts has become a trend with terrorists in pursuance of their political or religious aims, making the seemingly isolated attempts at bombings, assassinations, and hijackings a part of the bigger pattern. With terrorists developing newer facilities for attack along with improving their existing capabilities, they have gained a stronghold in several countries to the point of uprooting civilians from their homes and settling their own regime in those areas. Able to adapt to newer methods and techniques of counter-terrorism, terrorists reduce the predictability factor, further complicating the security operations of nations.

The adaptive capabilities of terrorists are well-demonstrated in their use of technology to their own advantage. The clichéd yet extremely effective use of digital pictures to hide and exchange information, or the encryption of data embedded in seemingly simple communications, has enabled terrorists to carry out their plans without fear of detection. Backed by sufficient fund-flow, terrorists today are capable of increasing their abilities and sophistication in every aspect of their operations, thus matching the counter-terrorism measures by governmental agencies across the world with equal or, at times, exceeding prowess. [174] The increasingly easy availability of weapons, technology, and trained personnel, coupled with soaring corruption and lawlessness in certain nation states, has exacerbated the situation.

Today, most parts of Afghanistan, Pakistan, and the Middle East have turned into hotspots for terrorist activities and a hub for engaging newer recruits into the mission of "jihad," filling the power vacuum in regions of democratic disparity with their own diktats and engaging in large-scale human

---

173 What is Terrorism? http://www.terrorism-research.com/
174 Future Trends in Terrorism. http://www.terrorism-research.com/future/

rights violations. [175] Awakening from its slumber, the world has finally realized the dire need to contain and ultimately eliminate terror forces in order to establish peace.

The measures for counter-terrorism are not new; the formal commencement of such measures in the modern state was seen with the adoption of first resolution by the United Nations Organization in 1972 on the subject of international terrorism, which focused on the prevention of international terrorism and on studying the causes behind individuals engaging in such acts. [176]

However, earlier attempts focused on countering terrorism through understanding what it entails and then acting accordingly. While this holds true even today, nonetheless governmental agencies the world over are engaged in more proactive approaches to containing the threat of terrorism in their respective nation-states.

Since the 1960s, the practices of the United Nations suggest that despite the failure of a single universal definition of terrorism, there is, at least, a consensus among the international community that terrorism cannot be effectively addressed without international co-operation.

Lacking one single definition, international law includes various forms of counter-measures against acts of terrorism under different international conventions to ensure international co-operation in order to investigate, combat, and eliminate terrorist incidents in certain situations. [177] Therefore, the major anti-terrorism conventions are drafted within the framework of the UN and ratified by many states. Accordingly, at present, there are 12 international conventions addressing terrorism and related activities, each covering a specific type of criminal activity, including seizure of airplanes, political assassination, the use of explosives, hostage-taking,

---

175 Zafar, Abu. "Jihad is not terrorism, terrorism is not jihad," http://qz.com/316516/jihad-is-not-terrorism-terrorism-is-not-jihad/ - Elaborates about Jihad as a 'struggle' for the 'Cause of Allah'. But terrorists use the term for their own vested interests to coerce people into terrorism.

176 Ibid.

177 Cassese, A International Criminal Law (2003) Oxford, Oxford University Press, p. 120.

nuclear terrorism and assorted bombing, etc. [178]

The Rise of Extremist Groups: From al-Qaeda to Daesh

The phenomenon of radical Islamic fundamentalism and the characterization of the phenomenon as militant and radical have dominated the discourse on global politics and international relations in the twenty-first century. In academic discourse, fundamentalism is equated with a rejection of modernity and its secular variant in both democratic and non-democratic societies. The Concise Oxford Dictionary of Current English describes fundamentalism as the "strict maintenance of ancient or fundamental doctrines of any religion." [179] However, with the rise of extremists groups who commit acts of terrorism in the name of the Islamic religion, radical Islamic fundamentalism has been associated largely with terrorism and violent acts. Almost eight years ago, before the 9/11 attack on the World Trade Centre, the New York Times scathingly critiqued radical Islamic fundamentalism in the following words: "Muslim fundamentalism is fast becoming the chief threat to global peace and security as well as a cause of national and local disturbance through terrorism. It is akin to the menace posed by Nazism and fascism in the 1930s and then by communism in the '50s." [180]

In the twenty-first century, radical Islam and fundamentalism are seen by many as the paramount threat to universal

---

178 The 1963 Tokyo Convention on Offences and certain Other Acts Committed on Board Aircraft, the 1970 Hague Convention for the Suppression of Unlawful Seizure of Aircraft, the 1971 Montreal Convention for the Suppression of Unlawful Acts against the Safety of Civil Aviation, the 1973 New York Convention on the Prevention and Punishment of Crimes against Internationally Protected Persons, the 1979 Convention on the Physical Protection of Nuclear Material, the 1979 New York Convention against the Taking of Hostages, the 1988 Protocol for the Suppression of Unlawful Acts of Violence at Airports Serving International Civil Aviation, the 1988 Convention for the Suppression of Unlawful Acts against the Safety of Maritime Navigation, the 1988 Protocol for the Suppression of Unlawful Acts against the Safety of Fixed Platforms Located on the Continental Shelf, the 1991 Convention on the Marking of Plastic Explosives for the Purpose of Identification, the 1997 International Convention for the Suppression of Terrorist Bombing and the 1999 International Convention for the Suppression of the Financing of Terrorism.

179 http://law.unimelb.edu.au/__data/assets/pdf_file/0003/1681140/Evans.pdf

180 Hollingworth, Clare, "Another Despotic Creed Seeks to Infiltrate the West," 9 September 1993, The New York Times, URL: http://www.nytimes.com/1993/09/09/opinion/09iht-ed-clare.html.

security since the culmination of the Cold War. Radical Islam has led to the execution of hundreds in suicide bombing attacks across the world, killing thousands of Muslims and non-Muslims, including the attacks of September 11, 2001, when over 3,000 people perished in the al-Qaeda attacks ordered by Osama Bin Laden. [181]

An Overview of the Evolution of Radical Islam Terrorism from the Mid-20th Century

According to John Moore, three phases of evolution can be identified in the rise of radical Islam terrorism from the mid-20th century to the dawn of the 21st century. [182] He identifies the first phase, from 1969-1979, as "The Inception;" phase two, 1979-1991, as the "Rise of Afghan Jihad and State-Sponsored Terrorism," and; phase three, from 1991-2001, as "The Globalization of Terrorism." [183]

Phase I: The Inception (1969 -1979)

The first phase of terrorism in the Arab World was a reaction to Western transformations, and was ignited by the creation of Israel in 1948. During this period, there was a general belief that terrorism was an effective instrument in achieving political aims. The epicentre of terrorist activities was in Palestine and Israel, where Al Fatah and the Popular Front for the Liberation of Palestine (PFLP) began to target civilians outside of the immediate arena of conflict. [184] With the victory of Israel in the 1967 Arab-Israel War, Palestinian revolutionary groups moved from classic guerrilla-based warfare to that of explicit acts of terrorism, such as hijackings, kidnappings, bombings, and shootings, culminating

---

181 Milton- Edwards, Beverly *Islamic Fundamentalism Since 1945*, (2005) Abingdon: Routledge pg. 9.

182 Moore, John (2014), The Evolution of Islamic Terrorism: an overview, pbs.org, URL: http://www.pbs.org/wgbh/pages/frontline/shows/target/etc/modern.html

183 Ibid.

184 http://www.inquiriesjournal.com/articles/1500/2/the-political-rationality-of-terror-understanding-terrorism-as-the-result-of-organizational-goal-seeking

in the kidnapping and subsequent deaths of Israeli athletes during the 1972 Munich Olympic games.

Three major Palestinian terror groups dominated during this time period. The first of these was the Popular Front for the Liberation of Palestine (PFLP). The PFLP was a leftist Palestinian nationalist group that formed after the Arab states' overwhelming defeat in the Six Day War of 1967. The PFLP, which pioneered such terror tactics as airline hijackings, was formed in December of 1967 by George Habash. In 1968, the PFLP joined the Palestine Liberation Organization (PLO), the main umbrella organization of the Palestinian national movement, which was then committed to a strategy of "armed struggle." [185] The PFLP became the second-largest PLO faction, after Arafat's own al-Fatah. The PFLP sought to topple conservative Arab states, destroy Israel, and apply Marxist doctrine to the Palestinian struggle, which it saw as part of a broader proletarian revolution. [186] Once a key player in Palestinian politics, the PFLP lost influence in the 1990s and was side-lined as Yasser Arafat established the Palestinian Authority.

The second group, the Popular Front for the Liberation of Palestine-General Command (PFLP-GC), was established in April 1968 by Ahmed Jibril, a former captain in the Syrian Army. The group formed mostly around a nucleus of former Syrian army officers; they joined the PFLP, but split from it, after an internal struggle with George Habash and other PFLP leaders, with the intention of focusing more on fighting and less on politics. [187]

The third group, the Abu Nidal Organization (ANO), was an international terrorist organization formed by Sabri al-Banna that made its initial appearance after a split from

185 http://www.encyclopedia.com/politics/legal-and-political-magazines/palestine-liberation-organization-plo

186 Global Security (2016), Popular Front for the Liberation of Palestine (PFLP), URL: http://www.globalsecurity.org/military/world/para/pflp.htm.

187 Jewish Virtual Library (2016), Palestinian Terror Groups: Popular Front for the Liberation of Palestine – General Command (PFLP-GC), URL: http://www.jewishvirtuallibrary.org/jsource/Terrorism/pflpgc.html.

the PLO in 1974. [188] Following the October 1973 Arab-Israeli War, a rift was caused by a personality conflict between Yasser Arafat and al-Banna. Differences emerged over issues of the political reconciliation of the Arab-Israeli conflict, and with regards to the restriction of targets. In fact, the rift between Abu Nidal and Arafat was so intense that Abu Nidal was sentenced to death, in abstention, by Arafat. ANO was made up of various functional committees, including political, military, and financial. The group contends that both inter-Arab and intra-Palestinian terrorism are needed to precipitate an all-embracing Arab revolution that alone can lead to the liberation of occupied Palestine. [189]

Phase 2: The Rise of Afghan "Jihad" and State Sponsored Terrorism (1979-1991)

The Soviet invasion of Afghanistan and the subsequent anti-Soviet mujahedeen war, lasting from 1979 to 1989, stimulated the rise and expansion of terrorist groups, which were nurtured by the growth of a post-jihad pool of well-trained, battle-hardened militants. In many ways, this phase can be regarded as an initial phase of insurgency-related violence, and of the growth of international terrorism. This phase was marked by a distinct move toward urban-based attacks, with a subsequent increase in collateral casualties, as well as a change in targeting methodology—civilians became the target. This time of conflict with a Superpower in Afghanistan became a formative period for the proliferation of weapons and emergence of militant, radical fundamentalist Islam. The major radical Islamic terror groups formed during this period were:

> 1) Hezbollah, whose origins and ideology stem from the Iranian Revolution. The revolution called for a religious Muslim government that would represent the oppressed and downtrodden. According to Hezbollah, the United

---

188 http://www.cfr.org/israel/abu-nidal-organization-ano-aka-fatah-revolutionary-council-arab-revolutionary-brigades-revolutionary-organization-socialist-muslims/p9153

189 Global Security (2016), Abu Nidal Organization (ANO), URL: http://www.globalsecurity.org/military/world/para/abunidal.htm.

States was to blame for many of the country's problems. Israel was seen as an extension of the United States and a foreign power in Lebanon. The organization itself started in 1982 as part of the Iranian government's Revolutionary Guard Corps. Led by religious clerics, the organization wanted to adopt an Iranian doctrine as a solution to Lebanese political malaise. This doctrine included the use of terror as a means of attainting political objectives. [190]

2) Egyptian Islamic Jihad (EIJ), often known as al-Jihad or the Jihad group, was a Jihadi, Salafi militant organization founded in Egypt in 1979 by Muhammad 'Abd al-Salam Farraj. Farraj was originally a member of the Muslim Brotherhood, but split from the organization to form the EIJ, following the Muslim Brotherhood's renunciation of violence in the late 1970s. [191]

3) Palestinian Islamic Jihad (PIJ) originated among militant Palestinians in the Gaza Strip during the 1970s. It was committed to the creation of an Islamic Palestinian state and the destruction of Israel through holy war. Headed by Dr. Fathi Shqaqi and inspired by the Islamic Revolution in Iran, the Palestinian Islamic Jihad had a radical fundamentalist Sunni Muslim ideology, and sought the immediate "liberation" of Palestine. The Palestinian Islamic Jihad rejected any arrangement or agreement with Israel. [192]

4) The Islamic Resistance Movement, or Harakat al-Muqawama al-Islamiya (HAMAS), originated on December 14, 1987, and was founded in the Gaza Strip by Sheikh Ahmed Yassin, a prominent Islamic figure. Hamas was formed on the basis of two groups operating in Gaza which were officially registered as cultural and educational charities: an offshoot of the Muslim Brotherhood in the West Bank and Gaza Strip, and the Islamic Jihad in the Palestinian territories. The Hamas Charter, adopted in August 1988, laid the ideological foundation for the movement. The Charter states that the movement's purpose is the creation of a Palestinian state on the territory of today's Israel, the West Bank, and the Gaza Strip. One of the main demands of Hamas is the withdrawal of Israel from the territories it occupied in 1967. [193]

190 Jewish Virtual Library (2016), Hezbollah, URL: http://www.jewishvirtuallibrary.org/jsource/Terrorism/hizbollah.html

191 Stanford University (2016), Mapping Islamic Jihad, URL: https://web.stanford.edu/group/mappingmilitants/cgi-bin/groups/view/401

192 Global Security (2016), Palestine Islamic Jihad (PIJ), URL: http://www.globalsecurity.org/military/world/para/pij.htm

193 Sputnik (2014), Facts about Islamic Resistance Movement Hamas, URL: http://sputniknews.com/middleeast/20141214/1015826529.html

5) Al-Gamaat Al-Islamiyya (also known as, the Islamic Group, al-Gama'at, Islamic Gama'at, Egyptian al-Gama'at al-Islamiyya), most commonly referred to as the Islamic Group (IG), is an Egyptian Sunni Islamist movement seeking the abolishment of the current secular Egyptian government for the creation of an Islamic state. The organization began as a radical umbrella for militant student groups in Egypt and officially formed as a reaction to the Muslim Brotherhood's renunciation of violence in the 1970s. The group served as Egypt's largest militant organization, attracting primarily college students or young unemployed graduates from urban areas of Egypt. The group maintains a presence both at home and abroad. To gain support for their goal of establishing an Islamic regime, the organization perpetrated multiple violent attacks against the Egyptian government from 1992 through 1998. [194]

Phase 3: The Globalization of Terrorism (1991-2001)

This phase was marked by a distinct movement towards urban-based attacks, with a subsequent increase in collateral casualties, as well as a change in targeting methodology, which became focused on civilians.

The disintegration of Cold War states, coupled with a stability vacuum and the absence of a regular government, were major factors behind the globalization of terrorism that began growing in the 1990s. Afghanistan and the Balkan regions were the most affected by terrorist activities. This phase was also marked by Pakistan's policy sponsoring terrorism in Afghanistan and India. Pakistan viewed the Afghan state mainly as an irritant before the Soviet invasion, but after 1979, the stakes for Pakistan were thought to involve threats to its national security and integrity. Pakistan's championing of the Afghan resistance struggle and its embrace of refugees was motivated by geostrategic and domestic imperatives which led Pakistan's leaders to pursue several objectives during the course of the war. First, there was a deep concern within the Pakistani government that Moscow would instigate, through material support, ethnic separatist movements in Baluchistan and the North-West Fron-

---

194 START (2015), Al-Gama'at Al-Islamiyya (IG), URL: https://www.start.umd.edu/baad/
narratives/al-gamaat-al-islamiyya-ig

tier Provinces. Second, Pakistan wanted the early return of refugees to Afghanistan. [195] The government in Islamabad facilitated and supplemented the massive international aid program that sustained the refugee community, and a broad consensus held that the Afghans be allowed to stay until they could return with a sense of security. Managing the burden of refugees, however, left Pakistan dependent on the continued assistance of the international community. Increasingly, Pakistanis began to view the Afghan exiles as having an undesirable impact on their economy and society. Third, the Pakistani president, General Muhammad Zia ul-Haq, used the Afghanistan situation to help his martial law regime survive. Fourth, Zia ul Haq intended to use the war to portray itself as a frontline "Islamic state" in the defense of Islam against hostile forces. Fifth, Pakistan aimed to block the revival of Afghani nationalism and then create a post-war Afghanistan that would offer a friendly north-western frontier, which would assure the recognition of the Pakistan-Afghan border at the Durand line. [196]

Thus, Pakistan assisted the Islamic Resistance forces against the Soviet Union in Afghanistan, and in this it received massive support from the United States, and Saudi Arabia. An Afghan resistance sponsored by the regime of Zia and his allies, designed to discourage Soviet offensive ambitions in the region and wear down the Soviet army, also provided Pakistan with an opportunity to blunt Afghan nationalism. Secular and leftist parties, some of which had championed the idea of a Pashtun state, were deliberately excluded from participation in a mujahedeen alliance fashioned by Pakistan's premier intelligence agency, the Inter-Services Intelligence (ISI). [197] Through the 1980s, financial support for the mujahedeen was funnelled through the ISI. The ISI encouraged and sponsored armed Islamist groups in Pakistan linked to Afghan mujahedeen groups and helped create a string of training camps on the Pakistan-Afghan frontier.

---

195 http://ambijat.wdfiles.com/local--files/admin:manage/weinbaum.pdf

196 Weinbaum, M. G. (1991). "War and Peace in Afghanistan: The Pakistani Role." *Middle East Journal*, 45:1, 71-85.

197 Ibid.

Tribal areas thus became the assembly points for the volunteers to train and fight in Afghanistan and the transit points for the supply of weapons. In an effort to build sympathies for the anti-communist resistance, the ISI facilitated Saudi funding for mosques and madrassas. [198]

It must be mentioned that Hekmatyar was a favourite of the ISI and received major funding. The ISI is alleged to have backed Hekmatyar to topple the Tajik-dominated government in Kabul. [199] Hekmatyar also cooperated with the ISI in training foreign volunteers to fight in the Indian-held Kashmir in the early 1990s. Although all of the mujahidin had contacts and support groups in Pakistan, Hekmatyar's connections to both the Afghan refugees in Pakistan and the ISI were especially tight. [200] After Soviet forces left Afghanistan in the late 80s, Afghanistan plunged into an internecine civil war. With the ousting of the pro-Soviet regime from Kabul in 1992, attempts were made to establish a Mujahedin-based government in Kabul. Without any established agreement on how to share power, and with a number of candidates ready to get hold of Kabul, the early calm soon changed to an increasing infighting amongst the Afghan parties and changing of alliances, with disastrous consequences, especially for civilians. Local warlords established their rule in several places across the country, based on their merits as leaders in the resistance against the Soviets, and supported by control of arms and by an emerging opium industry. When the infighting among the Mujahedin parties started, Pakistan started the search for another partner in Afghanistan. The emerging Taliban movement from 1993 is closely linked.

Pakistan viewed the civil war as both an opportunity and a security threat. An unstable Afghanistan was perceived as a security threat that could coalesce into border conflict. At the same time, Pakistan saw an opportunity to promote fundamental Islamic groups that could serve its strategic in-

---

198 Ibid. at 25-38.

199 Institute for the Study of War. (2009). *Pakistan and Afghanistan*. Washington.

200 Felbab -Brown, V. (2014). *No Easy Exit: Drugs and Counternarcotics Policies in Afghanistan*. Washington DC: Center for 21st Century Security and Intelligence.

terests not only in Afghanistan, but also in the South-Asia region. In reaction to the anarchy and warlordism, Pakistan gave full support in all forms to the Taliban movement. The Taliban movement has its origin in a network of religious schools, established in Pakistan by another Islamist party, Jama'iyyat Ulama al-Islam. In the early 1990s, some 4000 madrassas sprang up all over Pakistan, especially near the Afghan border where two million Afghan refugees were living in camps. [201] These schools included not only refugee children, but also sons of wealthy Pakistani families. Such madrassas trained their pupils within a military and political framework. Out of them came the Taliban movement, under the supervision and responsibility of Pakistan's ISI. In August 1994, the Pakistani regime decided to use the Taliban in order to establish control over Afghanistan, where it intended to impose order and stability. [202] Throughout 1995, the collaboration between ISI and the Taliban strengthened, and changed in character, increasingly becoming a direct military alliance. The ISI was itself divided in this period of the Taliban's emergence about how to conduct its policy in Afghanistan. The ISI, during a long period of the anti-Soviet war, had been closest to Gulbuddin Hekmatyar, a Pashtun commander and an Islamist. By the 1990s, however, Hekmatyar was no longer effective, at least in the judgment of many within ISI. [203] The Taliban gradually proved themselves as the better client. They became more effective militarily, and it became increasingly clear that something about their austere discipline appealed to ordinary Pashtuns, at least in the south and east of Afghanistan.

Taliban's military triumph in Afghanistan, culminating in their takeover of Kabul in 1996, can be attributed to the fact that they were a proxy force, a client of the Pakistan army, and benefited from all of the material support that the Pakistan army could provide them. The Taliban remained an

201 https://www.greenleft.org.au/content/afghanistan-how-us-put-taliban-power
202 Erfat, Y. B. (2001, November 21). "Afghanistan: How the US Government put Taliban in Power." *Green Left Weekly*
203 http://www.pbs.org/wgbh/pages/frontline/taliban/pakistan/alliance.html

important client of the ISI right up until 9/11. [204] They were an ally of the Pakistan government, and the ISI maintained contact with them to support their governance, but also their military campaign in the Afghan civil war that persisted despite the Taliban's takeover of Kabul. The Taliban were also important to the Pakistan ISI in the late 1990s for another reason. The ISI also promoted terror groups against what it regarded as Indian occupation in Kashmir. The Taliban in Afghanistan provided logistical support, training, and other bases that the ISI could use to train and develop its Kashmir rebellion. [205] The main terror groups sponsored by Pakistan to usher violence into India were the Harakat ul-Mujahidin (HUM), Jaish-e-Mohammed (Army of Mohammed), and Lashkar-i-Taiba (Army of the Righteous).

However, the main terror group that posed a threat to global security was al-Qaeda. Al-Qaeda, Arabic for "the Base," is an international terrorist network founded by Osama bin Laden in the late 1980s. It seeks to rid Muslim countries of what it sees as the profane influence of the West and replace their governments with fundamentalist Islamic regimes. From 1989 until 1991, the group (hereafter referred to as "al-Qaeda") was headquartered in Afghanistan and Peshawar, Pakistan. In or about 1991, the leadership of al-Qaeda, including its "emir" (or prince) Osama bin Laden, relocated to the Sudan. [206] Al-Qaeda was headquartered in the Sudan from approximately 1991 until approximately 1996, but still maintained offices in various parts of the world. In 1996, Osama bin Laden and other members of al-Qaeda relocated to Afghanistan. At all relevant times, al-Qaeda was led by its emir, Osama bin Laden. Members of al-Qaeda pledged an oath of allegiance (called a "bayat") to Osama bin Laden and al-Qaeda. Those who were suspected of collaborating against al-Qaeda were to be identified and killed. [207]

Al-Qaeda had an inherent anti-American and anti-West

---

204 Ibid.

205 pbs, 2006

206 http://www.pbs.org/wgbh/pages/frontline/shows/network/alqaeda/indictment.html

207 Ibid.

outlook from its inception. This can be explained on account of the following reasons. Firstly, the West and the United States were considered as infidels, as they were governed in a manner inconsistent with the principles of Islam. Secondly, the United States of America was perceived as a major supporter of other "infidel" governments, most notably that of Israel. Thirdly, Al-Qaeda opposed the involvement of the United States armed forces in the Gulf War in 1991 and in Operation Restore Hope in Somalia in 1992 and 1993. In particular, al-Qaeda opposed the continued presence of American military forces in Saudi Arabia. Fourth, al-Qaeda opposed the United States government because of the arrest, conviction, and imprisonment of persons belonging to al-Qaeda, or its affiliated terrorist groups, or those with whom it worked. [208]

The August 1998 bombings of the United States embassies in Nairobi, Kenya, and Dar es Salaam, Tanzania, and the October 2000 U.S.S. Cole Bombings, were the major terrorist attacks carried out by Al-Qaeda in the 1990s. However, it was with the 9/11 attacks that al-Qaeda emerged as a global security threat.

The 9/11 Attacks and the Growth of Radical Islamic Terrorism

The September 11, 2001, hijacking of four United States airplanes—two of which were crashed into the World Trade Centre, and one crashed into the Pentagon—shook the global security order. The attacks on the Twin Towers were, for many people, the first time they learnt of al-Qaeda and its leader, Osama bin Laden.

The 9/11 attack cost al-Qaeda about a half million dollars to organize and execute, according to the United States 9/11 Commission report. The property damage in New York and Washington alone cost about $100 billion. The cumulative economic cost to the global economy has been estimated as high as $2 trillion. The attack led directly to the war in Afghanistan and indirectly to the war in Iraq. Brown Universi-

208 "Inside the Terror Network, Background Al Qaeda," pbs (2014), URL: http://www.pbs.org/wgbh/pages/frontline/shows/network/alqaeda/indictment.html

ty recently estimated the cost of those two wars at $4 trillion. [209]Seized by the success of 9/11, al-Qaeda has maintained its intent to conduct "spectacular" high-casualty attacks against the United States and its Western allies. The major attacks perpetrated by Al-Qaeda since 2001 are listed below:

• The April 2002 explosion of a fuel tanker outside a synagogue in Tunisia.
• Several spring 2002 bombings in Pakistan.
• The October 2002 attack on a French tanker off the coast of Yemen.
• The November 2002 car bomb attack and a failed attempt to shoot down an Israeli jetliner with shoulder-fired missiles, both in Mombasa, Kenya.
• The May 2003 car bomb attacks on three residential compounds in Riyadh, Saudi Arabia.
• The March 2004 bomb attacks on Madrid commuter trains, which killed nearly 200 people and left more than 1,800 injured.
• The July 2005 bombings of the London public transportation system.
• The February 2006 attacks on the Abqaiq petroleum processing facility, the largest such facility in the world, in Saudi Arabia.
• An October 2007 suicide bombing that narrowly missed killing former Pakistani Prime Minister Benazir Bhutto. Two months later, another bomber succeeded in killing the former prime minister; Pakistani officials blame Baitullah Mahsud, a top Pakistani Taliban commander with close ties to al-Qaeda.
• The attempted December 2009 bombing of a Detroit-bound Northwest Airlines flight.
• In December 2009, al-Qaeda of the Islamic Maghrib kidnapped two Italian citizens in Mauritania, claiming the abductions were to avenge Italy's

---

209 Reidel, Bruce (2011), The World After 9/11 – Part I , September 6, Brookings, URL: http://www.brookings.edu/research/articles/2011/09/06-after-911-riedel.

involvement in the wars in Afghanistan and Iraq. [210]

According to Abdel Bari Atwan, the author of *The Secret History of Al-Qaeda and After Bin Laden: The Next Generation*, The United States made a strategic mistake when it invaded Iraq by providing al-Qaeda with a safe haven and a means for recruitment. Al-Qaeda in Iraq was the first "franchise," with affiliates continued to increase in number across North Africa and the Middle East. [211] The leaders of these organizations swore allegiance, or bayat, to al-Qaeda leaders in Pakistan. In 2006, an organization that had existed under a different name in North Africa re-branded itself as al-Qaeda in Islamic Maghreb. By 2009 al-Qaeda added a Yemen contingent. In 2012, Somalia's Al Shabab established a relationship with the al-Qaeda core, while in 2013, Jabhat al-Nusra pledged their loyalty from Syria. [212]

The Killing of Osama bin Laden and Effect on al-Qaeda

On May 2, 2011, United States Navy Seals gunned down the dreaded terrorist and al-Qaeda chief, Osama bin Laden, at Abbottabad, a Pakistani city. Pakistani authorities claim that they had no knowledge of Osama's whereabouts. Abbottabad is a military town situated approximately 100-120 km from the Pakistani capital, Islamabad. Therefore, it is perplexing to believe the claims of Pakistani authorities that they had no knowledge of Osama's whereabouts in Pakistan. If Pakistan authorities were to be believed, then it surely exposed the ineffectiveness of the Pakistani military and intelligence establishments. The creditability of Pakistan's effort to fight terrorism further suffered a blow when the United States of America carried out a unilateral operation against bin Laden, despite the United States regarding

210 Jayshree Bajoria, and Greg Bruno (2012), al-Qaeda (a.k.a. al-Qaida, al-Qa'ida), June 6, Council for Foreign Relations. http://www.cfr.org/terrorist-organizations-and-networks/al-qaeda-k-al-qaida-al-qaida/p9126#p8.
211 Abdel Bari Atwan, *After Bin Laden: Al Qaeda, the Next Generation*, New Press, 2013
212 Ibid.

Pakistan as an important ally in the war on terrorism. [213]
The killing of bin Laden did not affect al-Qaeda in a negative way, and the organization continued to gain strength under
leaders such as Ayman al-Zawahiri—who vowed to continue jihad under the new leadership against "crusader America and its
servant Israel, and whoever supports them"—Khalid al-Habib,
Mustafa Hamid, and Matiur Rehamn. [214] In fact, it was in the
aftermath of the Arab Spring that fissures began to emerge within al-Qaeda. As the number of al-Qaeda groups grew across the
Middle East, it was inevitable that disagreements would emerge
over territory and control. Syria's Jabhat al-Nusra, "which was
formed in late 2011 as a branch of al-Qaeda in Iraq, broke with
their parent 'franchise' in 2013. Al-Zawahiri sent envoys and attempted mediation, but in January excommunicated al-Qaeda in
Iraq from al-Qaeda itself." [215]

The Rise of Daesh

The so called "Islamic State of Iraq and the Al Sham (ISIS/ISIL
- Daesh) [216] is predominantly a "jihadist" group seeking to im-
plant civil strife in Iraq and the Levant (the region spanning from
southern Turkey to Egypt and including Syria, Lebanon, Israel,
the Palestinian territories, and Jordan) with the now-achieved
aim of establishing a caliphate—a unitary, transnational "Islamic state" based on the principles of Sharia. The group emerged in
the vestiges of the United States led invasion to overthrow Sadd-
am Hussein and al-Qaeda in Iraq (AQI), and the insurgency that
followed provided it with lush ground to wage a guerrilla war
against coalition forces and their domestic allies.
    Led by an Iraqi called Abu Bakr al-Baghdadi, Daesh was orig-

---

213 http://nsarchive.gwu.edu/NSAEBB/NSAEBB410/docs/UBLDocument14.pdf

214 BBC (2015), Al-Qaeda's remaining leaders, June 16, URL: http://www.bbc.com/news/
world-south-asia-11489337.

215 Quince, Annabelle (2014), The franchised terrorism of al-Qaeda after Osama bin Laden,
April 8, ABC, URL: http://www.abc.net.au/radionational/programs/rearvision/5375448

216 It is a serious and unfortunate reality that terrorist groups, most notably the so-called
Islamic State of Iraq and the Levant (ISIL), use violent extremist propaganda to encourage
individuals to support their cause. This group is neither Islamic nor a state, and so will be
referred to as Daesh (its Arabic acronym) in this book.

inally an al-Qaeda group in Iraq—the Islamic State of Iraq (ISI). As the Syrian civil war escalated, its involvement in the conflict was at first indirect. Abu Muhammad al-Joulani, an ISI member, established Jabhat al-Jabhat al-Nusra in mid-2011, which became the main jihadi group in the Syrian war. Joulani received support and funding from ISI and Baghdadi. [217] Since the withdrawal of United States forces in late 2011, the group has increased attacks on mainly Shiite targets in what is seen as an attempt to reignite conflict between Iraq's Sunni minority and the dominant Shiite group. According to United Nations statistics, the total number of civilian casualties (including police) in Iraq inflicted by Daesh in 2013 was the highest since 2008, with 7,818 killed and 17,981 injured in 2013, compared to 6,787 killed and 20,178 injured in 2008. [218]

The activities of Daesh and its explicit agenda of spreading a unitary Islamic state globally have inevitably led to a comparison with al-Qaeda. Though the ideology of the two organizations is almost the same, and both groups have found tenuous common cause in military engagements, such as Iraq, their relations have been characterized by distrust, open competition, and outright hostility. In April 2013, overt enmity between Daesh and al-Qaeda broke out in full when Daesh leader Abu Bakr al-Baghdadi announced that he was extending the Islamic State of Iraq into Syria and changing the group's name to the Islamic State of Iraq and al-Sham. The major cause of the dispute between al-Qaeda and Daesh was over the question of the former merging with Jabhat al-Nusra, an al-Qaeda affiliate that has greater indigenous legitimacy in Syria, in April 2013. Al-Qaeda's top leader, Ayman al-Zawahiri, ruled against the merger of the two jihadi groups based in Syria and Iraq. In his letter, Zawahiri said Baghdadi was "wrong" to declare the merger without consulting or even alerting al-Qaeda's leadership. [219] He added that Syria was the "spa-

---

217 https://www.theguardian.com/world/2014/jun/11/isis-too-extreme-al-qaida-terror-jihadi

218 Tran, Mark (2014), Who are Isis? A terror group too extreme even for al-Qaida, June 11, *The Guardian*, URL: http://www.theguardian.com/world/2014/jun/11/isis-too-extreme-al-qaida-terror-jihadi.

219 Idachaba, Enemaku (2015), Islamic State Terrorist Organization: A Critical Study Of The Movement's Ideological Posture And Implications To Global Peace, Afro Asian Journal of Social Sciences Volume VI (1), URL: http://www.onlineresearchjournals.com/aajoss/art/166.pdf.

tial state" for al-Nusra, headed by Abou Mohammad al-Joulani, while Baghdadi's rule would be limited to Iraq. Baghdadi rejected Zawahiri's ruling and questioned his authority, his group's pledge of allegiance to al-Qaeda notwithstanding [220]

Despite their organizational differences, their objectives are broadly the same. In a report by *Reuters* dated July 9, 2014, it was highlighted that Daesh's plans for the establishment of a caliphate and, subsequently, a Sharia-driven government, were in the works years ago by an al-Qaeda group operating in Yemen. *Reuters* reported that it was shown an abandoned al-Qaeda notebook in Yemen that mapped out the "blueprint" for establishing an Islamic state. The notebook, with the name Abu al-Dahdah al-Taazi in red calligraphy on the first page, is one relic of what a local Yemeni governor called "a leadership camp" for al-Qaeda in the Arab Peninsula (AQAP). [221] The abandoned notebook features notes on weapons maintenance, topography, and elaborate diagrams for creating different ambushes. It also identifies the three stages of guerrilla warfare needed to create an Islamic state—a similar blueprint to the one Daesh seems to be following in Iraq and Syria. It covers everything from the principles of a raid—"Surprise, firepower, a sacrificial spirit, quick performance — to the ultimate goal: "Establishing an Islamic state that rules by Islamic Sharia law." [222]

Security experts now suspect that Daesh may turn out to be a greater threat for global security than bin Laden-led Al-Qaeda in the previous decade. Robert Ford, one of the foremost experts on the affairs of the Middle East and the former American ambassador to Syria, remarks that Daesh represents an immediate threat to the United States as it has the necessary financial and human resources that it can use to attack the United States and its allies in places like Europe, in the North Atlantic Treaty Organization

---

220 Ibid.

221 *NY Daily News* (2014), Abandoned Al Qaeda notebook found in Yemen features blueprint for creating Islamic state, July 8m URL: http://www.nydailynews.com/news/world/abandoned-al-qaeda-notebook-features-blueprint-creating-islamic-state-article-1.1858534.

222 Ibid.

(NATO) countries, as well as friends in the region. [223] Experts point out that Daesh has capabilities that exceed even the wildest dreams of the original founders of al-Qaeda. After capturing the city of Mosul and raiding the local government coffers, it now has over $400 million at its disposal. The 9/11 attacks only cost Al-Qaeda $500,000; ISIS has funds now adequate to execute the 9/11 attacks at least 800 times over. Today, Daesh membership is believed to number in the thousands, probably similar to al-Qaeda at its peak. However, experts point out that, while al-Qaeda was predominantly successful in bringing Arab Muslims from the Middle East to fight in wars in their own region or in South Asia, the magnitude of Daesh's terror network runs far deeper. Unclassified reports, and ISIS's own videos, confirm that it is having an unprecedented success in attracting Muslim men from the West to go and fight Jihad. Apart from security experts, a United Kingdom newspaper, *Express,* in its July 3, 2014 edition, cites the pronouncements of one double agent (a former Jihadi turned MI5 agent) Morten Storm, that Sunni Muslim extremists storming Iraq are a bigger threat to Britain than al-Qaeda, and that the West needs to wake up to the threat of fighters returning from Syria and Iraq. [224]

There is an urgent need for the international community to check Daesh in Iraq. In the crisis engulfing Iraq, the international community led by the United States and European Union should strive toward giving Iraq an inclusive government. This is the best means to reduce the influence of terrorism and extremism, and to restore normalcy in Iraq.

The USA PATRIOT ACT—Responding to the 9/11 Attacks

The Uniting and Strengthening America by Providing Appropriate Tools Required to Intercept and Obstruct Terrorism Act

---

223 Chotiner, Issac, "A Middle East Expert Explains Assad's Dangerous Charm, ISIS's Plans, and the Future of the Region An Interview With Robert Ford, the Former Ambassador to Syria," 10 July 2014, *New Republic,* URL: https://newrepublic.com/article/118623/qa-robert-ford-former-ambassador-syria-iraq-isis-iran.

224 *Daily Express,* "Isis is a bigger threat than Al Qaeda, reveals double agent," 3 June 2014 , URL: http://www.express.co.uk/news/world/486399/Al-Qaeda-Isis-Double-Agent-9-11-Attack-Terrorist-Fighters-Sunni-Muslim-Syria

of 2001 (USA PATRIOT Act), signed into law on October 26, represents the United States government's primary legislative response to the terrorist attacks of September 11, 2001. This law, signed by President George W. Bush for a limited period of four years, was renewed in early 2006, and then extended until June 2015. In brief, the Patriot Act strengthened the powers of government agencies (FBI, CIA, NSA, and military) [225] and reduced civil liberties.

The law provides that any intrusion into a computer system can be likened to an act of terrorism. The Act allows the Federal Bureau of Investigation to spy on the movement of electronic messages and retain traces of web browsing from anyone suspected of contact with a foreign power. In August 2006, a federal judge declared wiretapping unconstitutional and ordered the cease of the secret NSA domestic surveillance program. The law authorized the wiretapping of anyone with a near or distant relationship with a person alleged to be a terrorist. A provision authorizing the administration to have access to databases of libraries and booksellers was abolished by an amendment.

Critics of the United States of America PATRIOT Act have denounced the reduction of criminal defense rights and violation of privacy. They highlight the risks of encroachment of administrative authorities on the judiciary

A Brief History of the USA Patriot Act

The United States of America PATRIOT Act was signed in the aftermath of the September 11, 2001 attacks, expanding the powers of federal law enforcement agencies and investigating any persons suspected of having links with a terror network.

Only five days after the 9/11 terrorist attacks, Attorney General Ashcroft proposed new federal statutes and said that he would ask Congress to rewrite certain laws to enhance anti-terrorist efforts, including granting investigative agencies greater

---

225 Federal Bureau of Investigation (FBI), Central Intelligence Agency (CIA), National Security Agency (NSA)

surveillance authority. [226] In a meeting on September 19, 2001, Attorney General Ashcroft presented his proposed list of new and amended statutes to Congress and Ashcroft urged its immediate approval. Patrick Leahy (D-Vt.), the chairman of the Senate Judiciary Committee, and James Sensenbrenner, chairman of the House of Representatives Judiciary Committee—together with many of their colleagues—then wrote their own versions of the bill, which became S. 1510 and H.R. 2975. H.R. 2975 was introduced on October 2, 2001 and passed by the House on October 12th. S. 1510 was introduced on October 4th and passed the Senate on October 11th by a vote of 96 to 1. The bill for the Act was introduced in the United States of America House of Representatives on October 23, signed by the House on the 24th (by a vote of 98 to 1) and was signed by President George. W. Bush on October 26, 2001. [227]

President Bush remarked before the signing of the Act that it was an essential step in defeating terrorism, while protecting the constitutional rights of all Americans, as the Act gave intelligence and law enforcement officials important new tools to fight the present terrorist threat, and enforcement to identify, to dismantle, to disrupt, and to punish terrorists before they strike. Bush further said that the legislation was essential not only to pursuing and punishing terrorists, but also preventing more atrocities at the hands of the evil ones. [228]

Main features of the USA PATRIOT Act

The act comprises 10 categories, called "titles." Within these 10 titles, the major provisions of the USA PATRIOT Act included the following:

---

226 CNN =Ashcroft wants tougher anti-terrorism laws, 16 September 2001, URL: http://archives.cnn.com/2001/US/09/16/inv.ashcroft.congress/index.html

227 Standler, Ronald B (20080, A Brief History of the USA Patriot Act of 2001, URL: http://www.rbs0.com/patriot.pdf.

228 Whitehouse, George W. Bush, "President Signs Anti-Terrorism Bill, 26 October 2001, URL: http://www.whitehouse.gov/news/releases/2001/10/20011026-5.html.

Title I: Enhancing domestic security against terrorism

Section 101 established a Counterterrorism Fund in the United States Treasury to reimburse the Justice Department and other government agencies for losses incurred due to terrorism and for certain counterterrorism activities.

Section 102 declared that Arab Americans, Muslim Americans, and Americans from South Asia were entitled to the full rights of every American and that their civil rights and liberties must be protected.

Section 106 authorized the President, when dealing with "any unusual and extraordinary threat" to United States national security, foreign policy, or economy whose source is outside the United States to investigate, regulate, or prohibit the importing or exporting of currency or securities.

Title II: Enhanced surveillance procedures

Section 203 allowed the sharing of grand jury information with federal law enforcement, immigration, national defense, and intelligence officials when the matters involve foreign intelligence or counterintelligence information.

Section 213 allowed law enforcement to delay notice that may be required to be given of a search warrant if the "court finds reasonable cause to believe that providing immediate notification of the execution of the warrant may have an adverse result."

Section 215 allowed the Director of the Federal Bureau of Investigation "access to certain business records for foreign intelligence and international terrorism investigations" where such investigation is to be "conducted under guidelines approved by the Attorney General."

Section 224, titled "Sunset," stipulated that 16 sections and two subsections of the act would cease to have effect on December 31, 2005.

Title III: Anti-money-laundering to prevent terrorism

Section 311 allowed the Treasury Secretary to require domestic financial institutions to obtain certain record-keeping and background information from their customers.

Section 313 prohibited a financial institution from establishing or managing "a correspondent account in the United States for, or on behalf of, a foreign bank that does not have a physical presence in any country."

Section 318 prohibited money laundering through a foreign bank.

Title IV: Border security

Section 403 allowed the State Department and the Immigration and Naturalization Service access to criminal history and other records held by the Federal Bureau of Investigation.

Section 411 denied admissibility to the United States to an alien who was a member or representative of a terrorist organization.

Title V: Removing obstacles to investigating terrorism

Section 501 authorized the Attorney General to make funds available for the payment of rewards for assistance in combating terrorism.

Section 502 authorized payments to an individual who furnished information leading to the prevention of terrorism or the identity of someone "who holds a key leadership position in a terrorist organization" in the State Department's rewards program.

Section 504 authorized the federal officers who conducted electronic surveillance or physical searches to acquire foreign intelligence information, to consult with other Federal law enforcement officers, to coordinate efforts to protect against terrorist attacks or clandestine intelligence activities by a foreign power or its agent.

Section 505 allowed law enforcement easier access to

telephone, toll, and transactional records, financial records, and consumer reports.

Section 506 extended jurisdiction to the United States Secret Service to investigate computer fraud.

Section 507 authorized the Attorney General to collect education records from an educational agency or institutions that were relevant to certain government investigations by means of a written application to an appropriate court.

Title VI: Victims and families of victims of terrorism

Section 611 authorized payments to beneficiaries of public safety officers who were killed or who suffered catastrophic injuries while involved in the prevention, investigation, rescue, or recovery related to a terrorist attack within 30 days of receipt of certification.

Section 621 allowed donations to be made to the United States Treasury's Crime Victims Fund from private entities or individuals.

Section 624 provided for supplemental grants from the Crime Victims Fund to victims of terrorism within and outside the United States.

Title VII: Increased information sharing for critical infrastructure protection

Section 710 included "terrorist conspiracies and activities spanning jurisdictional boundaries" among the activities for which the Bureau of Justice Assistance can make grants and enter into contracts with local criminal justice agencies and non-profit organizations, and authorized $150,000,000 through 2003 for this purpose.

Title VIII: Terrorism criminal law

Section 801 created a prohibition of "terrorist attacks and other acts of violence against mass transportation systems."

Section 802 defined "domestic terrorism" as activities that "involve acts dangerous to human life that were a violation of the criminal laws of the United States or of any State; appear to be intended to intimidate or coerce a civilian population; to influence the policy of a government by intimidation or coercion; or to affect the conduct of a government by mass destruction, assassination, or kidnapping; and occur primarily within the territorial jurisdiction of the United States."

Title IX: Improved intelligence

Section 901 provides "assistance to the Attorney General to ensure that information derived from electronic surveillance or physical searches" under the Foreign Intelligence Surveillance Act "is disseminated so it may be used efficiently and effectively for foreign intelligence purposes."

Section 905 required that heads of federal law enforcement agencies were to disclose foreign intelligence information to the Director of Central Intelligence that was acquired in the course of criminal investigations.

Section 908 required the Attorney General, in consultation with the Director of Central Intelligence, to provide training in identifying and utilizing foreign intelligence information to federal officials who are not ordinarily involved with its use and to state and local officials who may encounter foreign intelligence in the course of a terrorist event.

Title X: Miscellaneous

Section 1006 prohibited the admissibility of an alien to the United States about whom the government has reason to believe is engaged in money laundering offences.

Section 1008 authorized a feasibility study of fingerprint identification and access to the FBI fingerprint database at overseas consular offices, and at points of entry to the United States, to identify aliens wanted in connection with criminal or terrorist investigations.

Section 1010: Gives temporary authority to the Defense Department to contract with local and state governments for performance of security functions at United States military installations until 180 days after the completion of Operation Enduring Freedom.

Section 1011 included telemarketing calls for charitable contributions along with calls for goods and services in the telemarketing fraud laws.

Section 1012 prohibited a state from issuing a license to operate a motor vehicle transporting a hazardous material unless the Secretary of Transportation determined that the individual does not pose a security risk warranting denial of the license.

Section 1016 established the National Infrastructure Simulation and Analysis Center to address critical infrastructure protection and continuity. [229]

Reauthorizations (2005) and the Sunset Provisions

To allay the concerns of legislators who had questioned the constitutionality of certain provisions, Section 224, titled "Sunset," stipulated that 16 sections and two subsections of the act would cease to have effect on December 31, 2005. [230] In 2005, a compromise was achieved when President Bush made 14 of the original sunset provisions permanent and extended two others, sections 206 and 215, to December 31, 2009. The act also extended the "lone wolf" provision of the Intelligence Reform and Terrorism Prevention Act of 2004, which permitted the Foreign Intelligence Surveillance Court (FISC) to authorize surveillance and physical searches aimed at foreign nationals who are "engaged in international terrorism or activities in preparation for international terrorism." [231]

The reauthorized version increased the powers of government agencies to carry out surveillance on a larger scale. After extending the provisions to February 2010 and then to February 2011,

229 Horowitz, Richard (2015), Summary of Key Sections of USA Patriot Act, URL http://www.rhesq.com/Terrorism/Patriot_Act_Summary.pdf.

230 https://www.britannica.com/topic/USA-PATRIOT-Act

231 https://www.fletc.gov/sites/default/files/imported_files/training/programs/legal-division/downloads-articles-and-faqs/research-by-subject/miscellaneous/ForeignIntelligenceSurveillanceAct.pdf

Congress adopted further extensions to May (sections 206 and 215) and December 2011 (the lone wolf provision). All three provisions were finally extended to June 1, 2015, by the PATRIOT Sunsets Extension Act of 2011, which was passed by Congress and signed into law by Pres. Barack Obama on May 26. [232]

Criticisms of the Act

Since its inception, the United States of America Patriotic Act has been subject to a number of criticisms. The American Civil Liberties Union (ACLU) objected to various provisions of the Act and charged that it was far too sweeping in allowing government law enforcement and other agencies to gain access to information that has traditionally been considered confidential and private and therefore not accessible to the government. [233]

First and foremost, critics allege that several parts of the act were unconstitutional and increased the powers of federal agencies beyond a permissible limit; the act violates the privacy provisions of the fourth amendment.

Secondly, critics of the Act argue that the provisions that authorize search and seizure of records requiring "only that the agent believe the records sought are related to [terrorist activity]," [234] and further, that targets are prohibited from disclosing that the FBI has sought or obtained information from them, infringes upon the right to freedom of speech.

Thirdly, the Act has been criticized for the lack of an effective judicial review mechanism. [235] The detainment of material witnesses and terrorist suspects without access to lawyers, hearings, or any formal charges are seen as erosions of the Fifth and Sixth Amendments, the rights of due process and trial by jury, respectively.

Democratic and Republican critics of the Patriot Act

---

232 Duignan, Brian (2014), USA PATRIOT Act, *Encyclopedia Britannica*, URL: http://www.britannica.com/topic/USA-Patriot-Act

233 Truman, Robert (2002), "Life With the USA Patriot Act: At the Crossroads of Privacy and Protection," *OLA Quarterly*, 8(4), URL: http://commons.pacificu.edu/cgi/viewcontent.cgi?article=1630&context=olaq

234 https://fas.org/irp/crs/RL31377.pdf

235 Ibid.

warned that its extraordinary surveillance powers would be used to investigate political dissent or low-level offenses rather than terrorism, and these apprehensions were realized in a 2007 report by the Inspector General of the Justice Department, who found "widespread and serious abuse" [236] of authority by the FBI under the Patriot Act. The report demonstrated numerous instances of direct and indirect surveillance of those who had no involvement in terrorist activity. These instances of abuse since 2002 counted to more than 1000. [237]

Provisions related to detention of immigrants have also come under harsh criticisms. Experts in America have criticized these provisions on the grounds that:

> Indefinite detention upon secret evidence—which the United States PATRIOT Act allows—sounds more like Taliban justice than ours. Our claim that we are attempting to build an international coalition against terrorism will be severely undermined if we pass legislation allowing even citizens of our allies to be incarcerated without basic U.S. guarantees of fairness and justice. [238]

To sum up, it can be said that the United States of America PATRIOT Act has given unprecedented powers to the US government and its organs to gather intelligence. Despite the Act facing vigorous criticisms from a major section of the academic fraternity, as well as from civil rights groups, the Act remains functional today with only minor changes to the original 2001 draft. The challenge still remains before the United States government to establish an adequate balance between security and civil liberty.

---

236 https://www.hrw.org/sites/default/files/wr2014_web_0.pdf

237 Grabiobowski, Ed (2016), How the Patriot Act works: Primary Criticisms of the Act, URL: http://people.howstuffworks.com/patriot-act2.htm.

238 Ramasastry, Anita (2001), INDEFINITE DETENTION BASED UPON SUSPICION:,How The Patriot Act Will Disrupt Many Lawful Immigrants' Lives, October 5, URL: http://writ.news.findlaw.com/commentary/20011005_ramasastry.html.

PART IV: MASS SURVEILLANCE— PRIVACY VS. SECURITY

Understanding the Balancing Challenge

"Those who would give up essential Liberty, to purchase a little
temporary Safety, deserve neither Liberty nor Safety."
– Benjamin Franklin

Do individuals have a divine right to privacy? In the book
The Limits of Privacy, Amitai Etzioni states that, "Most
people instinctively feel that privacy is to be cherished, but we
do not feel the other half of the equation – the need to give up
privacy for the good of common." [239] Etzioni argues that the
individual does not have a right to "absolute privacy;" [240] rather, it should be balanced with other rights. The purpose of as-
saulting another's privacy must be in order to combat a known
threat to the common good. For example, an employer should
not demand access to an employee's full medical records in
order ensure they are not being deceitful about their claims
to illness. The necessary invasions of privacy should involve
as little intrusion as possible, only requiring the documents
that are absolutely necessary. Once privacy is invaded, means
must be taken to minimize and treat undesirable side effects.

---

239 http://knowledge.wharton.upenn.edu/article/the-limits-of-privacy/

240 http://www.colinbennett.ca/wp-content/uploads/2012/06/Privacyin-the-Political-Sys-
tem.pdf

The problem lies in determining the middle ground between effective security and the invasion of privacy, and in deciding who should be trusted with society's personal information. The line between privacy and security is not so obvious. According to a claim of philosopher Jeremy Bentham, "Law is an invasion of privacy that must be justified on the grounds of necessary utility, in order to maximize happiness and minimize suffering." [241] Therefore, entities should employ a utilitarian perspective: private and government agencies should aim to achieve a balance by minimising the potential risks of managing delicate personal information, and maximising security.

Privacy is every person's "fundamental right," but when we try to interpret it from the security perspective, it becomes intricate and complicated. Privacy is our fundamental right, but we, as a nation, also strive to uphold the idea of national security to protect the safety of the entire country and all citizens. This debate has troubled our countries for years. Which is more meaningful and important for us as citizens: proper protection of our privacy or better security systems to protect us from terrorist attacks? Finding a perfect balance between these two concepts throughout history has proven to be nearly impossible. We can never strike a balance between privacy and national security. In recent years, we have, sort of, become adapted to the concept that sacrifice of privacy is the cost for better security. [242]

Starting in the 1960s, the United States government began digitalising its record systems and has since been making use of our generation's technologies to improve its efficiency and data collection capabilities. These new technologies have improved the security of the people significantly but can also be used to breach personal privacy and gather information regarding personal activities.

---

241 https://plato.stanford.edu/entries/bentham/

242 Lovejoy Kristen, Security vs. Privacy, Sep 2015(accessed online).
http://gsec.hitb.org/materials/sg2015/KEYNOTE%201%20-%20Kristin%20Lovejoy%20-%20
Our%20Daily%20Struggle%20to%20Balance%20National%20Security%20Interests%20
and%20Civil%20Liberties%20at%20the%20Ground%20Level%20.pdf

Edward Snowden—Revelations About Government Surveillance

In a world increasingly marked by security threats, the issue of the extent to which personal privacy should be sacrificed for security has assumed increasing significance. It cannot be denied that it is in the post-9/11 United States of America that the issue began and has continued to be hotly debated. In the post-9/11 era, under the USA Patriot Act, security has been far more proactive and intrusive in the United States than ever before.

On June 5, 2013, numerous confidential classified documents from the National Security Agency (NSA) were leaked to the press, revealing to the world the unbelievable extent of the surveillance being executed by United States intelligence agencies. A few days later on June 9, the name Edward Snowden surfaced as the identity of the whistleblower behind this revelation. The world was polarized in their opinion about him; the United States government charged him with espionage and theft of government property. The number of documents taken by him is still unknown; initially, NSA director Keith Alexander estimated that Snowden had copied anywhere between 50,000 to 200,000 documents. Now it is estimated that he copied around 1.7 million documents. These include phone call transcripts and global surveillance conducted by the NSA and the "Five Eyes"—an intelligence alliance comprised of Australia, Canada, New Zealand, the United Kingdom, and the United States. These countries maintain surveillance on their citizens and around the world.

In his interview, Edward Snowden revealed the American government's reactions in the wake of 9/11. Washington started a devastating war based on false information, and influential United States policymakers knew the pretext was false. [243] The documents released by Snowden showed that the NSA and other security agencies of America were collecting information, spying on the activities of people, and of other countries as well, through a surveillance system. The privacy of the American people was breached by America's Se-

---

243 https://www.wired.com/2014/08/edward-snowden/

curity Agencies in the name of improving national security. Snowden's documents revealed some shocking information. The NSA collects millions of Americans' phone records on a daily basis; it operates a program called PRISM, involving the surveillance of internet communications. In some cases, the agency can "incidentally" sweep up Americans' emails and phone calls without a specific warrant and store them for up to five years. [244]

Documents revealed by *The Guardian* shed some light on the extent of the agency's surveillance and suggest it is capable of consuming huge volumes of communications data. However, there is little evidence so far that supports any allegation that it can and does sweep up all global communications. An NSA tool named Boundless Informant, for instance, is used to record and analyze a significant portion of where the agency's intelligence is coming from. The tool showed that in March alone, the agency gathered, from across the world, 97 billion metadata records from computer networks and 125 billion telephone metadata records. Metadata is information about communications—who you are communicating with, where, and when—but not the content of the communications. A leak revealed by *The Guardian* in 2013 uncovered what national security officials called "an early warning system" for detecting terror plots. This involved an order, signed off by a judge of a secret court, compelling network provider Verizon to produce to the NSA electronic copies of all call detail records: that is 'telephone metadata' created by Verizon for communications between the United States and abroad or wholly within the United States, including local telephone calls. [245] The order also directs Verizon to continue production on an ongoing daily basis thereafter for the duration of the order. The order specifies that the records to be produced include session identifying information, such as the originating and terminat-

244 Gallagher Ryan, "Fact and Fiction in the NSA Surveillance Scandal," 26 June, 2013 (accessed online). http://www.slate.com/articles/technology/future_tense/2013/06/edward_snowden_fact_checking_which_surveillance_claims_were_right.3.html

245 Greenwald Glenn, "NSA collecting phone records of millions of Verizon customers daily," *The Guardian* (June, 2013) http://www.theguardian.com/world/2013/jun/06/nsa-phone-records-verizon-court-order

ing number, the duration of each call, telephone calling card numbers, trunk identifiers, International Mobile Subscriber Identity (IMSI) number, and comprehensive communication routing information. The sense that one gets from the order is that, more than the content of the call, what the government is looking for are network patterns. They are looking for how people are connected, trying to put timelines together, and trying to identify the locations of calls. This phenomenon of taking a bulk of data and finding patterns was much larger than previously thought. It can be assumed that the Verizon phone records acquired were being matched with an even broader set of data.

The government feels free to collect metadata about phone calls made in the United States because no one is said to have any genuine probability of privacy when it comes to this information, since customers already share it with their phone company. Meanwhile, the government opportunely asserts that the right to privacy is not involved when it collects communications and that the data would only be under scrutiny at such time as further examination was warranted. By this rationale, it would be acceptable for the government to gather and store a filmed video stream from peoples' bedrooms, so long as the streams were not being watched until the discovery of some compelling reason.

Data Mining and PRISM

The security breach by Snowden revealed that the government gathers billions of pieces of data from communication giants and then combs through the information for leads on national security threats; this is, in fact, data mining. According to a study by IBM, human beings create 2.5 quintillion bytes of data every day, which includes stored information, like photos, videos, social-media posts, word-processing files, phone-call records, financial records, and results from science experiments and data that normally exist for mere moments, such as phone-call content and Skype chats. This data is picked up by companies who use an algorithm to analyze the information for marketing purposes.

Snowden released a top-secret 32-page PowerPoint presentation describing software used by the FBI, CIA, and NSA that can search hundreds of databases for leads. [246] Snowden claims this program enables low-level analysts to access communications without oversight, helping them to avoid the checks and balances of the FISA court. America has been using data mining in the form of a clandestine surveillance program, which collects Internet communication from at least 9 companies, including AOL, Apple, Facebook, Google, Microsoft, Yahoo, Skype, YouTube, and Paltalk.

This program, code-named "PRISM," began in 2007 in the wake of the passage of the Protect America Act under the Bush Administration. [247] It was revealed that PRISM was the number one source of raw intelligence used for NSA analytic reports, and it accounts for 91% of the NSA's internet traffic acquired. PRISM was apparently established to provide in-depth surveillance on live communications and stored information about foreigners overseas. In statements, Apple, Facebook, Google, Microsoft, and Yahoo said that they only provide the government with user data required under the law. The tech companies have all denied that they have set up "back door access" to their systems for the United States government. The leaked NSA's documents make clear that the NSA has been able to obtain unilaterally both stored communications as well as real-time collection of raw data for the last six years, without the knowledge of users, who would assume their correspondence was private. If the NSA gets a tip, they vet it and then they mine the data for intelligence. For instance, they may notice an individual who has been watching a lot of terrorist propaganda and has been on a bomb-making website, and then makes a few purchases involving explosives or pressure cookers. This individual would be tagged and added to the suspect list.

Besides the invasion of privacy, another issue with govern-

246 "Edward Snowden: Leaks that exposed US spy programme"., BBC, Jan. 2014 http://www.bbc.com/news/world-us-canada-23123964

247 Sottek. T.C & Kopstein Joshua., "Everything you need to know about PRISM," The Verge (July 2013) http://www.theverge.com/2013/7/17/4517480/nsa-spying-prism-surveillance-cheat-sheet

ment data mining is the possibility of false positives. There is a high probability for error in this system where an algorithm is being used to identify potential terror suspects. Innocent people may be singled out to be questioned or put through duress because a computer program has erroneously flagged them as suspicious. From a resource perspective, false leads in the thousands could have agents running down useless leads. The case of Maher Arar, a telecommunication engineer, shows one such example. Maher Arar was recognized to have dual Syrian and Canadian citizenship and he was detained by United States government as a terrorist suspect. He was not associated with any terrorist group, as a Canadian enquiry confirmed, but the United States nonetheless still refuses to remove him from its watch-list. [248]

The surveillance program can be justified under section 215 of the Foreign Intelligence Surveillance Act, as amended by the USA Patriot Act, but it can also be claimed unconstitutional under the Fourth Amendment law of the European convention. The NSA's surveillance program was aimed at the collection of personal information, mainly non-content call information: information about who is contacting whom, time duration, and location of both the parties.

Massive amounts of long-term stored data have proven to reveal intimate details about a person's life that could never have been ascertained before. Many critics see this legislative act as Orwellian. George Orwell in *Nineteen Eighty-Four* depicted a harrowing totalitarian society ruled by a government called Big Brother that surveilled its public and demanded total obedience. Another bureaucracy of power is demonstrated in Kafka's novel, *The Trial,* which depicts a person unleashing sorrow after having been detained by the State without any valid reason. His information is used unethically by the State and he could not participate in how his information was used. The harms are abuse, frustration, and lack of transparency and accountability.

In the aftermath of Snowden's revelations, Obama announced a set of reforms designed to scale back the NSA sur-

---

248 https://infosecurity-magazine.com

veillance programs. He also ordered an end to the program that allows mass surveillance of telephone metadata. As of now, the intelligence community requires a court order to access any of the information they collect. Snowden revealed that America and the Five Eyes had been spying on leaders of other countries, and to this Obama called for an end to spying on foreign leaders, short of a compelling national security purpose. Companies like Yahoo and Google, whose data was being used, have now increased their security measures.

In a recent statement, British counter-terrorism official Stephen Phipson went on record to say that Snowden's leak changed how terrorist groups operate. Phipson said, "Our adversaries, the terrorists out there, now have full sight of the sorts of tools and range of techniques that are being used by government." [249] He claimed to have data showing a substantial reduction in the methods of communication used earlier by terrorists. The NSA was designed to protect America, but with Snowden revealing their methods of operation, the intelligence community felt that his exposure made it more difficult to save the country from terrorists. Central Intelligence Agency Director John Brennan has been critical of data collection methods in the United States of America and Europe. Mr. Brennan said that the "Islamic State and other terror groups had studied public disclosures on how US and other countries' agencies conduct surveillance. That has altered their methods and made them harder to catch." [250] The NSA's newest director, US Navy Admiral Michael S. Rogers, stated that while some terrorist groups had altered their communications to avoid surveillance techniques revealed by Snowden, the damage wasn't irreparable. Rogers said that Snowden's disclosures created "blind spots" in the NSA's surveillance by revealing United States strategies to monitor terrorism.

Osama bin Laden did not use email and avoided using phones because he did not want to be intercepted. What led to his capture was people on the ground and officials monitoring certain situations and behaviors, not tracking down email ac-

---

249 http://www.reuters.com/article/us-britain-snowden-idUSBREA3S0FQ20140429

250 Harnik, Andrew. "CIA Director John Brennan responds to a question as he speaks at the Global Security Forum," 16, Nov. 2015, *Associated Press.*

counts. The inconvenient truth is that terrorist networks know that phones and emails are not secure and avoid using them.

Central Intelligence Agency Director John Brennan has been critical of data collection methods in the United States and Europe. Mr. Brennan said that the "Islamic State and other terror groups had studied public disclosures on how United States and other countries' agencies conduct surveillance. That has altered their methods and made them harder to catch." [251]

Snowden's disclosures also created tensions between the United States and some of its close allies after it was revealed that the United States of Ameirca had spied on Brazil, France, Mexico, Britain, China, Germany, and Spain, as well as 35 world leaders. German Chancellor Angela Merkel, said that this "spying among friends" was "unacceptable." [252] Leaked documents published in 2014 appcarcd to show that the NSA had targeted 122 "high ranking" leaders.

Edward Snowden was Time Magazinc's man of the year; he has been celebrated in some quarters and called a traitor in others. He is hunted by America, and awaits life in prison if he ever returns. To his fans, he is lauded for his bravery in telling the truth at great personal risk. The intelligence community, however, questions the authenticity of Snowden's claims that he did not sell any information to Russia or China, two coun- tries that would do anything to get their hands on sensitive United States information. Given that all of his interviews were conducted in Hong Kong, and that he now has asylum in Russia, this question seems pertinent.

The world's citizens, thanks to Snowden, now know that they could be monitored at any time and nothing is truly pri- vate. As he said, "I do not want to live in a world where every- thing I do and say is recorded... My sole motive is to inform the public as to that which is done in their name and that which is done against them." [253] He will continue to impact the world one revelation at a time, and in a few years we will

251 Ibid.
252 Ibid.
253 Ibid.

know extent to which he has created changed. Regardless, thanks to Snowden, government agencies are being forced to strike a balance between security concerns and privacy.

In the modern era, technology has long been viewed as the source of many privacy concerns. Governments and private companies have at times employed technology outside of any legal framework and without regard to individual privacy. In the wake of Edward Snowden's leaks, lawyers and commentators have recognized that, while surveillance and information technologies have developed rapidly, the law of privacy has not kept pace with these changes. Although privacy law, at the international human rights level, is grounded in robust and pedigreed principles, it seems not to have been developed or adapted to fit the needs of 21st century society.

The United Nations framework also recognizes the right to privacy and is critical of government surveillance interfering with the privacy of citizens. In its resolution 68/167, the General Assembly requested the United Nations High Commissioner for Human Rights to submit a report on the protection and promotion of the right to privacy in the context of domestic and extraterritorial surveillance and/or the interception of digital communications and the collection of personal data. This report was to be conducted on a mass scale, and submitted to the Human Rights Council at its twenty-seventh session, and to the UN General Assembly at its sixty-ninth session, with views and recommendations, to be considered by member states. The result of this was a resolution titled, "Right to Privacy in a Digital Age" which was sponsored by more than 50 countries, including India, and approved unanimously by the 193 members. The resolution upholds the right to privacy for everyone and reaffirms the human rights core principle that individuals cannot be denied human rights simply because they live in a country different from the one that is placing them under surveillance.

The resolution calls upon states to end violations of privacy by ensuring that national legislation complies with obligations under international human rights law, and:

to review their procedures, practices and legislation regarding the surveillance of communications, their interception and collection of personal data, including mass surveillance, interception and collection, with a view to upholding the right to privacy by ensuring the full and effective implementation of all their obligations under international human rights law. [254]

The United Nations report also outlines the rights to an effective remedy against illegal surveillance. This right is laid out in the International Covenant on Civil and Political Rights which requires states to ensure that victims of violations of the Covenant have an effective recourse. Article 2, paragraph 3 (b) of the Covenant further specifies that State parties to the Covenant undertake:

to ensure that any person claiming such a remedy shall have his right thereto determined by competent judicial, administrative or legislative authorities, or by any other competent authority provided for by the legal system of the State, and to develop the possibilities of judicial remedy. [255]

The United Nations report recommends a greater role of multi-stakeholder engagement in order to address the concerns related to infringement of privacy due to surveillance, and calls for a dialogue involving all interested stakeholders, including member states, civil society, scientific and technical communities, the business sector, academics, and human rights experts.

Can Mass Surveillance be Ended?

Many activists around the globe came forward demanding freedom from surveillance. Levels of concern about government surveillance in democratic countries are now nearly as high as in non-democratic states with long legacies of perva-

---

254 http://www.ohchr.org/EN/Issues/DigitalAge/Pages/DigitalAgeIndex.aspx

255 http://www.ohchr.org/en/professionalinterest/pages/ccpr.aspx

sive state surveillance.

Edward Snowden recently discussed the failure of mass surveillance in providing security and averting terrorist attacks. In an interview with Dutch broadcasters, NOS, he suggested that if mass surveillance was a successful project, the Paris attacks could have been averted by the government. France passed one of the most intrusive, expansive surveillance laws in all of Europe, but it did not prevent the attack. He also talked about the Boston attack, of which the United States government was aware but could not do anything to stop. He claimed that, "The problem with mass surveillance is that you're burying people under too much data." This echoes arguments that others have made about the "base rate fallacy." [256]

After more than a decade of legal adventurism, secret presidential orders, and deceptive wordplay, policymakers and intelligence officials have erected a surveillance apparatus that can track the location of hundreds of millions of people, collect the phone records of the entire nation, and tap into the very backbone of the internet. [257] Apart from investing millions in spying and collecting data, nothing much has been achieved; moreover, the people of these nations have lost trust in investigative agencies and in terms of democracy and rights bestowed by the constitution.

The question of whether mass surveillance can be stopped remains a matter of debate. As long as the governments of these nations are of the opinion that mass surveillance is enhancing the security of their people, it will receive support from national authorities. Vigilantes are coming forward to demand freedom from authorities in their nation. People are conducting rallies to stand against mass surveillance, the revelation of which has created a wave of apprehension amongst the general population. Europeans have been more vocal in

256 Global Chilling: Impact of mass surveillance on international writers. (2015, January). PEN America, Pg. 5 …I think it's the second one…Meyer, D. (2015, January). Snowden: Paris showed mass surveillance doesn't stop terrorism. Retrieved from https://gigaom.com/2015/01/21/snowden-paris-showed-mass-surveillancedoesnt-stop-terrorism/

257 Sottek, T.C.. "End the Nightmare of mass surveillance," The Verge, (December 2013) retrieved from http://www.theverge.com/2013/12/12/5200142/end-the-nsa-nightmare

the matter and have reported such practices as a threat to their human rights.

Mass surveillance is not a venture of governments alone but a collaborative effort of various contributing companies. Activists and supporters of anti-surveillance forums have demanded that these companies work towards discontinuing ventures that support government surveillance initiatives. Many companies have understood their role in this matter and have deliberately weakened their services to the government as a result. To bring an end to mass surveillance, the government needs to be pressed for more transparency, and companies must make an effort to protect the privacy of the people they serve to a greater extent.

Governments must decide whether risking the trust of its citizens is worth the benefits of conducting mass surveillance, which has so far not proven sufficiently worthwhile. The United Nations and European Parliament have expressed their desire to eradicate the practice and have time and again demanded that the "Five Eyes" [258] alliance put an end to such practices, or devise policies to ensure the privacy of the majority of the population, only concentrating surveillance efforts on persons under warranted suspicion.

Privacy and Physical Surveillance

Whenever there is a discussion about the importance of privacy, surveillance is much discussed. The simple question is: who is watching us and why? Surveillance revolves around the monitoring of behavior and movement for the purpose of influencing, managing, and protecting. Mass surveillance is a systematic interference with people's right to privacy; the government can capture virtually all of the records of an individual. Closed circuit television cameras (CCTV) in public places have become a more commonplace phenomenon, but the monitoring of phones and computers are the main area of focus. There are no set limits to the government's broad access and power. States can amass data via optic cable in-

---

258 http://www.un.org/press/en/1998/19981210.ga9533.html

terception and read the contents of any unencrypted communication.

Camera surveillance, or close-circuit television, has received much attention since the bomb explosion on July 7, 2005 in London. Three bombs exploded on three underground trains and one bomb exploded on a bus in the city of London, killing fifty-two commuters. Identification of the suicide bombers was made possible by CCTV footage. United States House of Representatives representative Peter King of New York was impressed by surveillance cameras that could detain culprits, calling them "a great law enforcement method and device." [259] New York City Police Commissioner Ray Kelly went as far as refuting individual privacy for the sake of national security, saying: "The more cameras the better and I think the privacy issues have been taken off the table." [260] As a result of the London effect, the Homeland Security Agency demanded more CCTV cameras in the city, believing that video surveillance could be helpful to fight against terrorism and street crime.

CCTV is expected to deter terrorism by delivering the identity of terrorists. But terrorists' response to CCTV is not clearly predictable. Metal detectors have proven successful in reducing skyjacking. However, the propensity for terrorist attack is not decreasing. Camera footage may increase public attention to terrorist activities and might assist the attribution of attacks to specific networks. The United States routinely updates the authentication and identification of individuals, but it is also necessary to protect this stored data, data in transit, and to have some control over the release of data. Secrecy should be maintained in dealing with and processing this data. Surveillance is not only used to detect crime, it has many more potential uses. GPS transmitters can help dispatchers provide better service on the road. Iris scanning is a technological system that can dissect the cartographical record of an individual and whether he has previously entered a building without necessarily identifying the individ-

---

259 http://www.nytimes.com/2016/10/04/nyregion/despite-national-trend-new-york-police-are-slow-to-adopt-body-cameras.html?_r=0

260 https://www.theguardian.com/commentisfree/2013/jul/24/factchecking-ray-kelly-nypd-wsj

ual. Radio-Frequency Identification gives information about the clothes we wear and the money we carry and exchange. People are living in a society where nothing can really be hidden.

State audio and videotaping laws are facing challenges from pro-privacy organizations. United States of America courts concluded that the use of facial-recognition technology may hamper individual privacy and violate the Fourth Amendment prohibition of "unreasonable search and seizure."

DNA databases are also a subject of debate. They are used to trace people who are suspected of committing a crime; however, privacy concerns arise from the very personal nature of storing an individual's tissues and computerized DNA samples. In some countries, only the DNA of convicted criminals is stored, but in this case, the DNA of persons in the United States who are arrested, but not convicted, has been recorded. In some countries, a DNA database of the whole population has been proposed. In October 1998, the Federal Bureau of Investigation began a nation-wide DNA database mission in which DNA would be collected from all fifty states. DNA databases could also potentially be used to track those whose "crime" is an act of peaceful protest or dissent. It is also possible that, "in a state where freedom of speech or political rights are restricted, the police or secret services could attempt to take DNA samples from the scene of a political meeting to establish whether or not particular individuals had been present." [261] Although DNA analysis has led to notable advancement in crime scene investigation technology, DNA can be restored badly or the experts can make a mistake, and in that case an individual's privacy is at risk.

Privacy concerns fall into grey areas of the United States Constitution, which does not directly address privacy rights. To provide Americans with a constitutional right to privacy, the Supreme Court has merged First Amendment protection, i.e. the right to speech and to assemble, and the Fourth Amend-

---

261 http://dnapolicyinitiative.org/resources/dna-databases-and-human-rights/

ment, i.e. protection of individuals against illegal search and seizure. However, no right is absolute and the government does have some conditional right to invade one's privacy. Personal information will be the new currency of access and privilege. Technology determines most of what we do. A news story from the New Zealand Press set an example. According to the report, an employee was terminated because he refused to give his fingerprints. The company claimed that they needed the fingerprints of every employee to combat false time claims. The fired employee saw this request as an illogical invasion of his personal information, reminiscent of a master-slave relationship rather than a boss-employee relationship, so he did not give his consent. Also relevant is the case of the news reports on an alleged sex scandal of the former President of the Federation Internationale de l'Automobile, Max Mosley, who successfully took legal action against News Group Newspapers Limited for violating and damaging his privacy. [262]

Governments can breach the personal privacy of the people, but in doing so, they should be very careful, since they are dealing with a very sensitive issue. The government, especially the Security Agencies, should be very cautious while gathering the personal information of the people. The American Constitution, most specifically in the fourth amendment, provides clear regulations for wire-tapping, bugging, and other methods of communication surveillance, but it does not clearly regulate physical surveillance. As a result, there is a gap concerning what is and what is not illegal, which can potentially be exploited since there are no laws to protect privacy.

Assessing the Usefulness of Data Mining for National Security

Gone are the days when governments followed people on foot. Today, electronic monitoring is used on an unparalleled scale. Never in the history of humanity have our lives been such an open book to governments agencies.

The entire world descended heavily on America post-

---

262 Extra reference: www.equalityhumanrights.com; www.libertyhumanrights.org.uk; https://en.m.wikipedia.org; www.thegurdian.com; http://www.aclu.org

Snowden, each country aghast at leaked reports of America spying on them, but America has stood strong in saying it used all this data to circumvent any further terror attacks on American soil and even helped out other countries in the process with its refined intelligence measures.

Keith Alexander, director of the United States National Security Agency, claims that its digital archive is essential to monitoring terrorist activities and has stopped dozens of potential attacks, asserting that the program is not about spying on citizens, but rather using the data for national safety. "The perspective is that we're hiding something because we've done something wrong. We're not." [263] On the other hand, privacy activists counter that such deep data-mining is an unjustified invasion of personal privacy, undermining civil liberties and eroding longstanding constitutional protections.

Despite the backlash, the United States does make a good argument in support of Prism and its ability to help prevent terror attacks in the early stages. Critics still point out that terrorist masterminds have been becoming more technologically savvy and will find a way around these programs, but one cannot deny the usefulness of such a handy technology that could help find a needle in a haystack.

The NSA has constantly described Prism as "one of the most valuable, unique and productive accesses" [264] of intelligence, and boasts the service has been made available to spy organizations from other countries, including the Government Communications Headquarters (GCHQ), a British intelligence and security organization. [265] According to reports, the British agency generated 197 intelligence reports from Prism in 2012, marking a 137% increase in the number of reports generated from the year prior. Intelligence reports from GCHQ are normally passed to MI5 and MI6.

According to James Clapper, the director of national intelli-

---

263 http://www.jpost.com/printarticle.aspx?id=316867

264 https://www.theguardian.com/world/2013/jun/06/us-tech-giants-nsa-data

265 Hopkins Nick., "UK gathering secret intelligence via covert NSA operation," *The Guardian* (June 2013) https://www.theguardian.com/technology/2013/jun/07/uk-gathering-secret-intelligence-nsa-prism

gence in the United States of America, "Information collected under this program is among the most important and valuable intelligence information we collect, and is used to protect our nation from a wide variety of threats." [266] According to Mike Rogers, the chairman of the House Intelligence Committee, the NSA's phone-metadata collection program, part of which Clapper just declassified, helped prevent a "significant domestic terrorist attack" [267] within "the last few years." [268] Data Brokerage Company, Axciom Corp., has said that they also worked with the government after the September 2001 terrorist attacks, providing information about 11 of the 19 hijackers. United States officials say this tactic helped snare Khalid Ouazzani, a naturalized United States citizen who the FBI claimed was plotting to blow up the New York Stock Exchange. Ouazzani was in contact with a known extremist in Yemen, which brought him to the attention of the NSA. It identified Ouazzani as a possible conspirator and gave the information to the FBI, which "went up on the electronic surveillance and identified his co-conspirators." [269]

Surveillance allowed by the Patriot Act provided necessary tools for investigating defendants in the "Virginia Jihad" case. Eight individuals had been giving paramilitary training in Northern Virginia, at the centre of Dar al-Arqam's Islamic Center, and had been sending members to Pakistan and Afghanistan to terrorist training camps. These individuals were associated with a violent Islamic extremist group known as Lashkar-e-Taiba (LET) and had been tied to Al-Qaeda terrorist networks. The record obtained through FISA (Foreign Intelligence Security Act) was helpful in bringing charges against these individuals and prosecuting them.

Another example is the little-known Vermont Bomb Plot of 2002 where six "terrorists" had been planning to lay and detonate a bomb in four different locations at the Vermont centre.

---

266 https://www.theguardian.com/world/2013/jun/07/clapper-secret-nsa-surveillance-prism

267 http://theweek.com/articles/463450/what-know-about-prism-nsas-data-goldmine

268 Ibid.

269 http://abcnews.go.com/Blotter/nsa-claim-thwarted-nyse-plot-contradicted-court-documents/story?id=19436557

The government had the upper hand when the suspects discussed their plans prior to the event via email and in phone conversations. It is also worth noting that nearly 60% of foiled acts of terrorism have been stopped through monitoring.

Due to the very real threat of terrorism, many are not against surveillance, seeing the invasion of privacy as a trade off with security. In a poll a week after the Boston marathon bombings in April 2013, 78% of people said surveillance cameras were a good idea.

The United States federal government controls the world's biggest data bank. The NSA, specifically, is storing as much data as possible; the agency has built a data center in Bluffdale, Utah that is five times larger than the United States Capitol, all for the purpose of sifting through Big Data. [270] According to their website:

> The $1.5 billion-dollar, one-million-square-feet houses a 100,000 sqare-foot mission critical Tier III data center. The remaining 9,000,000 square-feet are used for technical support and administrative space. Our massive twenty building complex also includes water treatment facilities, chiller plants, electric substation, fire pump house, warehouse, vehicle inspection facility, visitor control center, and sixty diesel-fueled emergency standby generators and fuel facility for a 3-day 100% power backup capability. [271]

The website also goes on to say, "the center is designed to support the Intelligence Community's efforts to monitor, strengthen and protect the nation. Our Utah 'massive data repository' is designed to cope with the vast increases in digital data that have accompanied the rise of the global network." [272]

The $1.5 billion dollar center has fed perceptions that some factions of the United States government are determined to

---

270 NSA Web page: Domestic surveillance directorate
https://nsa.gov1.info/utah-data-center/
271 Ibid.
272 Ibid.

build a database of all forms of communication, including the complete contents of private emails, cell phone calls, and internet searches, as well as all types of personal data trails. The NSA website also goes on to say, "The steady rise in available computer power and the development of novel computer platforms will enable us to easily turn the huge volume of incoming data into an asset to be exploited, for the good of the nation."[273]

Today, information is currency, while data analytics is a booming field—the $1.15 billion revenue of Axciom is proof enough—and while harnessing the power of data analytics is clearly a competitive advantage, too much data mining can backfire and threaten the peace and privacy of the customers involved. Sometimes surveillance helps prevent terrorism, but there needs to be a perfect balance between secrecy in technological maneuvers, and adequately informed policing is essential for the checks and balances in the national security system. One cannot completely vilify and denigrate the efforts of the intelligence community in their attempt to keep the country safe, but at the same time citizens should not feel like their space and privacy is being blatantly violated by both corporate and security agencies.

There has to be a balance between security and privacy, nobody should infringe on the right to privacy, but at the same time, if an individual is planning to create chaos and harm innocent people, the country will sleep better knowing that the government has an eye on them. The government should focus on targeting terrorists and figuring out ways to prevent and derail threats to the nation or the world. Information is the most valuable

---

273 Ibid.

PART V: TERRORISM AND LAW POST-9/11

"The security of which we speak is to be attained by the development of international law through an international organization based on the principles of law and justice"
– Ludwig Quidde

The community in which we work and live today is more international than it has ever been in the past. This section focuses on the role of law within this international community and, more particularly, how it has been breached in recent times. International law is not the law of particular states; rather, it is a law that applies between the states, not within one country. The importance and significance of international law can be realized from the growing number of treaties between states, or between states and different international organizations. There are a vast number of areas where international law operates and controls, inclusive of the security and sovereignty of each and every nation.

The First and Second World Wars were the bloodiest wars ever witnessed by the people of the world. These two world wars, with the participation of almost all the powerful nations of the world, brought unimaginable devastation and havoc. As a result, the common people realized the need for strict international laws to put an end to these wars and provide the people with peace and security. The thought process or ideology of the people of that time was that international organizations and international law could replace war with peaceful international adjudication. International laws were formed, existing laws were strengthened, a number of treaties were signed between nations, and each and every nation took the vow to protect international security and national sovereignty.

Even when there is no country fighting with another nation, no world war being fought, there is still a threat, an elusive enemy lurking. This threat is gaining prominence and causing serious issues; it is trying to cause a wound so deep to mankind that it could never be healed. This threat is terrorism. In present day, the global network of terrorism is triggering disasters of unpredictable magnitude. The terrorists are blind with their ideology, and their hatred is too lethal to be counteracted by war machinery, or by the law and order enforcement agencies of various states. Terrorism is a global threat, and the terrorists are operating globally, causing irrevocable harm to mankind.

Terrorist attacks have become so common nowadays that it seems that "peace has become a subject to be discussed in conferences and summits and all endeavours to have it have been futile as violence has made its way to establish its diabolic might." [274] Its glaring threat was seen most poignantly in the recent terror attacks in Paris, in November of 2015. These attacks once again compelled us to think about our security and about strengthening international laws.

The recent terror attacks of — 2015 and 2016 — have made it very clear that there is a serious crisis of security in the world. I am providing here a list of the terror attacks which took place in this single year. Note that the chart does not list the thousands of monthly executions and attacks carried out by Daesh in Iraq and Syria.

Date: 7 January
Type: Car bomb
Dead: 37/38
Location: Yemen
Details: A car bomb detonated in front of a police academy in Sanaa killing 33 people and injuring 62.

---

274 http://gulfnews.com/your-say/your-view/terrorism-is-a-menace-to-humanity-1.1631709

Date: 10 January
Type: Suicide Bombing
Dead: 19+
Location: Nigeria
Details: At least 19 people were killed by a girl, aged 10, in a suicide bombing attack.

Date: 4-5 February
Type: Mass shooting, Bombing
Dead: 22
Location: Pakistan
Details: A militant group broke into a mosque and started shooting people. Three explosions were also heard in the mosque. 22 people were killed and at least 60 injured.

Date: 26 February
Type: Suicide Bombing
Dead: 19
Location: Nigeria
Details: A suicide bomber detonates himself near a market in the Northern town of Biu, Nigeria, killing 19 and wounding another 19 people; a second suicide bomber was caught and beaten to death by the crowd. Attack was attributed to Boko Haram.

Date: 20 March
Type: Suicide Bombing
Dead: 142
Location: Yemen
Details: Daesh militants in Yemen carried out four suicide bombings at the Badr and al-Hashoosh Shia mosques during prayers in the city of Sana'a mosque bombings.

Date: 1 April
Type: Mass Shooting
Dead: 147
Location: Kenya
Details: Six to ten gunmen associated with the radical Islamic terrorist group Al-Shabaab open fired at the Garissa University in Kenya. Christians were the main target of the attack, with the Islamic extrem-

143

ists separating the Muslims from Christians before executing them. Up to three hundred students are unaccounted for. One hundred and forty-seven students were reported killed, with fears the toll will rise, along with seventy-nine wounded.

Date: 13 May
Type: Attack
Dead: 45
Location: Pakistan
Details: A bus carrying Shia Muslims was attacked by six armed gunman who rode up in motorcycles. After the attack the bus driver drove straight to a hospital, where people said most of the riders were either dead, unconscious, and spattered in blood. Jundallah (claimed), Daesh (claimed), Tehrik-i-Taliban Pakistan (claimed)

Date: 25-29 June
Type: Massacre
Dead: 223-233
Location: Syria
Details: Daesh bombers detonated three car bombs in Kobanî, close to the Turkish border crossing.

Date: 1-2 July
Type: Massacre
Dead: 145
Location: Nigeria
Details: Kukawa Massacre: Boko Haram militants attacked multiple mosques. 84 men and boys were killed on the 1st at one mosque in Kukawa. 17 were wounded in the attack. 97 others, mostly men, were killed in numerous mosques on the 2nd with a number of women and young girls killed in their homes. An unknown number were wounded. Boko Haram claimed responsibility.

Date: 17 July
Type: Suicide Bomb
Dead: 130
Location: Iraq
Details: Khan Bani Saad bombing: A car bomb was sent to a crowded market in Khan Bani Saad in Iraq, 30 km north to Baghdad, during the

Eid al-Fitr celebrations. The explosion killed at least 100 (15 children among them) and injuring another 170 people and brought down several buildings. Daesh claimed responsibility and said 180 people were killed.

Date: 7 August
Type: Suicide Bomb
Dead: 50
Location: Afghanistan
Details: A lone suicide bomber attacked recruits outside a police academy. A truck bomb was set off in a residential area in the city. A block was leveled, leaving a thirty foot deep crater. At least 50 people were killed with more than 500 wounded. Responsibility for the attack has not been claimed, but the Taliban is suspected.

Date: 10 August
Type: Suicide Bomb
Dead: 50
Location: Iraq
Details: Bombings in the predominantly Shia areas of the Diyala Province killed more than 50 people and wounded more than 80. Daesh claimed responsibility for the attacks.

Date: 13 August
Type: Car Bomb
Dead: 76
Location: Iraq
Details: Baghdad market truck bombing: A refrigeration truck loaded with explosives was blown up in the center of a market in Baghdad's Sadr City. Followers of Shia Islam were targeted in the attack. Seventy-six were killed with two hundred and twelve wounded. Daesh claimed responsibility for the attack.

Date: 20 September
Type: Suicide Bomb
Dead: 145
Location: Nigeria
Details: Boko Haram executed a series of blasts, some of which were Suicide bombings, in the north eastern city of Maiduguri, targeting a

market and civilians in a mosque during night pray and a football match viewers, bringing the total number of casualties to at least 53 dead and over 90 wounded. The attack was said to be made using homemade weapons.

Date: 10 October
Type: Suicide Bombing
Dead: 102
Location: Turkey
Details: Two suicide bombers detonated near Ankara central station where a rally for peace supported by HDP was taking place. The attack left 102 dead and 508 injured.

Date: 13 November
Type: Mass Shooting
Dead: 130
Location: Paris
Details: Daesh - A series of co-ordinated attacks over approximately 35 minutes at six locations in central Paris. The first shooting attack occurred in a restaurant and a bar in the 10th arrondissement of Paris. There was shooting and a bomb detonated at Bataclan theatre in the 11th arrondissement during a rock concert. Approximately 100 hostages were then taken and overall 89 were killed there. Other bombings took place outside the Stade de France stadium in the suburb of Saint-Denis during a football match between France and Germany.

Date: 5 December
Type: Suicide Bomb
Dead: 27
Location: Chad
Details: Boko Haram - Three female suicide bombers attacked markets in different areas of the island Loulou Fou on the Chadian side of Lake Chad

Date: 8 December
Type: Suicide Bomb
Dead: 50
Location: Afghanistan
Details: Taliban Kandahar Airport attack: The Afghan defense minis-

try said 50 civilians and members of the security forces had been killed, along with 11 Taliban. A further 35 people were injured, it said. Taliban claimed responsibility. [275]

2016

Date: 1 January
Type: Suicide bombing
Dead: 15
Location: Afghanistan
Details: Suicide bomber detonated himself in a French restaurant called 'Le Jardin', located near a district with many foreign embassies and government buildings in Kabul, killing 15. Taliban claimed responsibility.

Date: 3 January
Type: Suicide Bombing
Dead: 15
Location: Iraq
Details: Two of the bombers detonated their vehicle-borne explosives at the western gate of Camp Speicher, a former U.S. base. The blasts killed at least 15 members of the security forces and wounded 22 others. The Islamic State claimed responsibility for the blasts and said it was aimed against Shi'ite Muslims.

Date: 4 January
Type: Suicide Bombing
Dead: 30
Location: Afghanistan
Details: Militant drove a truck packed with explosives to the armored gates of a compound for civilian contractors near Kabul's airport before being detonated, smashing windows and sending glass flying and badly damaging nearby houses. At least 30 Afghan civilians, including nine children, were wounded in the attack. Taliban claimed responsibility for the attack.

---

275 For further list of all the terrorist incidents which took place in 2016, including attacks by violent non-state actors, split up by month, check: https://en.wikipedia.org/wiki/List_of_terrorist_incidents_in_December_2015

Date: 7 January
Type: Suicide Car Bombing
Dead: 60
Location: Libya
Details: Suicide truck bomb was detonated at a police training camp al-Jahfal while around 400 young policemen were being trained in the Libyan town of Zliten, killing 60 people and wounding 200 others. No group claimed responsibility, but Daesh is suspected.

Date: 20 January
Type: Attack
Dead: 20
Location: Pakistan
Details: Bacha Khan University attack: Several gunmen, some equipped with suicide vests, opened fire on Bacha Khan University, killing 20 people and wounding another 20. At least four of the attackers were also killed during the attack. More than 200 students were rescued from the building. Tehrik-i-Taliban Pakistan claimed responsibility, and it was perpetrated by members of the Geedar-faction.

Date: 17 February
Type: Suicide Bombing
Dead: 30
Location: Turkey
Details: Ankara bombing: At least 30 people died and 61 were injured in the Turkish capital. The attack targeted the army buses near the central square of Kizilay.

Date: 29 February
Type: Suicide Bombing
Dead: 40
Location: Iraq
Details: The death toll in a suicide bombing in Iraq's eastern province of Diyala rose to 24. A further 55 people were wounded in the attack at a funeral for a Shi'ite Muslim militia fighter in Muqdadiya, 80 km (50 miles) northeast of Baghdad.

Date: 6 March
Type: Suicide Car Bomb

Dead: 61
Location: Iraq
Details: A suicide bomber kills at least 60 people and wounds 70 others after ramming his explosives-laden truck into a security checkpoint at one of entrances to the Iraqi city of Hillah, south of Baghdad.

Date: 22 March
Type: Suicide Bombing
Dead: 32
Location: Belgium
Details: Brussels bombings: three coordinated nail bombings occurred in Belgium: two at Brussels Airport in Zaventem, and one at Maalbeek metro station in Brussels. In these attacks, 32 people and three suicide bombers were killed, and 340 people were injured. Daesh inspired attack.

Date: 25 March
Type: Suicide Bombing
Dead: 30
Location: Iraq
Details: Iskandariya suicide bombing: A suicide bomber blew himself up in a crowd after a local football game in a village near Iskandariya, in a mixed Sunni-Shiite area, killing at least 30 people and wounding more than 65. Daesh is suspected.

Date: 27 March
Type: Suicide Bombing
Dead: 72
Location: Pakistan
Details: Lahore suicide bombing: At least 72 people were killed, including 29 children and over 200 others people were injured in a suicide bombing that hit the main entrance of Gulshan-e-Iqbal Park, one of the largest parks in Lahore.

Date: 19 April
Type: Suicide Car Bomb
Dead: 64
Location: Afghanistan
Details: Kabul attack: A Taliban suicide bomb and gun assault on a

government security building during morning rush hour in central Kabul killed at least 64 people and wounded more than 320, in the most deadly single attack in the Afghan capital since 2011.

Date: 21 April
Type: Shooting
Dead: 250
Location: Iraq
Details: At least 250 Iraqi woman were executed by Daesh State fighters because they refused to become sex slaves.

Date: 30 April
Type: Suicide Car Bomb
Dead: 38
Location: Iraq
Details: April 2016 Baghdad bombing: A suicide bomber driving a car killed at least 38 people and wounded 86 others on April 30 in an attack claimed by Daesh on a group of Shi'ite Muslim pilgrims in a southeastern suburb of Baghdad, Iraqi police sources said. A second explosion near a Shi'ite militia checkpoint in the capital's Dora district killed two and wounded three others, police sources said.

Date: 1 May
Type: Suicide Car Bomb
Dead: 40
Location: Iraq
Details: Daesh attack - several children are among over three dozen dead after two suicide car bombs blast go off in different areas.

Date: 12 June
Type: Shooting
Dead: 49
Location: USA
Details: Orlando nightclub shooting: 49 people were killed when an alleged lone-wolf gunman entered the Pulse gay nightclub. Hostages were taken and the perpetrator, Omar Mateen, was shot dead by local SWAT units in an attempt to storm the building. The FBI classified the attack as an act of "domestic terrorism" motivated by Daesh.

Date: 30 June
Type: Suicide Bombing
Dead: 40
Location: Afghanistan
Details: At least 40 people were killed and 50 were injured after two Taliban suicide bombers attacked police cadets returning from a graduation ceremony outside of the capital Kabul.

Date: 1 July
Type: Shooting
Dead: 24
Location: Bangladesh
Details: Daesh Dhaka attack: A number of gunmen attacked a restaurant popular with foreigners in the wealthy Gulshan Thana area of Dhaka. At least twenty-two civilians, two police officers, and five attackers were killed in shoot-outs and dozens of hostages were taken.

Date: 3 July
Type: Bombing
Dead: 342
Location: Iraq
Details: Karrada bombing: At least 346 people were killed, and over 246 injured, in a series of coordinated bomb attacks in Baghdad. Early in the evening of July 3, a large car bomb exploded in the middle of a busy market, killing nearly 346 civilians. The blast occurred in the Baghdad neighborhood of Karrada, which contains Shia Muslims and a large Christian minority. A second car bombing in the district of Sha'ab killed at least 5 people and injured 16, while two more bombings killed at least two more people

Date: 6 July
Type: Suicide Bombing
Dead: 33
Location: Yemen
Details: Al-Qaeda in the Arabian Peninsula - Militants launched an attack against the airport army headquarters adjacent to Aden International Airport starting with two suicide car bombs. The militants then stormed the facility and engaged in a firefight with security forces. At least 25 security personal were killed and at least 8 were wounded.

Date: 7 July
Type: Suicide Bombing
Dead: 56
Location: Iraq
Details: Muhammad ibn Ali al-Hadi Mausoleum attack: At least 56 people were killed and 75 injured after a suicide car bomb blew up at the gate of the Mausoleum of Sayid Mohammed bin Ali al-Hadi. Gunmen then entered the mausoleum and started shooting at the people inside. Daesh claimed that they killed over 100 people.

Date: 14 July
Type: Vehicle assault
Dead: 86
Location: France
Details: A cargo truck was deliberately driven into crowds celebrating Bastille Day on the Promenade des Anglais in Nice, France, resulting in the deaths of 86 people and injuring 434. Daesh inspired attack.

Date: 23 July
Type: Suicide Bombing
Dead: 80
Location: Afghanistan
Details: Kabul bombing: Two suicide bombers targeted ethnic Hazaras at a rally in Kabul, killing over 80 people and wounding at least 230 more. Daesh claimed responsibility for the attack.

Date: 6 August
Type: Execution
Dead: 85
Location: Iraq
Details: At least 85 people were killed and hundreds kidnapped and held hostage after a massacre carried out by Daesh. Daesh also kidnapped over 3000 more people and executed 15 in the same city, before the event listed first.

Date: 8 August
Type: Suicide Bombing
Dead: 93
Location: Pakistan

Details: Taliban - Quetta attacks: A suicide bomb attack killed at least 93 people and wounded dozen others at a hospital in Quetta in southwest Pakistan, and injured around 120 more.

Date: 20 August
Type: Suicide Bombing
Dead: 54
Location: Turkey
Details: Daesh attack - Gaziantep suicide bombing: A suicide bomb attack at a Kurdish wedding ceremony near the Syrian border killed at least 50 and injured 94. The suicide bomber was aged 12 to 14, reports say.

Date: 29 August
Type: Suicide Bombing
Dead: 71
Location: Yemen
Details: Daesh - August 2016 Aden bombing: At least 71 people were killed in a suicide car bombing at a military facility in the southern Yemen city of Aden.

Date: 5 September
Type: Suicide Bombing
Dead: 58
Location: Afghanistan
Details: Taliban - September 2016 Kabul attacks: At least 58 people died in a double suicide attack in rush hour near the Ministry of Defence. Ninety-one people were also injured. A third explosion caused one death.

Date: 9 September
Type: Suicide Car Bomb
Dead: 40
Location: Iraq
Details: Baghdad bombings: Two car bombs exploded outside a crowded shopping center, killing at least 40 people, and wounding 60 more. Most of the victims were Shi'a Muslims. The attack was claimed by Daesh.

Date: 16 September
Type: Suicide Bombing
Dead: 30
Location: Pakistan
Details: Taliban - 2016 September Pakistan mosque bombing: A suicide bomber attacked a Sunni mosque in northwest Pakistan, killing at least 30 worshippers and wounding 28 others, officials said. Several children were also among those killed or wounded in the deadly attack. A breakaway Taliban group later claimed responsibility for the bombing.

Date: 15 October
Type: Suicide Bomb
Dead: 41
Location: Iraq
Details: Baghdad attacks: Suicide bomber targets mourning tent in Baghdad, kills 41.

Date: 24 October
Type: Suicide Bomb Shooting
Dead: 62
Location: Pakistan
Details: Daesh and Lashkar-e-Jhangvi: Quetta police training college attack, at least five militants stormed a police training center in Quetta and took between 200 and 500 cadets hostage. Three of the attackers were killed and at least 60 people were killed and 120 were injured. Several hostages escaped as well.

Date: 12 November
Type: Suicide Bombing
Dead: 55
Location: Pakistan
Details: Daesh - Khuzdar bombing: At least 55 people including women and children have been killed and above 100 injured when a suicide bomber went off in the crowded Shah Noorani Shrine in Hub town, Lasbela District, Balochistan, Pakistan.

Date: 18 November
Type: Suicide Car Bomb

Dead: 40
Location: Iraq
Details: Daesh - at least 40 people were killed and more than 60 wounded after a suicide car bomb attack targeted a police officer's wedding in Amiriyat al-Fallujah in Iraq.

Date: 21 November
Type: Suicide Bomb
Dead: 30
Location: Afghanistan
Details: Daesh - Kabul suicide bombing: At least 30 people have been killed and another 35 were injured in a suicide bombing at a Kabul mosque.

Date: 24 November
Type: Suicide Truck Bomb
Dead: 125
Location: Iraq
Details: Daesh -Hillah suicide truck bombing: A truck bomb killed at least 100 people in Hillah city.

Date: 9 December
Type: Suicide Bombing
Dead: 57
Location: Nigeria
Details: Boko Haram - Madagali suicide bombings: Officials say 2 explosions in Madagali a town Nigeria have killed 57 and injured 177.

Date: 10 December
Type: Suicide Bombing
Dead: 50
Location: Yemen
Details: Daesh - Aden suicide bombings: 50 Yemeni soldiers were killed and another 70 were injured in a suicide bombing attack.

Date: 10 December
Type: Suicide Car bomb
Dead: 45
Location: Turkey

Details: Istanbul bombings: Two bombs killed 44 and injured at least 155 people in Istanbul.

Date: 18 December
Type: Suicide Bomb
Dead: 52
Location: Yemen
Details: Aden suicide bombings: At least 52 Yemeni soldiers collecting their salaries at a base in northeast Aden were killed when a suicide bomber detonated. [276]

Urban Attacks: Madrid, London, Mumbai, and Paris Attacks

Terrorism is a complex phenomenon, defined as a type of asymmetric warfare that deliberately and indiscriminately employs violence against non-combatants and their sources of support in order to threaten or intimidate them for political purposes. According to United Nations Secretary General Ban Ki Moon, "Terrorism and violent extremism are global threats, transcending cultures and geographical boundaries." [277] The urban landscape now bears the brunt of major terrorist activities; public places—shopping malls, department stores, public squares, and public transportation—have become potential venues of attack.

In the last four decades, cities have been subject to more than 12,000 incidents of terrorism and incurred over 73,000 casualties. The proportion of urban to nonurban terrorism is staggering. Approximately three out of every four attacks and four out of five casualties occur in a city. [278] Since 9/11, urban regions in particular have been the targets of terrorist attacks.

H.V. Savitch identifies three dimensions behind the targeting of urban landscapes for terror attacks—territory, space, and logistics. The first dimension, pertaining to territory, entails that

---

276 For further list of all the terrorist incidents which took place in 2016, including attacks by violent non-state actors, split up by month, check: https://en.wikipedia.org/wiki/List_of_terrorist_incidents,_2016

277 United Nations (2016), Speakers Focus on Online Recruitment Activity, Need to Implement Relevant Resolutions as Security Council Debates Threat of Global Terrorism, April 14, URL: http://www.un.org/press/en/2016/sc12320.doc.htm.

278 Savitch, H.V. *Cities in a Time of Terror: Space, Territory and Local Resilience*, (2008) Armonk: ME Sharpe.

terrorists target urban centres because of their strategic value. A mass destruction at a strategic centre will not only lead to widespread destruction of life, but will also result in economic and commercial devastation. Moreover, an attack on a strategic urban centre instils the fear in citizens that no part of their country is safe for them.

The second dimension pertains to space; terrorists strike in spaces that strategically inflict a maximum amount of damage. Such spaces include transportation junctures, hubs for business, finance, politics, religion, and media, or other such places of strategic and symbolic value. Moreover, news of an attack on these strategic spaces will also spread like wildfire, causing the magnitude of the threat to increase manifold.

The third, logistical dimension of urban terrorism derives from its capacity for self-incubation, its ability to infiltrate into urban spaces, and its closeness to prospective targets. Cities are particularly well-suited for equipping terrorists with anonymity, safe houses, and supply depots in order to gain access to potential targets. [279]

The Madrid Terrorist Attacks (2004)

Course of Events: A total of ten bombs placed on four different trains were detonated during the terrorist attack in Madrid on March 11, 2004. Fourteen explosive devices had been prepared and put in rucksacks and sports bags which had then been placed on trains at Acalá de Henares station east of Madrid. Each bomb contained explosive material and a detonator which was connected to the alarm function of a mobile phone. The first bomb exploded at 7:39 am, after which a further nine bombs were detonated within a few minutes. Four bombs never exploded. The locations that were attacked were the central station, Atocha, and the stations at Santa Eugenia and El Pozo, plus the area around Téllez. The trains which were attacked at Téllez and El Pozo were each estimated to have between 1,000 and 1,800 passengers onboard. A total of 191 people were killed and more than

---

279 Ibid.

1,500 injured. [280] These were the deadliest attacks in the history of Spain and the most deadly attacks since the Pan Am flight 103 bombing in 1988. The Madrid bombings occurred three days prior to a national election. [281]

Responsibility for the Madrid Bombings: On April 13, 2004, an al-Qaeda claim of responsibility was made via videotape by a man speaking in Arabic with a Moroccan accent. Although the attacks were described as the artefact of an autonomous cell of self-radicalized individuals only inspired by al-Qaeda, the extensive criminal proceedings on the Madrid bombings rebut this proposition. The network responsible for the Madrid attacks developed from the fragments of an al-Qaeda cell formed in Spain a decade earlier. It was instigated following instructions from an operative of the Libyan Islamic Fighting Group (LIFG) and included members of the Moroccan Islamic Combatant Group (GICM), as well as two former members of the Algerian Armed Islamic Group and Egyptian Islamic Jihad. Although the network also included common criminals who radicalized into jihadists, this cell component was only a late addition. [282]

In October 2007, 18 Islamic fundamentalists of mainly North African origin, and three Spanish accomplices, were convicted of the bombings (seven others were acquitted), which constituted one of Europe's deadliest terrorist attacks in the years since World War II. [283]

Security Measures in the Aftermath of Madrid Terror Attacks: In response to the Madrid attacks, calls were made to reform the internal security architecture of the country. The Attacks in Madrid made it crystal clear that the combat against the menace of global terrorism had not received due importance from the government before the event, and that as a result, police infor-

280 Bolling et al. (2007) The Terror Attacks in Madrid, Spain, 2004 Kamedo-report 90, URL: https://www.socialstyrelsen.se/Lists/Artikelkatalog/Attachmen ts/9210/2007-123-36_200712336.pdf.

281 Mandrell, J. (2008). "It Couldn't Happen Here: A Cross-Cultural Rhetoric," *South Atlantic Quarterly,* 107:2 pgs 321–337.

282 Reinares, Fernando (2012), The Evidence of Al-Qa`ida's Role in the 2004 Madrid Attack, March 22, Combating Terrorism Centre: URL: https://www.ctc.usma.edu/posts/the-evidence-of-al-qaidas-role-in-the-2004-madrid-attack.

283 The Editors, *Encyclopaedia Britannica* (2016) "Madrid train bombings of 2004," URL: ⟨http://www.britannica.com/event/Madrid-train-bombings-of-2004.⟩

mation and intelligence services could not meet the prevailing needs. Also, it became clear that there were serious problems of coordination, both between police forces and within each of them. Since global terrorism was seen as a persistent threat to Spain, the Interior Ministry's first decisions were aimed at amending these weaknesses. A counter-terrorism plan was devised, aimed at preventing and responding to the different varieties of terrorism that pose challenges to Spain, though specific attention focused was on al-Qaeda-related terrorism. As part of strengthening intelligence capabilities, the decision was made to strengthen police central units of information and intelligence, as well as their branches deployed on the periphery of the country. To counter the threat of Islamic radicalization, the number of translators and interpreters working in the internal security structure, in Arabic and certain other highly relevant languages, such as Urdu, rose from 11 to 86 between April 2004 and November 2007. [284] At the European level, Spain has played an active role in the implementation of the European Union Action Plan for the Fight Against Terrorism, revised in March 2004, and was involved in the preparation of the European Union Strategy on the Fight Against Terrorism, whose final wording was adopted in late 2005. [285]

Since 2004, Spain has been part of the informal working group on "jihadist" known as the "5 + 5." The group brings together defense ministers or their designees from five European countries (Spain, Portugal, France, Italy, and Malta) and five Maghreb countries (Mauritania, Morocco, Algeria, Tunisia, and Libya). [286] Its mission is to exchange information and discuss the operational implications of the threat from violent Islamist extremists in the European theatre, including the threat posed by returning foreign terrorist fighters. Four of the group's members—Spain, Morocco, Algeria, and Portugal—held *Seaborder* 2014, a joint maritime exercise, in September. The full

---

284 Reinares, Fernando (2008), After the Madrid Bombings: Internal Security Reforms and the Prevention of Global Terrorism in Spain (WP), URL: http://www.realinstitutoelcano.org/wps/portal/web/rielcano_en/contenido?WCM_GLOBAL_CONTEXT=/elcano/elcano_in/zonas_in/international+terrorism/dt40-2008

285 Ibid.

286 http://www.timelines.ws/countries/FRANCE_G.HTML

group met in December in Granada and expanded its mission to include cyber-terrorism/cyber-recruiting. Spain's participation in the G-4 with Portugal, France, and Morocco also has an operational objective. The four countries freely exchange tactics and intelligence on counternarcotic, counterterrorism, and organized crime/illegal immigration. Spain continued its work with the Global Initiative to Combat Nuclear Terrorism and invited France and Morocco to participate in two nuclear attack simulations, one held in Spain and one in Portugal.[287]

The London Terrorist Attacks (2005)

Course of Events: The London bombings of 2005, also called the "7 July" attacks or "7/7" attacks, were coordinated suicide bomb attacks on the London transit system on the morning of July 7, 2005. At 8:50 am, explosions tore through three trains on the London Underground, killing 39 people. An hour later, 13 people were killed when a bomb detonated on the upper deck of a bus in Tavistock Square. More than 700 people were injured in the four attacks. The four bombers—characterized as "ordinary British citizens" in the subsequent investigation—carried out the attacks using inexpensive, readily available materials. These factors made advance-detection of the plot by authorities extremely unlikely and forced a change in British counterterrorism policy, which was previously focused on foreign threats. On the morning of the attack, three of the bombers travelled from Leeds, the site of the suspected bomb-making "factory," to Luton, where they joined the fourth bomber. The group, now carrying backpacks filled with explosives, boarded a train to London's King's Cross station. At about 8:30 am, the attackers entered King's Cross station and split up, boarding east- and westbound trains on the Circle Line and a southbound train on the Piccadilly Line. Twenty minutes later, simultaneous explosions struck trains at Russell Square (killing 26 and injuring more than 340), Aldgate (killing 7 and injuring more than 170), and Edgware Road (killing 6 and injuring more than 160). The fourth bomber then exited the Underground station and eventually boarded a crowded

---

287 United States Department of State (2015), Country Reports on Terrorism 2014 – Spain, URL: http://www.refworld.org/docid/5587c73e15.html.

bus en route to Hackney. He detonated his device, an estimated 10 pounds (4.5 kg) of high explosive, at Tavistock Square, killing 13 and injuring more than 100. [288]

Responsibility for the attacks: On the day of the London bombings, a claim of responsibility was made by a "previously unknown group" calling itself "The Secret Cell of al-Qaeda of Jihad in Europe" on an Islamic website. On the same day, a letter dated June 20th, allegedly from Osama bin Laden, was released, wherein the al-Qaeda leader said that the London bombings were part of a wider al-Qaeda summer offensive. A translation of the letter stated:

> Rejoice for it is time to take revenge against the British Zionist Crusader government in retaliation for the massacres Britain is committing in Iraq and Afghanistan. The heroic mujahideen have carried out a blessed raid in London. Britain is now burning with fear, terror and panic in its northern, southern, eastern, and western quarters. We have repeatedly warned the British Government and people. We have fulfilled our promise and carried out our blessed military raid in Britain after our mujahideen exerted strenuous efforts over a long period of time to ensure the success of the raid. [289]

Security Measures in the Aftermath of London Bombings: The London terror bombings were marked by an immediate change in anti-terrorism laws in the United Kingdom. The Terrorism Act 2006, a direct consequence of the attacks, provided for terrorism suspects to be held without charge for 28 days, an increase of 14. That legislation was followed by measures that allowed the Bank of England to freeze the assets of terrorism suspects. The Counter-Terrorism Act 2008, passed after the government failed in its attempt to increase detention periods to 42 days, allowed police

---

288 The Editors, *Encyclopaedia Britannica* (2016), "London Bombings of 2005," URL: http://www.britannica.com/event/London-bombings-of-2005.

289 Quinn, Joe (2010), London Bombings - The Facts Speak For Themselves, July 7, sott.net, URL: http://www.sott.net/article/124587-London-Bombings-The-Facts-Speak-For-Themselves.

to continue questioning suspects after they had been charged, required convicted terrorist to notify the police of their whereabouts, extended the jurisdiction of courts to overseas terrorism offences, increased some sentences, and has been interpreted as banning photographs of the police in public places. [290] There were changes in intelligence-sharing and data-gathering, including surveillance-photo-sharing between the intelligence department and the police departments. Measures were also taken to strengthen border security measures. [291]

The Mumbai Terrorist Attacks (2008)

Course of Events: The attacks on November 26, 2008, on Mumbai, were carried out by 10 gunmen who were believed to be connected to Lashkar-e-Taiba, a Pakistan-based terrorist organization. Armed with automatic weapons and hand grenades, the terrorists targeted civilians at numerous sites in the southern part of Mumbai, including the Chhatrapati Shivaji railway station, the popular Leopold Café, two hospitals, and a theatre. While most of the attacks, which began around 9:30 pm, ended within a few hours, the terror continued to unfold at three locations where hostages were taken—the Nariman House, where a Jewish outreach centre was located, and the luxury hotels Oberoi Trident and Taj Mahal Palace & Tower.

By the time the standoff ended at the Nariman House on the evening of November 28, six hostages as well as two gunmen had been killed. At the two hotels, dozens of guests and staff were either trapped by gunfire or held hostage. Indian security forces ended the siege at the Oberoi Trident around midday on November 28 and at the Taj Mahal Palace on the morning of the following day. In all, at least 174 people, including 20 security force personnel and 26 foreign nationals, were killed. More than 300 people were injured. Nine of the 10 terrorists were killed,

---

290 Cobain, Ian , "London bombings: the day the anti-terrorism rules change," 7 July 2010, *The Guardian*, URL: http://www.theguardian.com/uk/2010/jul/07/london-bombings-anti-terrorism.

291 BBC (2015), 7 July London bombings: 15 changes to anti-terror planning, July 7, URL: http://www.bbc.com/news/uk-33388286

and one (Kasab) was arrested. [292]

Responsibility for the attack: An unknown group calling itself Mujahideen Hyderabad Deccan claimed responsibility for the attacks in an e-mail; however, the e-mail was later traced to a computer in Pakistan, and it became obvious that no such group existed. The manner in which the terrorists had reportedly singled out Western foreigners at both of the luxury hotels and at the Nariman House led some to believe that the radical Islamist militant group al-Qaeda was possibly involved. This appeared not to be the case after the lone arrested terrorist, Ajmal Amir Kasab, provided substantial information regarding the planning and execution of the attacks. Kasab, a native of Pakistan's Punjab province, told investigators that the 10 terrorists underwent prolonged guerrilla-warfare training in the camps of Lashkar-e-Taiba. He further revealed that the team of terrorists had spent time at the headquarters of a second and related organization, Jamaat-ud-Dawa, in the city of Muridke, before traveling from Punjab to the port city of Karachi and setting out for Mumbai by sea. [293]

The Mumbai attack is an example of state-sponsored terrorism. Sayed Zabiuddin Ansari, the suspected Laskhar-i-Taiba operative who was arrested by Indian authorities in 2012 for his alleged role in the 2008 Mumbai terror attacks, admitted that during the first 24 hours of the siege, he was in a control room in Karachi, Pakistan, from which Lashkar operatives gave orders to the gunmen in Mumbai. [294] However, despite a series of evidences presented by India, Pakistan continues to deny its role and complicity in the attacks.

Security Measures in the Aftermath of Mumbai Attacks:
Coastal security was identified as one of the priority areas of security reform after 26/11, with its utter and comprehensive

---

292 The Editors, *Encyclopaedia Britannica* (2016), "Mumbai Terrorist Attacks of 2008," URL: http://www.britannica.com/event/Mumbai-terrorist-attacks-of-2008.

293 Ibid.

294 Khan, Azmat (2012), New Evidence of Pakistan's Role in the Mumbai Attacks?, June 28, pbs, URL: http://www.pbs.org/wgbh/frontline/article/new-evidence-of-pakistans-role-in-the-mumbai-attacks/.

vulnerability demonstrated in the Mumbai attacks. Due to the coordinated efforts of all concerned, all these measures are now in place and overall maritime security is much stronger than before. The Indian Navy has been the lead agency in this regard and is assisted in this task by the Indian Coast Guard, Marine Police and other Central and state agencies. At the apex level the National Committee for Strengthening Maritime and Coastal Security (NCSMCS), headed by the Cabinet Secretary, coordinates all matters related to Maritime and Coastal Security. Joint Operations Centres (JOCs), set up by the Navy as command and control hubs for coastal security at Mumbai, Visakhapatnam, Kochi and Port Blair are fully operational. These JOCs are manned 24×7 jointly by the Indian Navy, Indian Coast Guard and Marine Police. Coastal patrolling by Navy, Coast Guard and marine police has increased sharply over the last few years. At any given time, the entire west coast is under continuous surveillance by ships and aircraft of Navy and Coast Guard. As a result, potential threats have been detected and actions have been taken to mitigate them in good time. [295]

The Paris Terror Attacks (2015)

Course of Events: On November 13, 2015, six simultaneous terrorist attacks took place throughout Paris. According to various sources, 129 people were killed in the attacks (including 89 in the Bataclan concert hall) and more than 350 were injured. At least 7 terrorists were involved in these "organized multifaceted" attacks which included mass shootings, hostage takings, and suicide attacks. These were carried out by eight ISIS operatives (according to another version, nine). Seven of them were killed during the attacks and one (or two) escaped. Six were killed by detonating their explosive belts. Several shot Kalashnikov assault rifles before they detonated the belts. One of them was shot and killed by the French police. [296]

---

295 Government of India (2014/), Initiatives to Strengthen Coastal Security, Ministry of Defense, November 25, URL: http://pib.nic.in/newsite/PrintRelease.aspx?relid=111871

296 Mer amit Intelligence and Terrorism information Centre (2015), ISIS Terrorist Attack in Paris Initial Overview and Implications (Updated to November 16, 2015) , November 17, URL: http://www.terrorism-info.org.il/Data/articles/Art_20910/E_210_15_938363285.pdf.

Responsibility for the Attack: The "Islamic State" (Daesh) has claimed responsibility for the Paris attacks. The suicide operations and the synchronous nature of these attacks are consistent with the modus operandi of salafi-jihadi militant groups such as Daesh and al-Qaeda. France's military incursion in the Middle East, including recent bombing campaigns against Daesh positions in Syria and Iraq, has put the country on the radar of jihadi terrorism. Daesh noted that "in the blessed attack of Allah, the squad of Caliphate soldiers shot and defeated Paris, the capital of abomination and perversion, which carried the flag of the Cross in Europe." [297] It also claimed that the attack had been carried out by "eight brothers wearing explosive belts" [298] and equipped with rifles, who attacked carefully chosen targets in the heart of the capital of France. Daesh also issued a video of a French-speaking operative calling on the masses [of Muslims] to swear allegiance to Abu Bakr al-Baghdadi, the leader of ISIS, and to carry out more terrorist attacks in France. [299]

Security Measures in the Aftermath of Paris Attacks: In response to the earlier Charlie Hebdo attacks, French authorities had reinforced security measures through the length and breadth of the country. Security personnel were deployed at all strategic locations, including popular tourist sights, transportation hubs, state borders, and other state infrastructure. The country was further securitized following the Paris attacks; more restrictive border controls were introduced, spontaneous identity checks were conducted, and there was an increase in widespread disruptive security operations. The state of emergency, which was intended to only last 12 days, was extended several times. Under this advisory, security forces are enabled to undertake extraordinary countermeasures that bypass judicial review in order to combat terrorism threats. These measures include warrantless searches, house arrest, extensive surveillance, and seizure of property and

---

297 http://www.terrorism-info.org.il/en/articleprint.aspx?id=20910

298 Ibid.

299 Mer amit Intelligence and Terrorism information Centre (2015), ISIS Terrorist Attack in Paris Initial Overview and Implications (Updated to November 16, 2015) , November 17, URL: http://www.terrorism-info.org.il/Data/articles/Art_20910/E_210_15_938363285.pdf.

data. Government officials have even gone so far as proposing to strip convicted dual-nationality terrorists of their French citizenship. [300]

From Madrid to Paris: Terrorism Continues Unabated

Over the last decade, although the main focus of terror groups has been the West, the terrorists have also spread their networks into Asia and Africa. In these attacks, it is clear that there is a level of sophistication and meticulous planning and execution on the part of the perpetrators of terrorism. More importantly, when we compare the Mumbai attacks with the Paris terror attacks, there is an eerie degree of similarity between the two. Multiple teams coordinated and simultaneously attacked different places. Hotels, stadium, and cafes were targeted. Both attacks took place at night. The AK-47 was the weapon of choice in both cases and trained gunmen fired randomly at crowds. [301] Another similarity in the attacks was the targeting of the Jewish community, showing that anti-Semitism has been prevailing as part of Islamic extremism. [302] These attacks also confirm that radicalization now appeals to a much wider audience (by age and social background) than before.

To combat terrorism, a range of counterterrorism policies have been implemented in various forms around the world, ranging from major wars and outright repression, to surveillance to counter online jihadi propaganda. However, certain measures need to be followed to counter the terror threat more effectively. Firstly, there needs to be an internationally agreed upon definition of terrorism in the wake of more fluid, dynamic, and complex terrorist threats. Counter-terrorism agencies have grad-

---

300 Tshabaala Kutloano, Terrorism in France: The security dynamic in the aftermath of the 2015 Attacks, 4March 2016, opinion.red24.com, URL: https://opinion.red24.com/2016/03/04/terrorism-in-france-the-security-dynamic-in-the-aftermath-of-the-2015-attacks/.

301 *Business Insider,* "Paris Attacks: The eerie similarity between Mumbai 26/11 and Paris 13/11," 14 November 2015, URL: http://www.businessinsider.in/11/articleshow/49780606.cms

302 Mishra, Mritunjaya (2015), New York, Madrid, London, Mumbai, Paris, and now Copenhagen, February 16, The Times of India, URL: http://blogs.timesofindia.indiatimes.com/mind-the-gap/new-york-madrid-london-mumbai-paris-and-now-copenhagen/

ually departed from a reactive, investigative-driven response to a pro-active, intelligence-driven one. Secondly, there is an urgent need to check the spread of radicalization and identify the major targets. In this context, Kathy Gilsinan remarks that "Islamic terror groups appeal to audiences in a variety of ways—from emphasizing a supposed Islamic utopia to promoting gory videos. But what we know about the Paris and Brussels attackers emphasizes the importance of in-person relationships to recruitment." Charlie Winter remarks in a similar vein that recruitment by terror groups has more to do with relationships than with passive absorption of propaganda and, irrespective of the fact of whether they are operating online or offline, these terror networks act in a similar way and are offering similar things. [303]

However major the threat of terrorism may be today, history has shown that previous generations of terrorist groups have been defeated. If countering previous acts of terrorism required stoic action from the affected region, then the menace of global terrorism can be defeated by a concerted action on the part of the global community, and by identifying and taking actions against the states and groups that use terrorism.

Terrorism in Europe

European citizens have been thought to enjoy high levels of security compared to other parts of the world, but the recent Paris attacks have raised questions about the effectiveness of French security services and heightened public concern on the issue of terrorist activities in Europe. The deadly terrorist attacks in Paris challenged the fundamental ideals that construct the base of the European Union, which now seem to be on the verge of destruction. After the attacks, Europe enhanced and tightened its security arrangements; at present, all of the European Union member countries are struggling to produce stricter counter-terrorism measures.

The *Charlie Hebdo* attacks in Paris in January 2015 that ended the lives of 17 people spurred much debate on the issues of ter-

---

303 Cited by Gilsinan Kathy, "ISIS and the 'Internet Radicalization' Trope," 8 December 2015, *The Atlantic*, URL: http://www.theatlantic.com/international/archive/2015/12/isis-internet-radicalization/419148/

rorism, Islamophobia, and radicalisation, as well as the European Union's counter-terrorism policies and their effectiveness in tackling terrorism. A number of policy agendas and proposals were proliferated, starting with the signing of a Joint Statement in Paris on January 11, 2015 by the Ministers of Interior and Justice of the European Union's member states. After the catastrophic terrorist attacks in Paris the following November that led to the death of 130 civilians and injury of more than 350, François Hollande, President of France, called for legislative reforms. According to Hollande, amendments to the Constitution would create "an appropriate tool... without having to resort to the state of emergency" [304] to the member states of the European Union to tackle Terrorism, both at home and abroad.

Riga Joint Statement

After the January attacks in Paris, the European Union Counter-Terrorism Coordinator (CTC) scheduled an informal meeting with the Home Affairs Ministers and the Law Enforcement Authorities, which was held on January 29, 2015 in Riga. The outcome of this meeting was the much debated adaptation of "Riga Joint Statement," which proposed a set reforms and amendments to European Union counter-terrorism measures. The "Riga Joint Statement" made the following proposals:

1. The creation of a European Union Passenger Name Record (PNR) framework without further delay;

2. The establishment of close cooperation between private sectors and other intelligence bureaus, like European Police Office (EUROPOL) and domestic security agencies, to "encourage them" to remove "terrorist and extremism content from their platforms;" and

3. A smooth information exchange system between European Union security agencies. [305]

---

304 http://time.com/4115712/france-paris-attacks-hollande-constitution-amendment/

305 http://www.consilium.europa.eu/en/policies/fight-against-terrorism/foreign-fighters/

According to the Director of the European Police Agency, Europol, the threat from Daesh and radical Islam are the most serious since 9/11, for three reasons. First, in comparison to other terrorist groups, Daesh and Al-Qaeda, two of the most active terrorist groups operating in the European Union, aim for mass casualties, as opposed to targeted or symbolic killings. Secondly, these two terrorist groups have designated Europe as their prime target. Lastly, a large number of Europeans have joined Daesh.[306] According to the Director of Europol:

up to 5,000 European citizens have left for Iraq or Syria. Although most of them are either dead (about 40% according to one study) or still in the Middle East (about 40% as well), a significant minority of them has returned to Europe. Not all of them are returning to Europe with malicious intentions—many of these "foreign fighters" are simply fed up with or traumatized by their experience. Yet, some do come back to Europe with intentions either to recruit new members or to commit violent actions. These individuals present a very serious threat, as illustrated by the Paris attacks. These "foreign fighters" are the priority of law enforcement agencies in Europe. The enforcement agencies in Europe. The majority of arrests related to terrorism in Europe last year were related to jihadi groups. [307]

Terrorism is nothing new in Europe. Almost all of the member countries of the European Union have witnessed activity from domestic terrorist groups, like separatist groups, as well as international terrorist groups. These groups have carried out operations in Europe since the early 1900s. Thus, in Europe, there is a long history of terrorism as well as counter-terrorism.

The European Union's strategic commitment to its people is: "To combat terrorism globally while respecting human rights,

---

306 http://www.nato.int/docu/review/2015/ISIL/ISIL-Nuclear-Chemical-Threat-Iraq-Syria/EN/index.htm

307 http://reshaping-europe.boellblog.org/2015/12/04/after-paris-five-questions-on-counter-terrorism-in-europe/

and make Europe safer, allowing its citizens to live in an area of freedom, security and justice." [308] The European Union's counter-terrorism strategy is founded upon four strands in order to prevent its citizens from joining terrorist groups:

> first, by tackling and resolving the causes that lead to radicalization and recruitment of people in Europe; secondly, to enhance and tighten security systems for better protection of its citizens; thirdly, to counter-strike at terrorists across borders and globally, to disrupt their support network, and to cut off their access to funds and arms; and, fourthly, to improve co-ordination between government departments to manage and reduce or minimise the consequences of a terrorist attack. [309]

Although the primary responsibility for tackling terrorism lies with the member states of the European Union, the Union contributes by strengthening national capabilities, promoting co-operation between its member states for the development of a collective capability, and by promoting international partnership. The four strands of the European Union's counter-terrorism strategy constitute a proportionate and comprehensive response to the threat of terrorism. Despite these strict counter-terrorism measures, the terrorists involved in the deadly 2015 attacks exploited loopholes in the European Union's security services. In the wake of these attacks, European security experts expressed the view that the flaws and loopholes in the European Union's counter-terrorism laws were conspicuous, and that they saw no clear plan or intention for fixing them. "We lack the most obvious tools to deal with this threat," [310]

Maintaining tight security in Europe is not an easy task since the laws and institutions of the continent have facilitated its citizens' free movement and freedom of religious practices. This freedom has allowed the citizens of this continent to be exposed to radical preaching at home, even before going to Syria or Iraq

---

308 http://www.consilium.europa.eu/en/policies/fight-against-terrorism/
309 Ibid.
310 Ibid.

to receive training and to participate in the activities of terrorist groups. As a consequence, European security experts are quite sure that the occurrence of another large scale terrorist-attack is inevitable. According to a senior European intelligence official: "We have to figure out what went wrong and fix it as soon as possible. Because one thing is for sure: Islamic State will try to hit Europe again." [311]

All European Union member states enhanced and tightened security across borders, railways, and all over the continent, after the Paris attack. After the attacks, the President of France, Francoise Hollande announced a state of emergency. The emergency was initially for three months, but was later extended. However, as a member of the European Union, France cannot isolate itself from the continent and it has to work according to the security practices and laws of other European Countries. Belgium has a loophole in their security systems; their internal security is dysfunctional "because of the historical tensions between the French-speaking Walloons and the Flemish segment of the population,"[312] and terrorist groups like Daesh and other radical organizations exploit this situation for their own advantage. Another significant loophole in European security services is that, while the domestic security agencies of the member states function properly, they lack coordination.

European security agencies suffer from poor coordination with other intelligence bureaus, having "no comprehensive, shared list of suspected extremists or a European Union-wide biometric database." [313] The Washington Post notes that:

> The Paris terrorist attacks offered a cruel demonstration
> of Europe's weak and incoherent security. The crossed
> unguarded European Union borders freely and frequent-

---

311 https://www.washingtonpost.com/world/europe/paris-attacks-reveal-fatal-flaws-at-the-heart-of-european-security/2015/11/28/48b181da-9393-11e5-befa-99ceeb-cbb272_story.html?utm_term=.6851bdb967c5

312 http://www.homelandsecuritynewswire.com/dr20151209-paris-attacks-expose-weaknesses-in-europe-s-security-structure

313 https://www.washingtonpost.com/world/europe/paris-attacks-reveal-fatal-flaws-at-the-heart-of-european-security/2015/11/28/48b181da-9393-11e5-befa-99ceeb-cbb272_story.html?utm_term=.14172e8ebbbb

ly, with at least five of them also traveling to Syria and back. Most of the nine attackers had already been flagged as potential security threats — but then, so had tens of thousands of others, including 20,000 in France alone. The Paris terrorists were careful not to stand out or give law enforcement a reason to arrest them. [314]

According to Bernard Squarcini, a former head of France's domestic intelligence service, "The systems of European security that at one time were useful and effective are no longer adapted for this threat." [315]

After the 9/11 attack, American security officials not only adopted strict counter-terrorism measures, but also vowed to do everything and anything it took in order to prevent the recurrence of another deadly attack—the effectiveness of such measures are clearly visible. The terror attacks in Paris should likewise serve as a wake-up call for the European Security Agencies. The attacks mark an appropriate occasion to review the age-old security laws and counter-terrorism measures of Europe and minimize their vulnerability by initiating proper coordination amongst all the security agencies. Europe has a number of structural holes in its security networks. The European security structure, specifically its security systems and counter-terrorism laws, are no longer effective; these laws should be amended to prevent a repeat of the Paris attacks.

The Paris attacks also threatened the concept of a unified Europe, since the institutional structures of the European Union are not capable enough to tackle and confront the local security concerns of the countries. After the Paris attacks, France's President suspended the Schengen Agreement, a treaty which led to the creation of Europe's borderless Schengen Area, indefinitely. This significant preventive counter-terrorism measure has grave consequence. According to the Schengen Agreement: "The free movement of persons is a fundamental right guaranteed by the

---

314 http://www.homelandsecuritynewswire.com/dr20151209-paris-attacks-expose-weaknesses-in-europe-s-security-structure

315 https://www.washingtonpost.com/world/europe/paris-attacks-reveal-fatal-flaws-at-the-heart-of-european-security/2015/11/28/48b181da-9393-11e5-befa-99ceeb-cbb272_story.html?utm_term=.0fe17fe3c4f4

European Union to its citizens. Schengen cooperation enhances this freedom by enabling citizens to cross internal borders without being subjected to border checks." [316] With France's decision to suspend this agreement, the dream of a borderless Europe faces a huge challenge.

European Union Counter-Terrorism Policies

At present, the European Union's counter-terrorism policies are facing two fundamental challenges. Firstly, after the Paris attacks, use of large-scale surveillance and tracking of European Union citizens' activities—which have been proposed by the domestic security agencies of European Union—stand in contravention of the Schengen Agreement. Secondly, the current urgency to adopt contentious measures like an European Union PNR system—i.e. European Union Passenger Name Record—constitute a challenge to European Union democratic rule of law. [317] The Lisbon Treaty (2009) has endowed the European Parliament and the Court of Justice of the European Union (CJEU) with the responsibility of ensuring the democratic accountability of the European Union's counter-terrorism policies and scrutinizing their effectiveness. European Parliament and CJEU have expressed concern over the use of large-scale surveillance since this is not in compliance with the Human Rights Laws of the continent.

The recent initiatives and steps taken by the European Union Parliament and the European Union member states, in the aftermath of the Paris attacks, should be carefully and properly scrutinized by the European Parliament and the Court of Justice of the European Union (CJEU) before implementation. A significant aspect of the new set of initiatives, which have been proposed by the representatives of the European Union member states, European institutions, and law enforcement officials, is that these new measures raise a number of challenges to the European Union's democratic rule of law. These measures need to comply with the European Union's Human Rights Law; the

---

316 https://ec.europa.eu/home-affairs/what-we-do/policies/borders-and-visas/schengen_en

317 http://www.europarl.europa.eu/RegData/etudes/BRIE/2016/580904/EPRS_
BRI(2016)580904_EN.pdf

implementation of such laws could cause infringement of the fundamental rights of the European Union's citizens. Secondly, since these reforms provoke much controversy and debate, the effectiveness of these measures should be critically evaluated and examined.

European Union policy-makers and security professionals should implement a cautious approach and a rational and non-emergency-induced way of policy-making on counterterrorism responses. Otherwise, the European Union contribution to the Paris events will lead to more insecurity and legal uncertainty rather than security. In light of the experience and lessons learned from the rapid adoption of similarly contested measures in the past following terrorist events, it will also ultimately face rule of law and judicial accountability by relevant Courts, which will cause unrest and a disproportionate amount of effort to 'clean up' the situation at a later stage.

Terrorism in Canada

Terrorism in Canada has been manoeuvred by individuals for political violence, the attacks in Saint-Jean-sur-Richelieu and Ottawa in October of 2014 clearly established that Canada is not immune to terrorist acts. [318]

A terrorist activity in Canada is defined as:

> An act or omission undertaken, inside or outside Canada, for a political, religious or ideological purpose that is intended to intimidate the public with respect to its security, including its economic security, or to compel a person, government or organization (whether inside or outside Canada) from doing or refraining from doing any act, and that intentionally causes one of a number of specified forms of serious harm. [319]

---

318 https://www.publicsafety.gc.ca/cnt/rsrcs/pblctns/2016-pblc-rpr-trrrst-thrt/index-en.aspx

319 Building Resilience against Terrorism: Canada's Counter-Terrorism Strategy. http://www.publicsafety.gc.ca/cnt/rsrcs/pblctns/rslnc-gnst-trrrsm/index-eng.aspx - More about the nature of Terrorism in Canada

The threat to Canada's security comes from domestic extremism and international terrorist groups affiliated with radical Islam. With several groups acknowledging Canada to be a legitimate target for violent incursions, their actions on international lands, under the premise of saving Islam from attacks by the West, prove to be a substantial threat to Canadian security.

Daesh remains the frontrunner in the spectrum of Sunni extremism. Many members of the Islam community in Canada have become concerned that the youth can become radicalized by the extremist ideology of Daesh to use violence against their own country. The radicalization of such violent extremists remains an active threat across Canada with many of them engaged in fostering connections with like-minded extremists abroad.

The increased availability of the internet has helped these domestic and international extremists to promulgate their propaganda, raise funds for their activities, and establish connections with other individuals or groups who are engaged, or have the potential to engage in, violent extremist activities. With sophisticated tools for networking, it has become child's play for these groups to reach out to individuals and exploit vulnerabilities in their own favour.

Domestic "issue-based" extremism forms another facet of security threat to Canada. Although not as widespread in scale and scope as in numerous countries, this form of extremism still poses a threat to Canada's security when it surpasses the process of lawful protests and engages in violence. Revolving around causes of the likes of anti-capitalism, animal rights, and environmentalism, this form of extremism requires constant vigilance as a means to rein in protests and violent activities.

The worst terrorist attack in the history of Canada remains the 1985 bombing of Air India Flight 182 by radical Sikh extremists, which claimed 329 lives, including 280 Canadians. Canadian authorities determined that the main suspects were members of the radical Sikh militant group known as Babbar Khalsa who wanted to retaliate against India for the operation carried out on the premises of the Golden temple. After the most expensive trial in Canadian history, costing nearly $130 million CAD, Inderjit Singh Reyat, a Canadian national, remains the only person convicted of involvement in the bombing. Singh Reyat pleaded guilty in 2003 to manslaughter and was sentenced to 15 years in prison. [320]

While attacks on Canada by terrorist groups remain a dominant threat, significant concerns are also raised with regard to the Canadians who endorse violent conflicts in other countries, or to foreigners present in Canada using the country for financing, refuge, or for the recruitment of militants. A foreign conflict of great magnitude, especially one involving Canada's allies, poses an equally vital threat to Canada as a direct attack on the country itself. [321]

International terrorist threat is not a new phenomenon for Canada, the threat posed by Daesh and its affiliate groups has become a pressing concern for the country. [322] Realizing that it has no more essential obligation than the protection of the country and its citizens, the Canadian government must reflect on ongoing strategies meant for security and counter-terrorism. Ensuring the security of the country is a key priority which cannot be undertaken by the federal government alone; an effective strategy partnered with various governmental agencies and departments is much needed. A multifaceted approach involving efficient cooperation between all levels of government, coupled with civil society, is prerequisite for meeting the security needs of the people living in Canada, as well as the Canadians living abroad. Likewise, security cannot be sustained without any assistance from international allies.

Building Resilience Against Terrorism, Canada's first strategy for counter-terrorism, was designed to assess the nature and scale of threat, and sets forth basic principles and elements that underscore governmental counter-terrorism activities. [323] The elements of this strategy aid in evaluating, as well as prioritizing, the efforts of the

---

320 http://www.theglobeandmail.com/news/national/rcmp-says-1985-air-india-bombing-investigation-active-and-ongoing/article25071447/

321 Building Resilience against Terrorism: Canada's Counter-Terrorism Strategy. http://www.publicsafety.gc.ca/cnt/rsrcs/pblctns/rslnc-gnst-trrrsm/index-eng.aspx - More about the impact of international terrorism on Canada

322 Remembering Air India Flight 182. http://www.publicsafety.gc.ca/cnt/ntnl-scrt/cntr-trrrsm/r-nd-flght-182/index-eng.aspx

323 https://www.publicsafety.gc.ca/cnt/rsrcs/pblctns/rslnc-gnst-trrrsm/index-en.aspx

government for security. The premier goal of the strategy remains the countering of "domestic and international terrorism in order to protect Canada, Canadians and Canadian interest." [324]

As the name suggests, the core function of this strategy is to build the resilience of the country against terrorism with the ultimate goal of enabling individuals and communities to stand up to sectarian ideologies. The strategy also focuses on such counter-terrorism tactics which find inspiration from rule of law, human rights, and adaptability of actions.

The four "mutually-reinforcing" components—Prevent, Detect, Deny, and Respond—form the building blocks of this strategy and are meant to guide every governmental activity in this regard. In the area of Prevention, activities are focused on determining the motivating factors which cause or may lead a person to indulge in terrorist activities. [325]

The element of Detection focuses on recognising the terrorists and their supporters, their calibre and their action plans. Investigation and analysis of intelligence data plays a key role in this aspect. It is also dependent on information sharing and collaboration with several partners, both domestic and international. [326]

Denying as a facet of the counter-terrorism strategy concentrates on efforts on the part of law enforcement agencies which, on availability of effective means, can deny opportunities and means to terrorists for engaging in their nefarious plans. The action plan for this involves mitigating vulnerabilities by aggressively intervening with the help of intelligence agencies in the planning of any terrorist activity. [327]

Responding means engaging in a response proportionate to a terrorist attack, if and when one occurs. It encompasses a rapid and organized response to an attack so as to mitigate its effects. It also focuses on reducing the brunt of the terrorist attack and ensuring a prompt return to routine life. A seamless cooperation

---

324 Building Resilience against Terrorism: Canada's Counter-Terrorism Strategy. http://www.publicsafety.gc.ca/cnt/rsrcs/pblctns/rslnc-gnst-trrrsm/index-eng.aspx - More about the counter-terrorism strategy.

325 Building Resilience against Terrorism: Canada's Counter-Terrorism Strategy https://www.publicsafety.gc.ca/cnt/rsrcs/pblctns/rslnc-gnst-trrrsm/index-en.aspx

326 Ibid.

327 Ibid.

between law enforcement agencies and intelligence agencies is crucial for the success of all these elements in addressing the threat of terrorism.[328]

The fundamental necessity for countering terrorism remains an important goal of every nation which cannot be sustained without effective international partnerships and an integrated approach by all governmental and law enforcement agencies at each level of functioning, the private sector, and also the citizens.

The partnership of government agencies with citizens is as important as their collaboration with key international allies and partners. Informing citizens of the imminent threats in a forthright manner fosters in them a greater understanding of the need of undertaking certain actions, thus garnering their support in the process.

Another decisive element that Canada could exploit in the struggle to maintain security is to expand its efforts from existing operations targeted at individuals engaged in militant activities, to preventive measures aiming at curtailing potential militants. Reinforcing security through such preventive measures is mainly focused on preventing vulnerable persons from being influenced to engage in terrorism.

Keeping pace with the proliferation of sophisticated ammunitions and ever-evolving cyber milieu, the strategy for Canadian security must be adaptable, not only to contain existing threats but also to identify emerging developments. The strategy for security must be in consonance with advancing technology, changing globalization trends, increasing networking communities, and accelerated flow of ideas and resources around the world.

Canada's open and democratic society, along with its generous social and legal networks, entices terrorist organizations to pursue financial, social, and logistical support within the country. The advanced technological and financial sectors are like an icing on the cake for militant groups seeking resources and support for their agendas. It is a flexible approach which can set Canada on the path of security by helping it adapt to the growing threats.

A strategy focused on anticipating the threats will help Canada to concentrate its efforts on prevention, as well as to address the dynamics which make individuals vulnerable to falling prey

---

328 Ibid.

to such ideologies. Addressing these issues will also lend a helping hand in organizing efforts to deal with a security-breach if and when one occurs.

A key precept when formulating security strategies or dealing with threats is that terrorists are people living amongst us who adapt their techniques and modus operandi according to the milieu. When faced with counter-terrorism efforts, using newer forms of technologies, responding to events which are of interest to them, and creating novel organizational structures are no longer arduous tasks for them.

Dealing with such adept terrorist groups requires a flexible approach, competent enough to be streamlined as per the demands of any particular situation. This approach can only be integrated if the factors contributing to terrorism are taken into account and used in favour of counter-terrorism efforts.

Preventing or eliminating the proliferation of weapons, chemical and nuclear, is another step that should receive due consideration. A variety of domestic efforts, conventions, treaties, and multilateral initiatives should be introduced aimed at ceasing the proliferation of such weapons and at the ultimate disarmament of terrorist organizations. [329]

With attacks by the Daesh in various nations, and the rising extremist groups, it is time for Canada to re-organize its security and foreign policies under an umbrella concept of "sustainable common security." Sustainable security shifts the focus towards the "long-term impact and consequences" of the country's policies, as well as the "underlying basis of insecurity, conflict and desperation."[330]

The basic argument of sustainable security remains that all consequences of insecurity cannot be controlled, but efforts must be undertaken to resolve the causes. In simple terms, focus should be aimed at curing the disease, not treating the symptoms.

Globalization has brought the good and the problematic to all nations of the earth, it is therefore imperative that cooperation

---

329 Non-Proliferation and Disarmament. http://www.international.gc.ca/arms-armes/index. aspx?lang=eng

330 H. Peter Langille. September 25, 2015. http://rabble.ca/news/2015/09/17-ways-new-government-could-address-canadian-security-issues

is adopted among states, based on a shared approach against the formerly "competitive pursuit of national security at the expense of national security at the expense of others." An integrated approach will ensure cooperation of various nations and ensure that potential threats are addressed before they manifest as a security concern.

Acknowledging the dynamics between explicit violence (violent conflicts, war), structural violence (exclusion, exploitation), and cultural violence (as apparent in divisive politics, patriarchy, and extremism), sustainable common security furnishes a comprehensive approach to security issues while addressing both environmental and human requirements. It suggests a cosmopolitan international network with equitable and effective institutions at each level of functioning. [331]

To ensure security of the country, Canada needs to commit to augmenting its states' capacity for the prevention of terrorist activities and to provide a response. The government ought to realize that Canada's security is invariably linked to its international counterparts and thus it remains essential for Canada to rally against prominent international challenges through a series of coordination and leadership programs, involving a range of military and police personnel, as well as civilians. Maintaining coherence among foreign policies, militaries of various nations, and development issues is the key to addressing security threats potentially harmful to Canada. [332]

Realizing that there is no greater obligation for any government than to protect its citizens, the Canadian government has set out to undertake the safety of its citizens in a unified and coherent manner. Reconsidering the effects of its foreign and domestic policies on the safety of the nation, the newly appointed ministers have begun efforts to make their contribution Canada's security concerns.

A strategic framework and efficient action plan in this regard will help Canada remain prepared to contain a potential security

---

331 In search of Sustainable Security. By Gayle Smith. June 19, 2008. https://www.americanprogress.org/issues/security/report/2008/06/19/4550/in-search-of-sustainable-security/ - More about the concept of Sustainable Security

332 Promoting Stability and Security. http://www.international.gc.ca/development-developpement/priorities-priorites/security-securite.aspx?lang=eng

threat or to respond to a security breach. With focus on diverse global events and cooperation, Canada can formulate a strategy which is adaptable not only in dealing with threats but also in understanding emerging trends of the long-term global challenge presented by terrorism.

Terrorism and Social Media

Recently, some terrorist organizations, like Daesh, are using social media to recruit people. A large number of countries are quite worried regarding this potential terrorist approach. The terrorist organizations have developed a system and strategy where they are pushing out images, videos, and communications on a daily basis. Social media is being used by the terrorists as a means of reaching out to their followers all over the world. According to a report published by an Indian newspaper, Daesh has been using social media as an integral component to disseminating its ideology of violence and terror. By virtue of its large number of supporters and highly organized tactics, Daesh has been able to exert an outsized impact on how the world perceives it by disseminating images of graphic violence while using social media to attract new recruits and inspire lone actor attacks. It is estimated that the average age of new Daesh recruits is around 24; this age group is proficient in making use of social media sites like Twitter, Facebook, Instagram, and Whatsapp. A 2014 study by the noted American-based think tank, Brookings Institute, noted that "at least 46,000 twitter accounts traced in the last quarter of the year had distinctive sympathetic and ideological overtones identifiable with the ideology of Jihad". [333] According to the study, "the largest cluster of location-enabled accounts (28 percent) was found in Iraq and Syria, mostly in areas either controlled or contested by Daesh. More than twice as many users reported coordinates in Syria than in Iraq." [334] For these reasons, several countries are talking about not only spying on social media, but even banning the use of these sites. Britain's Prime Minister, David Cameron, wants to ban messaging apps, which can

---

333 http://www.newdelhitimes.com/is-using-social-media-to-propagate-its-ideology123/
334 Ibid.

be used by what he calls "suspected terrorists." [335] Is it a justified response or a necessary over-reaction? Responding to the Paris attacks, he said that, "there should be no means of communication which the government cannot read." [336] Cameron wants new laws to allow security services that could read the encrypted communications sent by members of the republic, such as apps like Facebook or Whatsapp.

In the context of the digital Jihad waged by Daesh on the West, United States and European officials are calling for expanded government surveillance. CIA director John Brennan has called for the empowerment of surveillance agencies and has termed the Paris attacks "a wakeup call." In the United States political spectrum, there are many strong advocates of the surveillance programs. Former Florida Governor Jeb Bush has asked to restart the National Security Agency's metadata surveillance program—a key part of the Patriot Act that President George W. Bush signed into law following the 9/11 attacks. Republican Representative Joe Barton even went to the extent of asking the Federal Communications Commission (FCC) if they could shut down websites that host Daesh content, an unprecedented move that would see the FCC take a role in regulating the internet. [337]

It has been posited that terrorists are now communicating over PlayStation 4 consoles. There is no question that terrorists will want to adopt services with stronger encryption, and Western intelligence will want more intrusive legislation and more powerful computers. This is a false dichotomy between privacy and security.

Counter-Terrorism Measures and Sovereignty Rights

The first major terrorist attack which took place in the US—the 9/11 terrorist attack—showed the vulnerability of the world's most powerful nation and its advanced security technique. It

335 http://arstechnica.com/tech-policy/2015/01/uk-prime-minister-wants-backdoors-into-messaging-apps-or-hell-ban-them/

336 http://www.aljazeera.com/programmes/insidestory/2015/01/paris-attacks-security-v-personal-privacy-2015114184616303870.html

337 http://www.independent.co.uk/life-style/gadgets-and-tech/news/texas-republican-lawmaker-joe-barton-calls-for-social-media-to-be-shut-down-to-stop-isis-a6738421.html

shocked the world that a super-power like America had failed to save the twin towers. After this, security systems were given pivotal importance and new advanced technologies were introduced. The question that remains unanswered is: should every nation give importance to its security systems only after the occurrence of terrorist attacks? There is also another side to it. After 9/11, America began ignoring territorial sovereignty or sovereign rights of other countries and initiated operations in several parts of the world, wherever they felt that the dangers associated with terrorism existed. Two years after 9/11, America's invasion of Iraq took place:

> The Iraq War was a protracted armed conflict that began with the 2003 invasion of Iraq by a United States-led coalition. The invasion regime toppled the government of Saddam Hussein. However, the conflict continued for much of the next decade as an insurgency emerged to oppose the occupying forces and the post-invasion Iraqi government. An estimated 151,000 to 600,000 or more Iraqis were killed in the first 3–4 years of conflict. The United States officially withdrew from the country in 2011 but became re-involved in 2014 at the head of a new coalition; the insurgency and many dimensions of the civil armed conflict continue. [338]

In 2015, when a Russian war plane was shot down by Turkish terrorists at the Turkey-Syria border, Russian President Vladimir Putin's comments included:

> This incident stands out against the usual fight against terrorism. Our troops are fighting heroically against terrorists, risking their lives. But the loss we suffered today came from a stab in the back delivered by accomplices of the terrorists. [339]
> IS has big money, hundreds of millions or even bil-

---

338 https://www.rijksoverheid.nl/documenten/rapporten/2010/01/12/rapport-commissie-davids

339 https://www.rt.com/news/323262-putin-downing-plane-syria/

lions of dollars, from selling oil. In addition they are protected by the military of an entire nation. One can understand why they are acting so boldly and blatantly. Why they kill people in such atrocious ways. Why they commit terrorist acts across the world, including in the heart of Europe. [340]

Russian Prime Minister Dmitry Medvedev said:

Turkey's actions are de facto protection of Islamic State [...] This is no surprise, considering the information we have about direct financial interest of some Turkish officials relating to the supply of oil products refined by plants controlled by ISIS. [341]

When America takes action, other countries feel licensed to do so. And this is what is happening all over the world nowadays. It is being observed that most of the countries in the world have stopped paying due respect to international law, and their acts quite often breach it.

A similar but less devastating incident also took place in 2015 in Russia. On the morning of December 13, a Russian frigate, Smetlivy, which was anchored off the Greek island of Lemnos, spotted a Turkish fishing boat heading towards it some 1,000m (3,000ft) away. It fired what the Russian Defense ministry called "warning shots" at the Turkish vessel to avoid a collision. [342] This was a violation of international law, as has been stated in Article 2, paragraph 4, of the United Nations Charter.

In the context of international law and security, the issue of surveillance should be discussed briefly. Intelligence gathering and sharing arrangements are quite common all over the world. International law does not have any express prohibition of one state observing the activities of another state, if certain conditions are fulfilled. Thus international law does not prohibit sur-

340 Ibid.

341 Ibid.

342 http://www.huffingtonpost.co.uk/2015/12/13/russia-fires-warning-shot-as-turkish-vessel_n_8798486.html

veillance, but the domestic or national laws of a state are against any form of surveillance. All states enjoy sovereignty over their land territory, and no nation has the right to invade that sovereignty. This issue of surveillance was not seen as a serious issue until 2001, when an incident involving the United States in China brought the issue to attention. A United States of America Navy AP3 surveillance aircraft conducting surveillance activity outside of the territorial limits of China, but within the 200 nautical mile exclusive economic zone of China, collided with a Chinese fighter plane, causing the crash of the United States fighter plane and loss of its pilot. After the incident, China argued that America's act was against international law and that the United States had no due regard for the security interests of China. In reply, America argued that the surveillance was meant for peaceful purposes, the act was in no way illegal, and that the surveillance was conducted with due regard to China's right of sovereignty and security interests. The United Nations took the position that routine surveillance activity did not constitute use or threat to use of force under international law, and hence was consistent with the peaceful purpose provision of United Nations conventional law. In the context of cyber surveillance, regional rules continue to apply; as long as there is no physical trespass into the territorial regions of the state, then there is no prohibition. In addition to these, there is also satellite surveillance, which has been approved by international law. Thus, there are various forms of surveillance which do not breach international law but still raise serious questions regarding security. These surveillances invade the security of different states.

In the matter of surveillance, the activities of drones should be given a proper mention here. The drone, a military revolution, marks the beginning of modern—or in other terms, future—warfare. These drones work not only as surveillance tools, but as arms which help in attacking targeted areas. Presently, a large number of drones are operating all over the world, collecting data and attacking terrorist bases. In 2003, there were two United States drone strikes on militant targets in Pakistan. In the same year, a United States drone aircraft fired on two leaders of Somalian organization Al-Shabab, who, according to the reports of military officials, were expanding their mission outside of Somalia, and working more closely with Al-Qaeda. More recently, a United States drone attacked a terrorist base in Syria on November 19, 2013. Also in 2013, using both American and Russian drones, Iraq military blasted Daesh in Tikrit. On July 8, 2015, at least 45 civilians were killed in United States drone attacks in Afghanistan's Logar province, a part of the capital city, Kabul. [343] The drones are operating all over the world, counter-attacking terrorists in each and every corner. These drone attacks, on one hand, are proving beneficial in destroying terrorist base camps in different parts of the world; at the same time, these attacks are raising critical questions regarding the security interests and the security concerns of particular states.

In the context of international law and the security argument, we should always keep in mind that international law is both enabling and constraining, and any country wishing to benefit from its enabling qualities also must comply with its constraints. It is these constraints—those which restrict countries from interfering with and controlling the internal issues of other countries—which have been neglected over time. It is a fact that compliance with international law legitimates a government's actions domestically and internationally, but this has never been duly observed, as is shown by the aforementioned incidents. Failure to comply with international law will harm national as well as international security systems, and this is what is happening currently. Another significant issue that arises from this analysis is that America's actions have inevitable ripple effects: whenever they try to push the barriers of international law, other countries feel licensed to follow suit. This is what has happened and is happening all over the world. International laws and international organizations are, to a certain extent, incapable of restricting the activities of countries in this context. As a consequence, both countries and terrorist organizations are taking advantage, and international law is continuing to be breached. [344]

---

343 https://www.thebureauinvestigates.com/2016/01/07/get-the-data-a-list-of-us-air-and-drone-strikes-afghanistan-2016/

344 The Bureau's complete data sets on drone strikes in Pakistan, Yemen and Somalia". Bureau of Investigative Journalism, 6 June 2015. Also: Gilbert Burnham, Riyadh Lafta, Shannon Doocy, and Les Roberts, "Mortality after the 2003 invasion of Iraq: a cross-sectional cluster sample survey."

Counter-Terrorism in the USA in the 21st Century

In the 21st century, the emergence of a number of non-state actors—such as terrorist networks, drug cartels, and maritime piracy networks—and intra-state conflicts (civil wars) have assumed importance as new-age threats to the national security of present day countries, including the United States. In particular, the rise of extremist groups such as Daesh have posed a direct threat to United States internal security. This threat takes the form of a direct terror attack, or the indirect threat of cyber-jihad. Further, the Syrian Crisis and the resultant refugee inflow into the United States of America have further aggravated the threat of pro-extremist elements entering the country and spreading their radical terror network. The United States has chalked out a diverse set of strategies to combat each of these threats.

1.Addressing the Threat of Terrorism

Currently, the United States is facing its greatest level of threat from terrorist groups since 9/11. According to the Federal Bureau of Investigation Director James Comey, there are more terrorist organizations desiring to attack the United States than there were at the time of the 9/11 attack. The ability of terrorists to have safe havens from whence to gather resources, people, and to plan increases the risk of their ability to mount a sophisticated attack. [345] Daesh has been increasing its sleeper operations in various regions of the United States. Fears of Daesh in America may be justified by a new 2015 map, which shows the locations by state. Not only can Daesh be seen in California, but the terrorists are apparently operating in states like New York, Minnesota, Texas, and others. The new report also challenges the stereotype that these Daesh terrorists are most likely to be Arab

---

[345] Scott, Eugene, FBI director: U.S. facing greatest threat from terrorist groups since 9/11, 9 December 2015, CNN, URL: http://edition.cnn.com/2015/12/09/politics/terrorist-threats-fbi-director-9-11/.

or Middle Eastern men. [346] Daesh has already recruited supporters in the United States with the intent of executing domestic
attacks in America. The key evidences for these are mentioned in
a research report from Threat Knowledge Group, dated November 2015. These evidences are cited verbatim below to gauge the
magnitude of the Deash threat to the United States:

- 82 individuals in the United States affiliating with ISIS
  have been interdicted by law enforcement since March
  2014 (including 7 unnamed minors and 4 killed in the
  course of attacks).

- More than 250 individuals from the United States have
  joined or attempted to join ISIS in Syria and Iraq, according to the Final Report of the Task Force on Combating Terrorist and Foreign Fighter Travel published by
  the U.S. House of Representatives Homeland Security
  Committee in September 2015.

- The FBI currently has nearly 1,000 on-going ISIS probes in the
  United States, according to a recent report by Judicial Watch.

- ISIS is recruiting within the United States at about three
  times the rate of Al-Qaeda.

- Ali Shukri Amin, a 17-year-old Islamic State (IS) supporter from Manassas, Virginia, recently sentenced to 11
  years in prison for conspiring to provide support to ISIS,
  had nearly 4,000 Twitter followers, under the alias, 'Am-
  reeki Witness.' [347]

- Ahmad Musa Jibril, an Arab-American Islamist preach-
  er living in Dearborn, Michigan, had 38,000 Twitter followers before his site went silent. A report by the International Centre for the Study of Radicalisation (ICSR)
  found that 60% of surveyed foreign fighters in Iraq and
  Syria followed Jibril on Twitter. [348]

---

346 Frye, Patrick, ISIS in America, 4 December 2015, *Inquisitor*, URL: http://www.inquisitr.
com/2609896/isis-in-america-2015-map-terrorist-threats-in-california-new-york-minneso-
ta-not-arab-middle-eastern-men/.

347 Gorka, Sebastian and Katharine Gorka (2015), ISIS: The Threat to the United States,
Threat Knowledge Group: URL: http://threatknowledge.org/isis-threat-to-usa-report/

348 http://threatknowledge.org/isis-threat-to-usa-report/

According to a United States of America Homeland Security Department's terror threat snapshot released in February of 2016, six terror-related arrests in five different states had already occurred that year. Arrests have been made for four types of acts—plotting attacks, travelling overseas, lying to authorities, and weapons charges. [349] According to Michael McCaul, Homeland Security Committee (HSC) Chairman:

> Islamist terror threat remains alarmingly high as recent arrests and terror plots demonstrate. ISIS recruits wage war in our communities, while thousands of deadly fighters trained in Syria stream back into the West – some of them infiltrating massive refugee flows. This year is on track to be as dangerous as – if not worse than – 2015 for the American homeland and national security. [350]

Daesh has set up a cyber-caliphate group as a sect of its hacking division and has launched a global cyber jihad. Cyber Caliphate was set up by Junaid Hussain from Birmingham, England, and urged its followers to take control of hacked Twitter accounts to spread Daesh propaganda. Most of the victims appear to be based in Saudi Arabia, though were also feared to be British. The group posted details of more than 54,000 Twitter accounts, including passwords. Junaid Hussain also exposed the personal information of hundreds of United States military and government personnel and, on behalf of the Daesh Hacking Division, in early August 2015, published names, emails, passwords, and phone numbers of more than 1,480 members of the Air Force, Marine Corps, National Aeronautics and Space Administration (NASA), FBI, State Department, and the Port Authority of New York and New Jersey. [351] The group urged "lone wolves" to "pro-

---

349 Homeland Security Committee (2016), Terror Threat Snapshot, February 2016, URL: http://inhomelandsecurity.com/february-terror-threat-snapshot-6-terror-related-arrests-in-5-states/.

350 Homeland Security Committee (2016), McCaul Releases February Terror Threat Snapshot , February 2016, URL: https://homeland.house.gov/press/chairman-mccaul-releases-february-terror-threat-snapshot

351 http://motherboard.vice.com/read/when-isis-calls-you-out-by-name

cess the info and assassinate," [352] according to tweets sent out by Hussain's account, which was suspended shortly afterward. Junaid Hussain, also known as Abu Hussain al-Britani, was killed by a United States drone strike in Syria. Since Hussain's death, Cyber Caliphate, which briefly took control of a Pentagon-owned Twitter account in January, kept a low online profile for some time before emerging on twitter in November with the message: "We are back." [353] The key strength of IS has been its ability to decentralize its social media, which has allowed its supporters to operate their own ministries of information. [354]

This "cyber jihad" of Daesh is not merely confined to hacking online accounts and classified information. The latest target on the radar of Daesh cybercrime activity has been power companies in the United States. In October of 2015, United States law enforcement officials revealed a series of cyber-attacks in which Daesh attempted to sabotage the American electrical system. The disclosure was given at a conference of American energy firms which were meeting about national security concerns. Caitlin Durkovich, assistant secretary for infrastructure protection at the Department of Homeland Security, warned company executives that "ISIS is beginning to perpetrate cyber-attacks." [355]

In order to act against dynamic threats, minimize risks, and maximize the ability to respond and recover from terrorist attacks and disasters of all kinds, the United States Department of Homeland Security has taken a number of initiatives. DHS defines domestic terrorism as any act of violence that is dangerous to human life or potentially destructive of critical infrastructure or key resources committed by a group or individual based and operating entirely within the United States or its territories without direction or inspiration from a foreign terrorist group.

---

352 Ibid.

353 www.newdelhitimes.com/isis-cyber-jihad-in-usa123/

354 Gallagher, Ian, ISIS 'cyber caliphate' hacks 54,000 Twitter accounts and posts phone numbers of heads of the CIA and FBI in revenge for the drone attack that killed a British extremist, 8 November 2015, *Daily Mail*, URL: http://www.dailymail.co.uk/news/article-3308734/ISIS-cyber-caliphate-takes-54-000-Twitter-accounts-Terrorists-hack-social-media-site-spread-vile-propaganda.html

355 Pagliery, Jose, ISIS is attacking the U.S. energy grid and failing), 16 October 2015 , CNN Money, URL: http://money.cnn.com/2015/10/15/technology/isis-energy-grid/

The act is a violation of the criminal laws of the United States or of any state or other subdivision of the United States and appears to be intended to intimidate or coerce a civilian population, or to influence the policy of a government. Some of the measures, designed specifically against terrorism are mentioned in detail below:

a) Nationwide Suspicious Activity Reporting (SAR): This initiative provides law enforcement with another tool to help prevent terrorism and other related criminal (SAR): This initiative provides law enforcement with another tool to help prevent terrorism and other related criminal activity by establishing a national capacity for gathering, documenting, processing, analysing, and sharing SAR information. [356]

b) Countering Violent Extremism—there are three major objectives this policy:

i. Understand Violent Extremism: support and coordinate efforts to better understand the phenomenon of violent extremism, including assessing the threat it poses to the nation as a whole and within specific communities;

ii. Support Local Communities: bolster efforts to catalyze and support community-based programs, and strengthen relationships with communities that may be targeted for recruitment by violent extremists; and

iii. Support Local Law Enforcement: deter and disrupt recruitment or individual mobilization through support for local law enforcement programs, including information-driven, community-oriented policing efforts, which for decades have proven effective in preventing violent crime. [357]

---

356 Institute for Intergovernmental Research (2016), Nation-wide SAR Initiative, URL: https://nsi.ncirc.gov/default.aspx.
357 Official Website for the Department of Homeland Security (2016), Countering Violent Extremism, URL: https://www.dhs.gov/topic/countering-violent-extremism

2. The Syrian Refugee Influx and the Threat of Terrorist Infiltration

Syria's civil war has resulted in the largest number of refugees and asylum-seekers to the United States in recent years. According to Bloomberg, the United Nations High Commissioner for Refugees (UNHCR), which determines refugee status, has referred 18,000 Syrian refugees for possible settlement in the United States. [358] Top United States counterterrorism officials have allayed concerns that intelligence on the ground in Syria is insufficient to thoroughly vet individuals traveling to the United States from the conflict zone. It is difficult both to confirm that Syrian asylum-seekers are who they claim to be, and to determine that they do not have ties to terrorist groups. Departments and agencies responsible for the security of the refugee vetting process have explained that additional screening measures have been put in place to ensure that Syrian refugees do not have ties to terrorism. [359]

A number of security measures have been implemented in the United States on the pretext of the refugee influx to mitigate the potential influx of radical and extremist elements. Firstly, the United States of America National Counterterrorism Centre, the State Department, and other security agencies screen the candidate in an interagency check for potential security risk. Then, refugees' fingerprints and photographs are taken in the camps and screened against FBI and Homeland Security databases. The refugee's name is run through law enforcement and intelligence databases for terrorist or criminal history. Some go through a higher-level clearance before they can continue. A third background check was introduced in 2008 for Iraqis but has since been expanded to include all refugees ages 14 to 65. The refugee's fingerprints are screened against FBI and Homeland Security databases, which contain watch list information and past immigra-

---

358 Bathke, Benjamin, How Canada and the U.S. compare on Syrian refugees, 2 December 2015, cbcnews, URL: http://www.cbc.ca/news/canada/syrian-refugees-canada-united-states-comparison-1.3340852

359 Homeland Security Community (2015), Syrian Refugee Flows Security Risks and Counterterrorism Challenges Preliminary: Findings of a House Homeland Security Committee Review, November, URL: https://homeland.house.gov/wp-content/uploads/2015/11/HomelandSecurityCommittee_Syrian_Refugee_Report.pdf.

tion encounters, including if the refugee previously applied for a visa at a United States embassy. Fingerprints are also checked against those collected by the Defense Department during operations in Iraq. Syrians face another security layer called the Syria Enhanced Review. [360]

Secondly, there is a rigorous medical check-up and an overseas cultural reorientation through which refugees develop realistic expectations about life in the United States. [361] Thirdly, a Customs and Border Protection officer reviews refugee documentation and conducts additional security checks at one of five United States airports designated for refugee admissions. [362]

Finally, the refugee is resettled in a local community by a national sponsor agency, and each refugee receives an allowance (around $1,000) to meet basic needs for the first 90 days from the local resettlement agency, which also offers community orientation, assistance with social security and Medicaid, English classes, and job search services. [363]

3. Recommendations for United States Policy to Combat the Daesh Terror Threat

Firstly, security policies should be linked with socio-cultural policy. It has been observed that it is primarily the younger generation that is more vulnerable to radical Islam extremist propaganda. Therefore, the government must extend help to all those who are countering the "Jihadi" propaganda. [364]

Secondly, through surveillance programs, radical Islam ideologues in society must be identified and all their means of com-

---

360 Park, Haeyoun and Larry Buchanan, Why It Takes Two Years for Syrian Refugees to Enter the U.S, 20 November 2015 , *New York Times*, URL: http://www.nytimes.com/interactive/2015/11/20/us/why-it-takes-two-years-for-syrian-refugees-to-apply-to-enter-the-united-states.html?_r=0

361 Cultural Orientation Resource Centre (2016),
Overseas CO URL: http://www.culturalorientation.net/providing-orientation/overseas

362 Ibid.

363 Bathke, Benjamin (2015), How Canada and the U.S. compare on Syrian refugees, December 2, cbcnews, URL: http://www.cbc.ca/news/canada/syrian-refugees-canada-united-states-comparison-1.3340852

364 http://www.idsa.in/system/files/jds/jds_10_2_2016_countering-the-threat-of-radicalisation.pdf

munication must be blocked. Moreover, these ideologues must be dealt with in the same way as the terrorists.

Thirdly, there must be an effective utilization of open source intelligence. Currently, one of the most underutilized sources of information about future terrorist plots is open-source intelligence. If effectively utilized, open source intelligence can certainly help indicate the possible modalities of the attack and the appropriate response. [365]

United Nations Global Counter-Terrorism Strategy

Terrorism is no longer a state-bound problem; it has transcended international borders and morphed into a global threat to world peace and security. An integrated approach with the cooperation and involvement of all nations is required to face this endemic threat on all levels of its functioning.

The foremost step in this direction was taken when all member states of the United Nations agreed to adopt the United Nations Global Counter-Terrorism Strategy on September 8, 2006. The strategy was formed as a unique global instrument meant to "enhance national, regional and international efforts to counter terrorism." [366] The ratification of this strategy by all nations sent a strong message that terrorism in any form or manifestation is unacceptable. It also paved the way for undertaking practical steps to prevent the promulgation of terrorism.

Law enforcement alone will not curb the menace that is terrorism; deterrence is as important a component of justice and peace-keeping. Deterring potential terrorists through strict vigilance not only gains citizens' confidence in government, but also instils a threat into the minds of extremists engaging in violent activities or in recruitment of militants for their missions.

While terrorist groups aim to produce widespread fear through their acts of violence so as to obtain worldwide attention and influence governmental decisions and legislations, social media and modern systems for communications inadvertently aid these

---

365 http://www.globalcenter.org/wp-content/uploads/2016/07/AMansWorld_FULL.pdf

366 United Nations General Assembly adopts Global Counter-Terrorism Strategy. http://www.un.org/en/terrorism/strategy-counter-terrorism.shtml

groups in planning their horrendous acts of violence. They also aid the terrorist effort to pervert the impressionable minds of others, especially youth, with their misguided agendas, usually hinging on an idealized concept of "jihad". [367]

Counter-terrorism measures launched by each nation must commence with the fundamental act of denying the terrorists access to resources to carry out attacks or to engage other people in their missions. Cooperation with other nations while obliging with international law is the only way forward in this regard, as isolated attempts will simply urge such groups to expand their zone of influence outside a fixed area, providing them safe haven abroad.

Concentration should not only be fixed on terrorists but also on their affiliates, who support or facilitate the attempts at terror through participation in planning, financial help, perpetration of their agendas, etc. The apprehension and prosecution of all such individuals, directly or indirectly involved in terrorist acts, or their extradition from other nations is possible by strengthening cooperation and coordination among nations.

The combating of crimes linked with terrorism (arms trade, drug cartels, money laundering, etc.) must supplement national-level measures meant for counter-terrorism mechanisms. The fight against terrorism can be enhanced by embodying such comprehensive international standards which coordinate efforts against terrorism at all levels of functionaries to evolve into a common international program.

While terrorists expand their presence through Twitter, Facebook, and other such social media, government agencies must also match strides with terrorists and use the internet as a tool. The internet can help detect the activities of such groups online, and help prevent the manifestation of those activities into real life. The involvement of potential militants can also be detected by surveillance of the internet to help prevent them from being influenced or involved into such activities.

Stepping up efforts and increasing cooperation to maintain security and detect any breach in it requires coordinated planning, from restricting the proliferation of arms and ammuni-

---

367 Why Youth join al-Qaeda? http://www.usip.org/sites/default/files/SR236Venhaus.pdf

tions to enforcing stricter security measures at airports, or from maintaining an exhaustive database of terrorists and suspects to keeping in check the vulnerable targets who may be coerced into joining militant groups.

While international cooperation remains mandatory to tackle terrorism, voluntary contributions must also be made to build the resilience of civilians, and of the nation as a whole, to cope with any tumultuous event in the face of a terrorist attack. Ensuring the confidence of citizens in the government, and maintaining effective coping mechanisms by the government, form a crucial part of the counter-terrorism strategy of any nation, and must not be compromised by focusing solely on assaults on terrorists. [368]

In a scenario where the durability of terrorism in itself poses a threat to society, a multifaceted inter-governmental strategy is the way forward towards a peaceful world. The fundamental essence to countering the persistent threat of terrorism remains an integrated approach among nations, with an adaptable strategy which not only reacts to emerging threats, but also identifies potential threats to contain them before they surface.

To What Extent Should National Security Override Privacy?

When governments talk officially about human security, it is mainly about protecting people from terrorists. Today we are living in a society still feeling the impact of the Cold War and internal threats rather than social reform; the term "national security" has been given importance in the discourse of international relations. Shortly after the 9/11 attacks, the American federal government changed several policies regarding security. There were changes in airport/flight security, Homeland Security, enhanced border security, etc. President George Bush signed the Patriot Act, which was extended by President Barrack Obama in 2011. The federal government gave orders to the National Security Agency (NSA) to extract personal data about US citizens;

368 United Nations General Assembly adopts Global Counter-Terrorism Strategy. http:// www.un.org/en/terrorism/strategy-counter-terrorism.shtml - More about measures to prevent and combat terrorism by UN.

thereby, cellphone records, mailing and corporate data, and even individual location data has become subject to NSA surveillance without any legal protocols. Citizens of the US showed respect to the government shortly after the unforgettable 9/11 attack, but the revelations of Edward Snowden shattered their confidence because he exposed that the NSA's activities directly devalued the United States Constitution Fourth Amendment. Where human safety is at stake, there should not be any abusive behavior on the part of the government, whose primary responsibility is to protect its citizens.

The debate over the referent object of security is not new. Kant, Hobbs, Rousseau, and Montesquieu are the philosophers who believed in the pluralistic approach of security and privacy. Hobbs believes that protection is the absolute responsibility of the State, whether from a local thief or an invading army; people should put their individual rights into the hands of their country, their protectors, and in this sense, security can override privacy concerns. This traditional state-centered security was seen at the time of the Cold War, but with the fall of Berlin Wall, it became clear that without macro-level security, citizens are not necessarily safe.

Security has been defined from both 'subjective' and 'objective' perspectives. Objective security refers to the damages, whereas subjective security refers to the feeling of security, or the absence of fear that values are being threatened. [369] Traditional security only focuses on the security of the state, but the security of people also includes cultural identity, economic welfare, environmental health, and political rights. Privacy reflects inherent values such as human dignity, autonomy, individuality, liberty, and social intimacy. In modern day society, the co-existence of national security and individual privacy seems like an oxymoron.

There always prevails a clash between national security and individual privacy. Each administration has tried to build a bridge of mutual exclusiveness between the two goals: by promoting human rights at the expense of national security, and by protecting national security by side-stepping international hu-

---

369 http://www.elesme.gr/elesmegr/periodika/t32/t32_05.htm

man rights. After 9/11, George Bush's "National Security Strategy" spoke of a "commitment to protecting basic human right" and also took a vow that "defending our nation against its enemies [would be] the first and fundamental commitment of the Federal Government." [370] Generally, human right is seen as subordinate to national security; without national security there would be no society at all.

Terrorism is a great threat to humanity and has a multitude of negative effects on human life, so a broad and firm prevention strategy is needed for the security of a nation in general, and the security of citizens in particular. For the Commission on Human Security (CHS), human security is to "protect the vital core of all human lives in ways that enhance human freedoms and human fulfillment [and] protecting people from critical (severe) and pervasive (widespread) threats and situations." [371] The International Commission of Global Governance, in 1995, first proposed the extended version of global security, acclaiming that "Global security must be broadened from its traditional focus on the security of states to the security of people and planet." [372]

Security has been at the core of European policies since the seventeenth century. Security of the state was achieved through military and chivalric policy, but over time the approach to security has changed so that, now, laws and policies are enacted to protect individual privacy or the privacy of the nation from foreign nationals. There is a paradigm shift of referent object from state, nation, community, and society, to individual. The nation, in past, gave importance to disease, poverty, calamity, violence, and human right abuses; privacy was violated only to protect citizens from natural disasters and terrorism. However, since the development of high technologies, the sole aim of the administration is the integrity of the nation, with little care given to intrusion of human privacy. The question thus arises: is it constitutional to discard individual privacy in the name of security?

---

370 President of United States of America, National Security Strategy http://www.whitehouse.gov/nsc/nss/

371 http://www.un.org/humansecurity/sites/www.un.org.humansecurity/files/human_security_in_theory_and_practice_english.pdf

372 Rothschild, Emma- "what is Security", an article published by the MIT press at page 63. http://www.jstor.org/stable/20027310.

In ethical terms, as the European view goes, human security is not only a 'system' but a 'method' to promote stability and security and progressive integration of the individual within their relationship to their state, religion, and community. Human security provides the individual with freedom, liberty, and justice.

Article 9 of the Universal Declaration of Human Rights stated that no one shall be subject to arbitrary arrest, detention, or exile, but during a time of emergency, freedom is the first right to be curtailed. Each year, all of the European countries are confronted with the practice of arbitrary detention. Post-9/11, citizens were being fed by ideologies. Citizens trust the government and the promise of security, but with possession of great power, the government proves to be destructive of human privacy. While it is true that the absolute privacy of the individual cannot be offered by government, there is a stated fact in the constitution that the government cannot invade individual privacy without 'reasonable' cause. Regardless, the United States government has illegally kidnapped, detained, and tortured numbers of prisoners. Security and power would be synonymous terms if security could be attained only through the accumulation of power.

How can citizens be sure that the government is committing no wrongdoing in terms of their informational databases? For example, adding or eliminating entries for the wrong reasons. What rights does the individual have regarding the use of their personal information? Under European Union law, personal data can only be stored legally under strict conditions. Every day, a vast amount of personal data is subject to transfer over national borders. Individuals may not agree to have their personal data sent abroad if they were uncertain about the levels of protection in other countries. In January 2012, the European Commission proposed a comprehensive reform of data protection rules in the European Union. The fundament of this reformation is to give citizens back control over their personal data.

The European Union has been considering the coexistence of security and privacy in different ways that could enhance safety through the use of smart and cutting-edge technology. In this regard, the first step taken by the European Union, a funded project called "Scalable Measures for Automated Recognition

Technologies" (SMART) [373] is highly appreciable. Almost two hundred countries have approved this system. It looks at information sharing and automation of police databases in line with legal implications and norms. SMART is also outlining weaknesses, safeguards, citizen's attitudes, and relevant laws. The system also helps with providing guidelines to ensure maximum privacy and data safeguarding. The project team is working to facilitate four areas, namely border control, close circuit television, mobile devices, and e-government.

Kim Taipale warned against the danger of moving from an analog world to a digital one. [374] In this world, security is based on identity, and the problem with this system is that the administration has to survey an individual at all times. Ironically, if the authorities identify a criminal, they cannot track the person because there is no single wire to tap. This makes it seem unnecessary that they have access to everyone's communication records. The danger is that once privacy has been eroded, it is not easy to reclaim, and once the systems designed to erode it have been installed, they are hard to revoke.

It should be noted that the European constitution has used the term "human rights" in the broader sense; protecting individuals from foreign threats could never be the sole aim. It offers security from hunger, national calamity, fatal disease, poverty, and freedom from fear and freedom from want. National security may override privacy as far as privacy issues are concerned, but the European Constitution has never given permission to absolute freedom. Citizens are the responsibility of the nation and in order to protect them, the nation may go beyond privacy concerns. But, where national security seems to be oppressive and totalitarian, dominating people's lives on the basis of power, there proves the vulnerability or the ambiguousness in the term 'national security.' People need to embrace the view that one idea

373 http://smartsurveillance.eu/index.php?option=com_content&view=article&id=47&Itemid=54

374 https://www.infosecurity-magazine.com/magazine-features/can-security-and-privacy-co-exist/

can support the other. [375]

Whilst freedom is an inherent part of modern-day society, it is just as important, if not more, for national security to be preserved. If that leads to probing our emails, monitoring our phone calls, or surveilling our internet activities, it is still important for us to be guaranteed that safety. In the present scenario, a nation, city, or community could be targeted at any time; it is important to gather as much information for these monitoring devices as possible to prevent attacks and other atrocities. Freedom remains a key institution in society, but let us remember that without these integral interventions we would have no society in which to live. An effective and secure nation is a necessary condition for human security, validating Hobbes' statement that "life without state is solitary, poor, nasty, brutish and short." [376]

375 www.justice.gov/archive/ll/highlight.htm; also Solove J. Daniel, Nothing to hide: the false tradeoff between privacy and security, (2011); Wolfers Arnold, National Security as an Ambiguous Symbol, 1952 and Oberleitner, Gerd , Human Security: A Challenge to International Law?, June 2005

376 Thomas Hobbes, Leviathan: or The Matter, Forme and Power of a Common Wealth Ecclesiasticall and Civil, (Chapter XIII, paragraph 9) (online: accessed 2 April 2012): http://oregonstate.edu/instruct/phl302/texts/hobbes/leviathan-c.html#CHAPTERXIII

PART VI: HUMAN RIGHTS IN AN ERA OF TERROR AND SURVEILLANCE

Introduction to Human Rights in the Context of Terrorism and Counter-Terrorism

"Peace is not so much a political mandate as it is a shared state of consciousness that remains elevated and intact only to the degree that those who value it volunteer their existence as living examples of the same... Peace ends with the unravelling of individual hope and the emergence of the will to worship violence as a healer of private and social disease."
- Aberjhani, The American Poet Who Went Home Again

It is not as surprising as it would have been a few decades ago that human rights have become an issue of concern with the growing surveillance and abuse of civil rights in the present discourse of terrorism and the efforts made to counter terrorism. Some rationales query whether observance of human rights is necessary when viewed empirically, especially when it comes down to a nation's safety. Some argue armed conflict as the most convincing approach. The debate is on-going and is unlikely to cease.

Over the past decade, many governments, mostly Western, have taken steps to draw together a wide range of different objectives and institutions under the concept of 'national security.' This trend is driven by two simple ideas. First, countries and their citizens face many different types of security threats, and they all need to be taken seriously and given due attention and priority. Second, government has many different types of policy instruments that can be used to manage this range of security threats, and they can and should all be used in the most cost-effective combination to address the full range of security challenges. From these two ideas comes a third, where the governments should view the security threats they face—and the responses they make to them—holistically, and unite them under an overarching National Security Strategy. These three ideas collectively give rise to the idea of national security.

Since the 9/11 terrorist attacks, and with the recent reiterating Daesh attacks, be it in Beirut, Paris, or other countries, authorities around the world have become more alarmed and cautious, resulting in increased security measures to prevent any future catastrophe. Over a million video surveillance cameras, biometrics, data mining, genomics, micro-sensors, and other emerging technologies are used worldwide, with many government organizations deploying forms of electronic surveillance and tracking devices to monitor public places and human activities. These have been deployed with the agenda of preventing crime from occurring, detecting crime as it occurs, reducing citizens' fear of crime, aiding criminal investigations after a crime has occurred, making better use of public safety resources, and, most importantly, countering terrorism.

Though these high-tech security systems seem like a simple solution to crime and terrorism, there is also a much darker side. With immense command and authority comes the power to abuse. Such a system gives the government incontestable power and influence which can be used, in certain cases, to blackmail, discriminate, or differentiate. If history has been any indication, power eventually corrupts and is finally abused, resulting in engagement with unlawful activities. Hence the paradox that while a nation's security is essential in protecting human rights, it also, at the same time, can become its biggest threat. International human rights law is flexible when it comes to its scope and application, making it adaptable to a variety of situations, capable of growth and evolution, but this very flexibility also makes it vulnerable to misuse and erosion. In this discourse, human rights become marginalized to an extent where they become obscured. The notion of "equality of esteem," which forms the core of all human rights, faces a great threat when national security systems result in judgment of individuals based on their culture or faith, and that information is used to categorize them as "good" or "bad." This disturbing concept creates a moral dilemma in which human rights are seen not as a subject concerned with the powerless individual, but rather as an idea which takes the humanity out of the "human rights," becoming more about the values than the people. [377]

Democracy has taken a battering in several countries post-9/11, where efforts to combat terrorism have managed to spawn human rights abuses on a large scale. These policies have endangered the civil rights that lay at the core of democracy and, therefore, the fight against terrorism poses an ironic dilemma in which counter-terror legislation threatens to destroy the very rights and values it strives to protect. The major violations include mass surveillance and drone-targeted aerial killings, without any clear justifications for these programs and instead hiding behind the asserted need for secrecy. Through the Snowden revelation and the on-ground reports of civilian casualties in the targeted killings, governments now face major public scrutiny. The slaughter of civilians in Europe by terrorists prompted global horror and outrage but still not enough to convince the world leaders to protect "human rights" by putting an end to such unethical and unlawful deeds.

Today, the world post-9/11 has changed remarkably and seems to be suffering from a collective memory loss. The Eastern bloc during the Cold War served as an example which presented the dangers of infringing on democratic rights. This collective memory loss began in 2001 with a paradigm shift, where the political will of Western democracies in the 1990s was to strengthen and prioritize human rights at home and abroad was replaced by increasing human rights compromises in the name of counter-terrorism and national security.

Many European states, including Denmark, struggle with

---

377 Yusuf Salma, Protecting Human Rights while Countering Terrorism, (Feb 14,2012): http://www.e-ir.info/2012/02/14/protecting-human-rights-while-countering-terrorism/

balancing their national counter-terror policies and international human rights requirements. In the European context, this is exemplified by the European Convention on Human Rights (ECHR), which is signed by most European states, giving the European Court of Human Rights a jurisdiction over creating a balance between the rights of individuals and the response to terrorism. Denmark ratified the Human Rights Convention in 1955 and has since been obliged to comply with these international standards. Are the basic human rights of terror suspects then guaranteed by European-wide human rights legislation or is it merely up to individual states to decide how they go about their terrorism-related trials? The use of secret trials as a legal instrument has often been justified in the name of protecting a nation's values and national security. To have a closed trial in order to protect the name of the accused is not a new concept. However, these European policies are more about protecting the nation's security than the accused, as proclaimed.

America has dealt another blow to human rights protection law worldwide. At the beginning of his second term in January of 2013, President Obama did little to alter his disappointing record on national security issues. Though to his credit, upon taking office, he banned torture and closed CIA detention centres where suspects were forcibly confined for months or years—two of the most shameful practices of the Bush administration in response to the September 11, 2001 attacks. Yet he has also refused to prosecute anyone for those abuses. He also has obstructed efforts to investigate them and provide compensation for victims. In addition, the government has done little to fulfil its promise to close the Guantanamo Bay detention centre and has continued to try suspects before fundamentally flawed military commissions, despite their dismal past records. To make matters worse, he has expanded his predecessor's plans in two important arenas of targeted killing, often by drones, and mass government electronic surveillance. With respect to drones, the Obama administration has not followed its own stated policies or made clear what legal framework it believes governs specific strikes. Though it has formally abjured the Bush administration's "global war on terrorism," the Obama administration has affirmed being in an armed conflict with the Taliban, al-Qaeda, and "associated forces" with no geographic boundaries. It has engaged in targeted killings in Pakistan, Yemen, and Somalia, shamelessly saying it is at war with these armed groups or claiming national self-defence. But, given the erratic (at best) violence involving the United States in many of these places, it is far from clear that the more permissive laws of war even apply. And even if they do, civilians have been killed illegally under that legal framework without any United States inquiry or known compensation to the victims or their families. The separate and more restrictive body of international human rights law allows the use of lethal force as well but in far more narrow circumstances: only if absolutely necessary to meet an imminent lethal threat. That would make even more of the deaths caused by drones unlawful.

Obama, in a May speech, suggested that the use of the rules of war should end at some unspecified time, and outlined policies governing drone attacks to limit civilian casualties that are, in many respects, closer to human rights law than the laws-of-war rules that the CIA and military claim to follow. But in the announcement, nothing seems to be clear regarding if any of them are being followed or even considered. Citizens continue to be killed, and the administration still refuses to accept responsibility for all of them, and instead hypocritically denies any involvement, excepting a few cases. The United States government seems to be in no hurry to validate the legitimacy of its use of drones for attacks as, for the moment, it stands practically alone in using them. This will soon change and Washington will regret the precedents it has set of empowering administrations to label anyone believed to be a threat as a "combatant" subject to attack under the laws of war, rather than abiding by the more protective standards of human rights law.

Human rights have wrongly been narrowed down to mean the protection of individual privacy and protection from violent threats. However, the phrase covers a much larger turf, including economic security, food security, health security, environment security, personal security, community security, political security, and freedom from fear and want. The Commissioner for Human Rights at the Council of Europe has warned intelligence services, pointing out that national security concerns, including the fight against global terror, do not justify intelligence services' covert operations which discriminate on a global scale.

The awareness of a world law of human rights implies there is a structure of intercontinental authority—a world state of some sort—to enforce this law. Of course, there is nothing of the sort. Relatively, we have an odd display of international establishments claiming the authority to lay down the law, without the control to see it through.

Even a domestic court depends on supervisory authorities to impose its decisions on the ground. In countries where there is some respect for law, executive officials do feel obligated to uphold court rulings. After all, courts are part of the same government and the reputation of the government as a whole is at stake when its courts are defied. When it comes to international courts, however, no national government has quite the same stake in upholding the court's authority. North Atlantic Treaty Organization forces in the Balkans have been notoriously sluggish about apprehending war criminals sought by the special tribunal in The Hague. Had a NATO commander or soldier been indicted, it is extremely unlikely that the United States or any other NATO country would have allowed him to be tried by the tribunal. If the ICC comes into existence and proceeds to issue arrest warrants, how many governments will stir to catch their own nationals or even nationals of states with which they want to stay on good terms? 378

With the end of the world wars and the Cold War, the world had hoped for the end of the barbarism, gross human rights abuses, genocide, civil war, mass starvation, mutilation, and slavery that the world experienced on a large scale. Instead, the world of the present century denies all the freedom that the cease of these wars promised. The world that was

---

378 Rabkin Jeremy, The Human Rights Agenda Versus National Sovereignty, (online: accessed 2001): https://freedomhouse.org/report/freedom-world-2001/essay-human-rights-agenda-versus-national-sovereignty

supposed to be immune to all these atrocities seems to have an inflating rate of abuse to civil rights with the current policies and programs. Just to be called a democracy is not enough when the very nation that gave you the freedom and liberty to exercise your rights then consistently takes them away without any clear notice or reason. This simulation of freedom seems to be a sham in a world where the government promises to abide by international laws of human rights, but instead creates an authoritarian world where freedom remains only a notion and exercising one's rights a vague idea.

There is no reason why the combination of national security and human rights should lead to moral conflict, yet we cannot seem to find reasons for their peaceful co-existence. At the very centre of the debate lies the dilemma exhibited by the conflicting demands of justice and liberty. Both express particular beliefs about how human beings might best achieve a condition of security, suggesting which values ought to be subordinated to others. The problem seems insusceptible to simple solutions, either yielding tyranny, subjugation, and destruction of human freedom, or else opens pores in national security, leaving nations vulnerable to infiltration.

Defining Human Rights

"All human beings are born free and equal in dignity and rights."
– Article 1, United Nations Universal Declaration of Human Rights.

The challenges of protecting and promoting human rights in the face of fast-paced technological developments and in times of terrorism are complex. The Universal Declaration of Human Rights, the milestone document for human rights across the world, recognizes the "inherent dignity and equal and inalienable rights" of every human being as the foundation of peace, freedom, and justice in the world. It advocates for the fundamental human rights of all members of the human family for the promotion of social progress and better standards of life.

Human rights, as the name suggests, are the fundamental

rights of human beings, inherent to all without discrimination of any kind. These are interrelated, interdependent, and indivisible rights to which all human beings are entitled without any discretion to their nationality, sex, ethnic origin, place of residence, religion, language, colour, or any other status. [379]

Human rights are those inalienable rights and fundamental freedoms of every human being which are applicable everywhere and at any given time, such as the right to equality, right to life, right to protection by law, right to privacy, right to education, etc. Not only do they bestow respect, dignity, and freedom upon an individual, but also oblige others to revere the dignity and freedom of that individual.

Human rights are the basic edifice of civil liberty. According to the United Nations:

> Human rights are rights inherent to all human beings, whatever our nationality, place of residence, sex, national or ethnic origin, colour, religion, language, or any other status. We are all equally entitled to our human rights without discrimination. These rights are all interrelated, interdependent and indivisible. Universal human rights are often expressed and guaranteed by law, in the forms of treaties, customary international law, general principles and other sources of international law. International human rights law lays down obligations of Governments to act in certain ways or to refrain from certain acts, in order to promote and protect human rights and fundamental freedoms of individuals or groups. [380]

According to James Nickel, human rights may be defined as:

> Basic moral guarantees that people in all countries and cultures allegedly have simply because they are people." Calling these guarantees "rights" suggests that

---

379 What are human rights? http://www.ohchr.org/EN/Issues/Pages/WhatareHumanRights.aspx

380 United Nations (2016), What are Human Rights, URL: http://www.ohchr.org/EN/Issues/Pages/WhatareHumanRights.aspx.

they attach to particular individuals who can invoke them, that they are of high priority, and that compliance with them is mandatory rather than discretionary. Human rights are frequently held to be universal in the sense that all people have and should enjoy them, and to be independent in the sense that they exist and are available as standards of justification and criticism whether or not they are recognized and implemented by the legal system or officials of a country. [381]

Human rights are universal in nature and are often expressed in the laws of each nation and in the form of international laws or treaties. The laws guaranteeing human rights lay down obligations for governments to act in specific ways or to refrain from particular acts, in order to protect the human rights and fundamental freedoms of citizens.

Privacy is recognized in multiple places as a human right. In 1950, the newly formed Council of Europe drafted an international treaty to protect human rights and fundamental freedoms, the treaty later came to be known as the European Convention on Human Rights (ECHR). [382] Currently there are 47 European states that are member of the Council of Europe [383] and are party to the convention. In addition, the Convention also established the European Court of Human Rights (ECHR).

Under Article 8 of the ECHR:

1. Everyone has the right to respect for his private and family life, his home and his correspondence.

2. There shall be no interference by a public authority with the exercise of this right except such as is in accordance with the law and is necessary in a democratic society in the interests of national security, public safety or

---

381 Nickel, James. (1987) *Making Sense of Human Rights: Philosophical Reflections on the Universal Declaration of Human Rights,* Berkeley; University of California Press: Pgs.562-562.

382 Formally the Convention for the Protection of Human Rights and Fundamental Freedoms

383 Council of Europe is separate from the 28-nation European Union and the Council cannot make binding decisions.

the economic well-being of the country, for the prevention of disorder or crime, for the protection of health or morals, or for the protection of the rights and freedoms of others. [384]

Article 8 is often considered to be one of the most open-ended provisions of the Convention, and with several actions taken by citizens of member states an enormous amount of jurisprudence has been defined and established privacy as a positive right of everyone.

The United Nations International Covenant on Civil and Political Rights (ICCPR) also protects privacy in Article 17: "No one shall be subjected to arbitrary or unlawful interference with his privacy, family, home or correspondence, nor to unlawful attacks on his honour and reputation. Everyone has the right to the protection of the law against such interference or attacks." [385]

With all countries having ratified one or more of the international instruments for human rights, ensuring these basic rights to every citizen has become a legal obligation to all countries. It is only in a scenario of emergency that such legal obligations can be exempted to suspend certain human rights of citizens as per due process.

Human Rights Abuses in the Context of Terrorism

The premise that all human beings are born free and are equal in rights and dignity forms the cornerstone of all international treaties and instruments which are meant to uphold and protect human rights. While many of these instruments came into existence in the aftermath of the atrocities witnessed during World War II and the Holocaust, it is the cases of atrocities along the same lines which have called the attention of the world to human rights. In today's times, the world has seen an increasing preponderance of torture, slavery, and war crimes in areas

---

384 http://www.echr.coe.int/Documents/Convention_ENG.pdf
385 International Covenant on Civil and Political Rights (ICCPR) of 1966

populated by terrorists.

It is no secret that, while pursuing such acts intended to achieve certain "imperative" goals, the seemingly unprovoked actions of terrorists only do harm and no good. The militant and repressive acts of terrorists violate the human rights of the victims, victimizing large numbers of people in a single act of terrorism. Terrorism not only threatens the peace and stability of a nation, but also jeopardizes the enjoyment of the citizens of their human rights. It is not only the security of the nation as a political entity which is put in peril by terrorist threats or activities, but also the security of any particular individual, national or alien, which forms her/his basic human right and consequently is an essential obligation on the part of the government.

With terrorists are unconcerned about the casualties resulting from their "missions," the colossal nature of their acts impacts not only the security of individuals, but also political, economic, psychological, and human rights aspects. The aggressive front of terrorism poses serious threats to the fundamental freedoms of people across the world, thus creating an atmosphere of fear and chaos.

Terrorist organizations like the Islamic State of Iraq and Syria create pandemonium in their regions of influence to the point of uprooting civilians from their homes; this remains in direct conflict with the provision of human rights instruments which declare that everyone has the right to freedom of movement and residence within the borders of each state, as provided in Article 13 of the Universal Declaration of Human Rights. [386]

With terrorism growing as a violent form of conflict, there has been an unprecedented surge in human rights violations, apart from the obvious risk to national security and international peace. Terrorism has become synonymous to these violations, attacking the values of the instruments which stand for human rights. Beyond the political and economic repercussions of terrorism, it also

---

386 Right to Freedom of Movement. http://www.claiminghumanrights.org/freedom_movement_definition.html

has a deep reverberating impact on the human rights and fundamental freedoms of civilians. The direct blow to human rights is the most disconcerting corollary of terrorism, due to the unsalvageable impact of its aftermath.

It is also observed that during times of such armed conflicts, the arbitrary deprivation of liberty or the life of individuals or groups of individuals is not uncommon. The sheer use of force or violence by terrorists more often than not takes a toll by claiming the lives of innocent civilians, or by snatching their right to liberty by imposing restrictions on their movement and day-to-day lives.

The right to life, which is also termed as "the supreme right," when violated leaves all other human rights redundant. With no derogation allowed for the most fundamental right of every human being, even in the case of emergency, the failed obligation on the part of each state to protect this right bears a direct correlation to the increased prevalence of terrorism in that state.

Another prominent human rights violation witnessed mostly in areas densely populated by terrorists is the employment of torture as a method to gain control over citizens or to gain information from them. The methods vary from confinement in cramped spaces, to hanging a person by their feet, from bodily mutilation, to rape, and other such degrading and inhuman treatments.

The Islamic State, for example, is known to confine people in cages for seemingly trivial acts, such as men being in the presence of women who are not his relatives, or smoking, or lying. [387] Public flogging for minor offences, amputating body parts of thieves, and beheadings for blasphemy, spying, or leaking information are not uncommon among Muslim extremist groups.

A gender-specific violation of human rights, which has been referred by some as "sexual jihad," is increasingly

---

387 Weiss Michael, "Inside ISIS's torture brigade ,"November 17, 2015 http://www.thedaily-beast.com/articles/2015/11/17/inside-isis-torture-brigades.html

gaining popularity among terrorists. [388] While some women voluntarily offer themselves sexually to the terrorists, the trend of forcing women into "sexual jihad" is increasing by the day, so as to motivate terrorists on their path of "jihad". [389] It is based on the premise that a woman who offers her body in the service of a man pursuing "jihad" will have reserved herself a place in paradise.

The violation takes an advanced form when women are bought and sold as slaves in slave markets by the militant groups. The slaves are viewed as nothing more than tools meant for the terrorists' pleasure, and their existence as human beings is disregarded from the very core. [390] In a newer low, Daesh has recently issued a fatwa, after re-interpreting old Islamic teachings in their favour, to regulate sex with slaves. [391]

Often it comes to notice that it is not just terrorists who indulge in human rights violations of civilians, but also the government of a nation faced with a preponderance of terrorist threats. Such states engage in torture and other degrading methods as part of measures for counter-terrorism, routinely disregarding the non-derogable rights of civilians suspected of taking part in terrorist activities. [392]

While terrorism minimizes the enjoyment of human rights by civilians, some groups are affected more by it than others. Since terrorist groups consist of militants sponsoring extremist tendencies and measures, the religious and cultural groups which hold beliefs against those favoured by the terrorists are more inclined to be on the receiving

---

388 Spencer, Robert. "Islamic State: Qur'an says women who engage in sexual Jihad will gain Paradise" September 13, 2015. http://www.jihadwatch.org/2015/09/islamic-state-quran-says-women-who-engage-in-sexual-jihad-will-gain-paradise

389 http://www.independent.co.uk/news/world/middle-east/isis-executes-19-women-in-mosul-for-refusing-to-take-part-in-sexual-jihad-10443204.html

390 Abu Talib, Muhammad. "Of misogynistic jihadists and their sexual jihad." August 11, 2015 http://blogs.tribune.com.pk/story/28972/of-misogynistic-jihadists-and-their-sexual-jihad/

391 Dearden Lizzie, "ISIS's fatwa on female sex slaves" December 29, 2015 http://www.independent.co.uk/news/world/middle-east/isis-fatwa-on-female-sex-slaves-tells-militants-how-and-when-they-can-rape-captured-women-and-girls-a6789036.html

392 Core Human Rights. http://nhri.ohchr.org/EN/IHRS/TreatyBodies/Page%20Documents/Core%20Human%20Rights.pdf

end of attacks, simply on the basis of the beliefs and values they hold.

Thus, terrorism as a threat not only to the security of a nation or its individuals, but also to their dignity and freedom, forms the basis of modern-day abuses in several countries. The right to life, prohibition of torture and inhuman and cruel treatment, prohibition of slavery and slave trade, freedom of religion, and the recognition everywhere of personhood before the law, are some of the most basic rights, the abuse of which by terrorists has left people in abysmal conditions across the world.

Today, the magnitude of human rights violations by terrorists is significantly high, especially in countries like Iraq and Syria which have witnessed, over the past few years, increasing stronghold of the Islamic State group. The instances of refugees from Syria thronging into other countries demonstrates the swelling cases of human rights violations and their colossal impact on people's lives.

While the causes or motives for engaging in terrorist activities may vary, the fact remains that such acts inevitably cause the obliteration of human rights. The terrorists' lack of fear of governments exacerbates the situation. The evident disregard of basic human rights principles by terrorists undermines the efforts of countries and instruments working for upholding human rights.

The actions of terrorists performed in the name of protest against tyrannical regimes that are supposedly strangling their fundamental rights is ironical to the very core. Extremist groups like Daesh allegedly fighting for religious liberty claim to follow the teachings of Islam, yet go against these very doctrines when they indulge in brutal massacres and beheadings, and other flagrant human rights violations, in order to force others into line with their beliefs.

The degradation of human worth and dignity caused by terrorist activities renders roadblocks to the enjoyment of freedom by society. The extent of terrorism is such that even the measures taken by states meant to counter the phenomenon do not adhere to the international and national laws which ensure the sanctity of human rights and freedoms of the civilians. [393] In such a scenario, the vision of instruments of human rights holds unprecedented importance; as history has witnessed, the trade-off between human rights and security benefits neither. Arbitrary arrests, mass killings, and restrictions on speech and freedom of movement, among others, are the cost paid by civilians as a corollary to the counter-terrorism measures in many states. Nation-states have been seen to compromise the human rights of suspects as a measure of political convenience in the struggle against terrorists. They misuse the tribulations inflicted upon civilians as a ruse to overlook the failed guarantee of human rights of persons suspected of terrorism and to vindicate the measures taken as part of their counter-terrorism strategy.

Further, a debilitated framework of human rights in a state magnetizes terrorists to the place as it provides an opportunity to them for mining new recruits among the aggrieved and disgruntled civilians. Thus, the fruition of fundamental human rights plays an essential task when terrorists are disabled from undermining the freedom of the citizens and the consequent strength of a nation.

As the guidelines of the Committee of Ministers of the Council of Europe on human rights and the fight against terrorism states, it is the obligation of a state, even during the fight against terrorism, to uphold and respect the human rights and fundamental freedoms of its citizens, failing which critically harms the solidarity of the society and democracy of the state. [394] With the violations of human rights increasing in the midst of increasingly challenging conditions, spearheaded by terrorist forces, the crusade to uphold the fundamental rights of each human being without any prejudice must take precedence. It is the obligation of international as well as national law to necessitate the sustenance of human rights in this fight. The derogation from principles of freedom of life, impartiality, independence, respect, and

---

393 John Wilson, and Ramana P.V. "Terrorism and Human Rights February 2007. http://www.observerindia.com/cms/export/orfonline/modules/policybrief/attachments/ trs_1171547246121.pdf

394 Guidelines on human rights and the fight against terrorism. https://www1.umn.edu/ humanrts/instree/HR%20and%20the%20fight%20against%20terrorism.pdf

humanity remains reprehensible even today, more so than ever, and it remains the duty of states to protect these fundamental freedoms of citizens in the face of a war, genocide, or terrorist incursion.

In today's challenging times, it has become more crucial than ever to address the marginalization of minority communities and discrimination on religious or ethnic grounds. While terrorists indulge in blatant human rights violations, it is the respect and sustenance of these very rights, along with cooperative action between nation states, which forms the bedrock of counter-terrorism measures around the globe.

The stringent enforcement of the law of the land alone does not and will not suffice in the fight against terrorism, unless it is accompanied by due attention and concerted efforts towards maintenance of the fundamental rights of citizens, in order to ensure their active participation. While on the one hand, terrorists engage in brazen violations of these rights, on the other hand, it is concentration on these very rights which will bolster counter-terrorism measures by enhancing cooperation from citizens and ensuring that strong support systems for these basic rights will deter terrorists from exploitation.

Necessary Limitations to Human Rights

Human rights are rights inherent to all human beings regardless of their origin, place of residence, sex, sexual orientation, nationality, ethnicity, colour, religion, language, or any other status, and we are all equally entitled to our human rights, collectively or individually, without discrimination. The concept or idea of a 'right' loses its value and meaning without the existence of a society; a society has the authority to control its members, and to prevent them from acting according to their own instinct and will. A society has the authority to impose certain limitations on its members' activities. Human rights play a vital role in democratic society, which becomes soulless and meaningless without them; "Human Rights are the jewels in a democracy's crown."[395] It is also true that, in a democratic society, certain limitations are

---

395 https://ecpr.eu/Events/PaperDetails.aspx?PaperID=7362&EventID=1

imposed on human rights for the sake of proper governance.

There are two kinds of limitations that are usually imposed on human rights; the first one is the limitation imposed on an individual's personal rights in order to recognise the right of other people, or to allow every individual to exercise their rights within a limit. This concept first took a definite form in France in 1789, in its *Declaration of the Rights of Man and the Citizen*. The second one is the limitation or limitations that a state can impose upon its citizens' human rights for ensuring a smooth and effective governance, for preserving its democratic nature, for maintaining public health and law and order, and for the greater cause. These limitations are imposed so that, while the state protects and upholds the people's individual rights, the citizens also protect the state, and its security and peace. Democracy is based on this relationship between human rights and the interests of the state.

When discussing the fundamental rights of people in a democratic society, a critical question arises about which is more important: human rights or national security. The Universal Declaration of Human Rights and the wider body of human rights instruments and norms are all meant to make human beings secure in freedom, dignity, and equality, through the protection of their basic human rights. Article 28 of the Universal Declaration of Human Rights is of crucial importance from this point of view. It provides that "everyone is entitled to a social and international order in which the rights recognized in the Declaration can be realized." [396]

According to United Nations Security General Kofi Annan, "We will not enjoy security without development, we will not enjoy development without security and we will not enjoy either without respect for human rights." [397] Kofi Annan emphasizes the necessity to strike a balance between the protection of human rights and the imposition of strict security laws. The two are not necessarily antithetical or inconsistent with each other, in fact or in principle. However, in this world of growing terrorism, the two concepts connote an almost insurmountable opposition. There is a call for "balance," but in reality, states are actually

---

396 http://www.un.org/en/universal-declaration-human-rights/
397 http://www.unfpa.org/resources/quotes-human-rights

retreating from human rights by detaching them from the issue of security. This challenge does not emerge from the recent terrorist attacks; rather, it was always there, existing at the centre of the liberal democratic enterprise. It is this challenge that not only gave rise to democratic politics but also resulted in a clash between the interests of the state and those of its citizens. Every democratic country confronts this clash, and to strike a balance is like a litmus test of the functionality of the modern state.

In the words of Irene Khan of Amnesty International, "There is no excuse for human rights abuse, whether in the name of security or in the name of liberation." [398] Kofi Annan also rightly stated:

> We must find ways of reconciling security with liberty, since the success of the one helps the other. The choice between security and liberty is a false choice… our history has shown us that insecurity threatens liberty. Yet if our liberties are curtailed, we lose the values that we are struggling to defend. [399]

If this is the relationship that exists between the two issues, then it is not that these two issues are irreconcilable; rather, it is a consequence of our collective inability or unwillingness to agree upon certain assumptions, terms, or rules.

After the 9/11 attacks, governments around the world—not only in the United States—reformed their security laws and created new strict counter-terrorism laws. In Australia, the government created 40 new laws, allocating more investigative powers to police, attorney generals, and security agencies—an unprecedented step for the Australian government. However, these new laws and legal reforms have been criticized all over the world. Those who expressed their concern over the possible violations necessitated by the introduction and practice of these new laws were often criticized as being "soft on terror."

---

398 http://www.azquotes.com/quote/605179
399 https://pdfs.semanticscholar.org/9edd/97224bb2978453e6ff5c08afc56dd9e6064e.pdf

Incorporating Human Rights into Counter-Terrorism

At its core, national security is about the government protecting the state and its citizens against all kinds of crises through a variety of power projections, such as political power, diplomacy, economic power, military might, etc. Safeguarding the nation is paramount, but at what cost? With nations going to extreme measures to protect themselves, human rights activists are fighting against human rights violations in the name of national security.

To cement the international status of human rights, the United Nations adopted the Universal Declaration of Human Rights (UDHR) at the United Nations General Assembly in 1948; this was partly in response to the atrocities of World War II. It is generally viewed as the preeminent statement of international rights and has been identified as being a culmination of centuries of thinking along both secular and religious lines.

The only time human rights can be pushed aside is during times of emergency, but even then, the four non-derogable human rights—the right to life, the right to be free from slavery, the right to be free from torture, and the right to be free from retroactive application of penal laws—cannot be violated. The charter also states that the emergency must affect the whole population and the threat must be to the very existence of the nation. The declaration of emergency must also be a last resort and a temporary measure.

Since 9/11, the United States has been on edge; likewise, worldwide, fear has spread of the unknown terrorists who operate in mountains and yet managed to rock the world to its core. A month later, United States troops began to invade Afghanistan in an attempt to dismantle al-Qaeda and eradicate the Taliban. Prisoners who were considered a valuable source of information were further questioned in the very controversial Guantanamo Bay, or "gitmo," an American detention centre in Cuba. The purpose of the camp was to detain extraordinarily dangerous people. At first, the Department of Defense kept the identities of the individuals held in Guantanamo a secret, but later they had to release the names. Though the Bush administration denies all charges of abuse and torture, there have been various reports concluding that the conditions and practices in Guantanamo Bay were cruel, inhuman, and degraded human rights. The policies, which allow for such violations, have endangered the civil rights that lie at the core of democracy, and therefore the fight against terrorism poses an ironic dilemma where counter-terror legislation threatens to destroy the very rights and values it strives to protect.

Besides the actual war and Guantanamo Bay, another consequence to 9/11 was the spike in government surveillance, mostly through a vast, clandestine network of phone and web surveillance. The twin tower attacks generated a massive change in the security policies of most Western democracies. In the attempt to fight terrorism and secure their citizens, states implemented extensive counter-terror measures. Not just America, but other countries too have begun to engage in increased surveillance, worried about possible terror attacks. While Americans were wary of surveillance, the actual extent was never known until revealed by Edward Snowden. A "black budget" report obtained from Snowden detailed the bureaucratic and operational landscape of 16 spy agencies and more than 107,000 employees that now make up the United States intelligence community. [400] Further audits reveal that the National Security Agency alone has annually collected as many as 56,000 emails and other communications by Americans with no connection to terrorism, and violated privacy laws thousands of times per year since 2008. However, the recent Paris and San Bernardino attacks revealed that, even with an immense network of surveillance programs, American and European governments were still not able to prevent the attacks. After Snowden, the NSA came under fire for invading the privacy of citizens in America and around the world. America received the brunt, but the truth is that Europe is no better; a report discovered that a person is 100 times more likely to be surveilled by their government if they reside in the Netherlands or Italy, and 30 to 50 times more likely if a French or Ger-

---

400 Ehrenfreund Max, " 'Black budget' leaked by Edward Snowden describes NSA team that hacks foreign targets" *The Washington Post*; [https://www.washingtonpost.com/world/national-security/black-budget-leaked-by-edward-snowden-describes-nsa-team-that-hacks-foreign-targets/2013/08/30/8b7e684c-119b-11e3-bdf6-e4fc677d94a1_story.html], 201.

man national, than if they are in the United States. Germany's Office of Criminal Investigation is allowed to use a computer virus to search IT systems and to monitor communications and collect data, all without the knowledge of users or service providers. Though they need a court order for it, companies can be kept in the dark about its deployment. While the NSA is restricted in the United States and has to follow laws concerning United States citizens, it has a free hand everywhere else.

We cannot make surveillance the enemy here. While attacks like the ones in Paris and California were not stopped, the NSA alone has thwarted more than 50 terror attacks. Intelligence agencies around the world have prevented more such attacks and have also played a key role in coordinating with government agencies to be hyper vigilant when the threat is real. While Paris was a letdown, a lot of good has come out of surveillance.

NSA director, Gen. Keith Alexander, testified at the House Intelligence Committee hearing in defense of the NSA's surveillance of phone records and internet communications, which had come under fire after Snowden revealed the program to be in breach of American civil liberties. [401] The breach revealed that the government operates under the authority of Section 215 of the United States of America Patriot Act, which allows the collection of Americans phone records, and Section 702 of the FISA Amendments Act, which authorizes foreign surveillance. At the hearing, the Deputy Director of the Federal Bureau of Investigation, Sean Joyce, spoke in the NSA's defense by citing instances where surveillance helped the war on terror. Joyce first quoted the case of Najibullah Zazi, who confessed to plotting to bomb the New York City subway system in 2009. Joyce confirmed that the NSA's internet surveillance program led officials to a suspect in Colorado who turned out to be Zazi. The Federal Bureau of Investigation took the necessary legal steps to identify and ultimately capture him, in concert with authorities in New York. "Without the 702 tool, we would not have identified Najibullah

---

401 Pema Levy; "The Four Times NSA Surveillance Programs Stopped An Attack"; *IBT* (2013) [http://www.ibtimes.com/four-times-nsa-surveillance-programs-stopped-at-tack-1312309]

Zazi," [402] Joyce said later in the hearing. Another instance was under Section 215's authority; according to Joyce, the NSA was able to track down a "previously unknown phone number of one of the co-conspirators." [403]

There is also the case of David Headley, an American in Chicago who played a huge role in the 2008 Mumbai terrorist attacks that shook India. Currently, Headley is testifying via video to an Indian court from a secret location in America, where he is being held. The FBI had received a tip about his involvement in the attacks when the NSA's 702 surveillance identified Headley as involved in a plot to bomb a Danish newspaper office that had published cartoons of the Prophet Mohamed considered offensive by some Muslims. "Headley later confessed to personally conducting surveillance of the Danish newspaper office," [404] Joyce said.

Joyce also testified as to how under the authority of Section 215 of the USA Patriot Act and Section 702 of the FISA Amendments Act, they had thwarted a plot to bomb the New York Stock Exchange. [405] The NSA monitored a known extremist in Yemen who was communicating with a man in Kansas City, MO. This information led the FBI to Khalid Ouazzani, his co-conspirators, and ultimately the plot to bomb the NYSE.

Cease of surveillance activity is thus not the answer. However, Amnesty International has singled out the United States as a country that is promoting anti-human rights when it comes to counter-terrorism; mainly with reference to Guantanamo and Snowden. America has denied any threat to human rights and has justified its measures, according to the 2015 National Security strategy document released by the White House. Obama's introduction in the report talks about America's economic strength as the foundation of their national security. [406] President Obama noted in his remarks that:

---

402 http://www.dailydot.com/layer8/fbi-prism-hearing-702-tool-subway-bomber/

403 https://www.eff.org/files/2015/04/29/alexanderselectintelcommittee_06182013_p5p60p61.pdf

404 http://www.ibtimes.com/four-times-nsa-surveillance-programs-stopped-attack-1312309

405 Ibid.

406 "National Security Strategy", White House (2015) [https://www.whitehouse.gov/sites/default/files/docs/2015_national_security_strategy.pdf].

Today, the United States is stronger and better positioned to seize the opportunities of a still new century and safeguard our interests against the risks of an insecure world. America's growing economic strength is the foundation of our national security and a critical source of our influence abroad. Since the Great Recession, we have created nearly 11 million new jobs. [407]

He talks about the progress made globally, and about moving on from the large ground wars in Iraq and Afghanistan that defined so much of American foreign policy over the past decade. Obama says that the United Sates currently possesses a military whose "might, technology, and geostrategic reach is unrivaled in human history." [408] He further notes that:

We have renewed our alliances from Europe to Asia. Now, at this pivotal moment, we continue to face serious challenges to our national security, even as we are working to shape the opportunities of tomorrow. Violent extremism and an evolving terrorist threat raise a persistent risk of attacks on America and our allies. Escalating challenges to cyber security, aggression by Russia, the accelerating impacts of climate change, and the outbreak of infectious diseases all give rise to anxieties about global security. [409]

Towards the end, he says:

We must be clear-eyed about these and other challenges and recognize the United States has a unique capability to mobilize and lead the international community to meet them. Any successful strategy to ensure the safety of the American people and advance our national security interests must begin with an undeniable truth—America must

---

407 https://www.whitehouse.gov/the-press-office/2015/02/06/fact-sheet-2015-national-security-strategy
408 https://www.whitehouse.gov/sites/default/files/docs/2015_national_security_strategy.pdf
409 Ibid.

lead. Strong and sustained American leadership is essential to a rules-based international order that promotes global security and prosperity as well as the dignity and human rights of all people. The question is never whether America should lead, but how we lead. [410]

Some very important points emerge here: he outlines the threats to America's safety, addresses America's ability to mobilize, and points to a leadership which promotes global security and prosperity as well as the dignity and human rights of all people.

Every country faces its own problems—for Japan, it is North Korea; for India, it is Pakistan; half the world is being rocked by the threat of Deash—but the key is to fight for national security while still preserving the human rights of all people.

President of the Human Rights and Equal Opportunity Commission, John Von Doussa, outlined a few measures that could be taken to achieve the necessary balance between national security and human rights. According to him, this balance is achieved by recognizing that sometimes it is necessary to limit individual rights to protect national security or respond to situations of public emergency. However, he is quick to say that the balancing exercise cannot be used to excuse the inexcusable, and some (non-derogable) rights cannot be suspended under any circumstances. [411]

Laws should not be passed which contemplate trespassing the fine line between security and tyranny, like allowing issuance of orders to shoot on sight or shoot to kill. Confessions that are borne out of torture should not be allowed or admitted into evidence.

Derogable rights can be infringed upon in accordance with human rights law; Article 4 of the International Covenant on Civil and Political Rights (ICCPR) sets out that certain rights may be justifiably infringed by states only "in times of public emergency which threatens the life of the nation." [412] In 2004, the United Kingdom's House of Lords accepted that the threat

---

410 Ibid.

411 https://www.humanrights.gov.au/news/speeches/incorporating-human-rights-principles-national-security-measures

412 http://www.ohchr.org/Documents/Publications/training9chapter16en.pdf

of terrorism might constitute a "public emergency." [413] International law permits protective action that limits derogable human rights only under very specific circumstances. While the UN believes that terrorism creates a state of emergency, it emphasizes that, even then, very specific conditions must be met.

After Guantanamo prisoners were released, there was an outcry about the prison's practices, which were said to include torture and denial of a fair trial. One former prisoner was Yaser Esam Hamdi, a United States citizen who was detained indefinitely as an illegal enemy combatant after being captured in Afghanistan in 2001. [414] Hamdi's father claimed that his son had gone to Afghanistan to do relief work and was trapped there when the United States invasion began. He cited his son's young age and lack of travel experience as reasons for his being trapped. After a lower court turned down Hamdi's father's petition for a fair process, he appealed to the highest court. [415] The Supreme Court reversed the decision and granted detainees who are American citizens due process and the ability to challenge their enemy combatant status before an impartial authority. Following the court's decision, on October 9, 2004, the United States government released Hamdi without charge and deported him to Saudi Arabia—where his family lived and he was raised—on the condition that he renounce his United States citizenship and commit to travel prohibitions and other conditions. This instance was particularly important, as it reiterated the need for a fair trial in the context of counter-terrorism action. For an accused to be granted the simple right to "be present for his trial and privy to the evidence against him, absent disruptive conduct or consent" is "indisputably part of customary international law." [416]

Citizens of the United Kingdom protested vehemently against their government for conducting secret trials in a terror-related case. After much protest, the two defendants were identified as Erol Incedal, a British national of Turkish origin,

---

413 http://www.publications.parliament.uk/pa/ld200405/ldjudgmt/jd041216/a&oth-2.htm

414 Hamdi Vs Rumsfeld", Legal Information Institute, Cornell University Law School (2004) [https://www.law.cornell.edu/supct/html/03-6696.ZD1.html]

415 Ibid.

416 Ibid.

and Mounir Rarmoul-Bouhadjar, a British national of Algerian origin. [417] The president of the Supreme Court launched a scathing attack on secret justice, saying it was "not justice at all." [418] Lord Neuberger said that hearing evidence behind closed doors was "against the principle of justice." [419] He also said that, other than in exceptional circumstances, judges should treat requests to hear cases in closed courts with "distaste and concern." [420] After a media uproar, a few journalists were allowed to sit in court, on the condition that they signed a non-disclosure agreement, and were warned of severe consequences should information about the trial be leaked. In October 2013, Erol Incedal, 27, from south London, was arrested after police shot out the tires of his Mercedes when he was pulled over near Tower Bridge in central London. [421] During parts of his trial which were not held in secret, the jury heard that a listening device inserted inside the car, thirteen days prior to his arrest, had captured Incedal's conversations about jihadist groups, his supposed love of the word terrorism, and his plan to purchase a gun. Both were convicted and jailed for possession of bomb-making manuals—possession of a document likely to be useful to a person preparing an act of terrorism—but were acquitted of charges of plotting a terrorist attack. The details of trial still remain sealed, until it is declassified. Many believe that the departure from the principle of open justice can never be justified. [422]

One way to incorporate human rights into national security is to ensure an independent judicial hearing with regard to upholding counter-terrorism laws. According to the United Nations High Commissioner, an important way of preserving the right to a fair trial is to retain "effective judicial control over qualifica-

---

417 Cobain Ian "Secret terror trial: two men jailed over bomb-making manual," *The Guardian* (2015) [http://www.theguardian.com/uk-news/2015/apr/01/secret-terror-trial-two-men-jailed-over-bomb-making-manual]

418 http://www.dailymail.co.uk/news/article-2344806/Secret-justice-justice-closed-court-requests-treated-concern.html

419 Ibid.

420 Ibid.

421 https://www.theguardian.com/law/2015/jul/01/secret-prosecution-of-terrorism-secret-raises-difficult-constitutional-issues

422 Ibid.

tions by the executive branch that certain information may not be disclosed in order to protect national interest." [423] While many cases might be time bound, and ensuring a trial before any sort of detention and charging would defeat the purpose of gathering intelligence and preventing terror attacks, those cases should also call for authorization by a judicial officer.

John Von Doussa, a prominent Australian Judge believes that one of the key ways to preserve human right in this climate of terror is by helping those affected by counter-terrorism laws to seek remedial action. [424] This is in keeping with Article 2 (3) of the International Covenant on Civil and Political Rights (ICCPR), which states that a person has a right to an effective remedy if his or her human rights are violated. If someone has suffered as a consequence of the misuse or abuse of counter-terrorism, then he/she should be able to seek a remedy, depending on the damage suffered, including compensation.

Regularly conducting independent reviews of counter-terrorism law operations ensure that the law purports to do what it says without any abuse or misuse, and that, in any case of misuse, remedial action is taken. Britain leads the way in these measures; the Secretary of State for the Home Department presented a report reviewing counter-terrorism laws in the United Kingdom Parliament. The report aimed to review counter-terrorism and security power, to ensure that the powers and measures covered by the review were necessary, effective, and proportionate, and that they met the United Kingdom's international and domestic human rights obligations. [425] Four points considered by the review were as follows; first was the detention of terrorist suspects before charge, and the hope to reduce the period of detention below 28 days. Second was the use of section 44: stop and search powers and the use of terrorism legislation in relation to photography. Third was the use of the Regulation of Investigatory Powers Act 2000 (RIPA) by local authorities and access to com-

---

423 https://www.humanrights.gov.au/news/speeches/incorporating-human-rights-principles-national-security-measures

424 http://www.austlii.edu.au/au/journals/JCULawRw/2006/6.html

425 "Review of Counter-Terrorism and Security Powers"; Secretary of State for the Home Department; United Kingdom (2011) [https://www.gov.uk/government/uploads/system/uploads/attachment_data/file/97972/review-findings-and-rec.pdf]

munications data. Fourth were the measures to deal with organizations that promote hatred or violence. [426] A very important aspect was extending the use of deportation in a manner consistent with legal and human rights obligations.

These counter terrorism laws were reviewed by a wide range of authorities, from lawmakers to intelligence agencies, police officers, government departments, and also human rights organizations, like Amnesty International and Justice and Human Rights Watch. After consultation, findings were published. The findings concluded that some areas of their counter-terrorism and security powers were neither proportionate nor necessary. Taken together, the recommendations do much to restore civil liberties while enabling the police and security services to effectively protect the public. Some changes were suggested, like maximum detention to be reduced from 28 days to 14; they wanted an end to the indiscriminate use of terrorism stop and search powers provided under Section 44 of the Terrorism Act 2000; also, they put an end to the use of the most intrusive RIPA powers by local authorities to investigate low level offences, and added a requirement that applications made by local authorities to use RIPA techniques must be approved by a magistrate. [427] They also provided additional resources to the police and security agencies to ensure that the new measures are effective in protecting the public and in facilitating prosecution. This process of routinely reviewing counter-terrorism laws keeps the process transparent and helps to ensure that civil liberties are not trampled in the name of fighting terrorism.

Stronger human rights laws help ensure that, in the hunt for terrorists, countries do not lose the core principles on which modern democracy was founded. For terrorist organizations, it is a very handy recruitment tool when democracies start losing the tolerant and just values for which they stand. Guantanamo Bay images have been used to recruit more vulnerable youth for terrorist activities. As put by Senator McCain: torture "serves as a great propaganda

---

426 Ibid.

427 https://www.liberty-human-rights.org.uk/human-rights/justice-and-fair-trials/stop-and-search/section-44-terrorism-act

tool for those who recruit people to fight against us." [428] This also echoes former United Nations Secretary General Kofi Annan, as already quoted. President Bush had once said that "defending our nation against its enemies is the first and fundamental commitment of the Federal Government." [429] Treating human rights as secondary is a mistake; national security and human rights are complementary and related, not in competition.

In Obama's speech on national security, he beautifully encases the above thoughts. [430] The President spoke about his duty to keep the country safe, but the need to preserve human rights; he condemned Guantanamo, calling it one of the biggest setbacks to America. He said "rather than keeping us safer, the prison at Guantanamo has weakened American national security." [431]

About the balance between human rights and national security, he said:

I believe with every fiber of my being that in the long run we also cannot keep this country safe unless we enlist the power of our most fundamental values. The documents that we hold in this very hall -- the Declaration of Independence, the Constitution, the Bill of Rights -- these are not simply words written into aging parchment. They are the foundation of liberty and justice in this country, and a light that shines for all who seek freedom, fairness, equality, and dignity around the world. I've studied the Constitution as a student, I've taught it as a teacher, I've been bound by it as a lawyer and a legislator. I took an oath to preserve, protect, and defend the Constitution as Commander-in-Chief, and as a citizen, I know that we must never, ever, turn our back on its enduring principles

428 https://www.whitehouse.gov/the-press-office/remarks-president-national-security-5-21-09

429 http://www.nytimes.com/2002/09/20/politics/full-text-bushs-national-security-strategy.html

430 Remarks by the President On National Security", The White House (2009)[https://www.whitehouse.gov/the-press-office/remarks-president-national-security-5-21-09]

431 Ibid.

for expedience sake. I make this claim not simply as a matter of idealism. We uphold our most cherished values not only because doing so is right, but also because it strengthens our country and it keeps us safe. Time and again, our values have been our best national security asset -- in war and peace; in times of ease and in eras of upheaval. I had to strike the right balance between transparency and national security. [432]

Human rights ensure national security and that is something which should never be forgotten, especially in times like these, when terror lurks around the corner.

Compliance with Human Rights in Counter-Terror Laws

The assurance of security from threats necessitates a multi-dimensional approach within the international order. This multi-dimensional approach does not treat the balancing of liberty and security in mutually exclusive compartments but regards the protection of human rights as an integral element of security. Counter-terrorism strategies not consistent with human rights law are considered to be unlawful as well as unethical. In 2005, UN Secretary General Kofi Annan emphasized:

> Human rights law makes ample provision for counter-terrorist action, even in the most exceptional circumstances. But compromising human rights cannot serve the struggle against terrorism. On the contrary, it facilitates achievement of the terrorist's objective—by ceding to him the moral high ground, and provoking tension, hatred, and mistrust of government among precisely those parts of the population where he is most likely to find recruits. Upholding human rights is not merely compatible with successful counter-terrorism strategy. It is an

---

432 Ibid.

essential element. [433]

In 2002, the Council of Europe Secretary General, Walter Schwimmer, pointed out:

> The temptation for governments and parliaments in countries suffering from terrorist action is to fight fire with fire, setting aside the legal safeguards that exist in a democratic state. But let us be clear about this: while the State has the right to employ its full arsenal of legal weapons to repress and prevent terrorist activities, it may not use indiscriminate measures which would only undermine the fundamental values they seek to protect. For a State to react in such a way would be to fall into the trap set by terrorism for democracy and the rule of law. It is precisely in situations of crisis, such as those brought about by terrorism, that respect for human rights is even more important and that even greater vigilance is called for. [434]

The international community has committed to adopting measures that ensure respect for human rights for all and the rule of law as the fundamental basis of the fight against terrorism, through the adoption of the United Nations Global Counter-Terrorism Strategy by the General Assembly in its resolution 60/288. The Counter-terrorism strategy outlined in the document sets out a plan of action spelling out key areas:

1. Measures to address conditions conducive to the spread of terrorism

2. Measures to prevent and combat terrorism

3. Measures to build states' capacity to prevent and combat terrorism and to strengthen the role of the United Nations system

---

433 Kofi Annan (2005), "A Global Strategy for Fighting Terrorism", Keynote address to the Closing Plenary of the International Summit on Democracy, Terrorism and Security, 8-11 March, Madrid, URL: http://summit.clubmadrid.org/keynotes

434 Council of Europe (2004), Guidelines on human rights and the fight against terrorism, Council of Europe Publishing: Strasbourg.

in this regard, and

4. Measures to ensure respect for human rights for all and the rule of law as the fundamental basis of the fight against terrorism. [435]

Moreover, universal treaties on counter-terrorism expressly require compliance with various aspects of human rights law. For example, the International Convention for the Suppression of the Financing of Terrorism stipulates in Article 15 that:

Nothing in this Convention shall be interpreted as imposing an obligation to extradite or to afford mutual legal assistance, if the requested State Party has substantial grounds for believing that the request for extradition for offences or for mutual legal assistance with respect to such offences has been made for the purpose of prosecuting or punishing a person on account of that person's race, religion, nationality, ethnic origin or political opinion or that compliance with the request would cause prejudice to that person's position for any of these reasons. [436]

While striking a balance between counter-terrorism operations and safeguarding human rights, the international community must thus remember the words of Thomas Paine, who stated: "He that would make his liberty secure must guard even his enemy from oppression for if he violates this duty, he establishes a precedent that will reach to himself." [437]

The human dimension of security which entails the protection of human rights and fundamental freedoms, along with promotion of strong democratic institutions and rule of law, is considered to be an important component in the global count-

---

435 United Nations (2008), Implementing the Global-Counter-terrorism Strategy, URL: http://www.un.org/ga/president/62/issues/cts.shtml

436 United Nations (1999), International Convention for the Suppression of the Financing of Terrorism, Adopted by the General Assembly of the United Nations in resolution 54/109 of 9 December 1999, URL: http://www.un.org/law/cod/finterr.htm.

437 Szurle, Christina (2011). Protecting Human Rights while Countering Terrorism a Decade after 9/11http://projects.essex.ac.uk/ehrr/V8N1/Szurlej.pdf.

er-terrorism measures devised by various states. According to a UN General Assembly Resolution dated September 20, 2006, "The promotion and protection of human rights for all and the rule of law is essential to all components of the Strategy, recognizing that effective counter-terrorism measures and the promotion of human rights are not conflicting goals, but complementary and mutually reinforcing." [438]

Human rights law makes it obligatory upon the states to respect, protect, and fulfil human rights. Respect for human rights means restraining from interfering with their enjoyment. Protection is focused on taking affirmative steps to safeguard that others do not impede the enjoyment of rights. The fulfilment of human rights requires states to implement apposite measures, including legislative, judicial, administrative or educative measures, in order to realise their legal obligations. A state party may be found accountable for meddling by private persons or entities in the enjoyment of human rights if it has failed to exercise due persistence in shielding against such acts.

Under international law, certain instruments have been devised to ensure the protection of human rights. Among them, the most important is the International Covenant on Civil and Political Rights adopted by the General Assembly of the United Nations on December 19, 1966, under which state parties have an obligation to take positive measures to ensure that private persons or entities do no inflict torture or cruel, inhuman, or degrading treatment or punishment on others within their power. Article 2 of the Covenant explicitly states that each state party to the present Covenant undertakes to respect and to ensure to all individuals within its territory and subject to its jurisdiction the rights recognized in the present Covenant, without distinction of any kind. Article 2 further obliges the states to ensure that: first, any person whose rights or freedoms are violated shall have an effective remedy, notwithstanding that the violation has been committed by persons acting in an official capacity; second, that any person claiming such a remedy shall have his right thereto de-

---

438 United Nations (2016), United Nations General Assembly Adopts Global Counter-Terrorism Strategy URL: http://www.un.org/en/terrorism/strategy-counter-terrorism.shtml#poa4.

termined by competent judicial, administrative, or legislative authorities, or by any other competent authority provided for by the legal system of the state, and to develop the state, and to develop the possibilities of judicial remedy; and, third, that the competent authorities shall enforce such remedies when granted. [439]

Governments all over the world can adopt or follow six principles while passing security bills in order to comply with human rights, as established by the International Conference on Terrorism, Human Security and Development: Human Rights Perspective in 2007 in Hong Kong. The first principle emphasizes that governments should never violate non-derogable human rights, i.e., the most important human rights, like "the right to life, the right to be free from torture and other inhumane or degrading treatment or punishment, the right to be free from slavery or servitude and the right to be free from retroactive application of penal laws (i.e. using a law to prosecute a crime that happened before that law was introduced)." [440]

The second principle is that the derogable rights can be breached or contravened only when it is in accordance with the International and National Human Rights Law. International Human Rights Law permits and allows governments to restrict and limit derogable human rights in certain prescribed circumstances. Article 4 of the ICCPR states that certain human rights, like the right to freedom of expression and the right to freedom of association, can be breached and contravened by states "in times of public emergency which threatens the life of the nation." [441]

The third principle is to recognize and respect the existence and the vital role of an independent judiciary that oversees the proper application and practice or exercise of counter-terrorism laws and powers. More specifically, the exercise of the new counter-terrorism powers and their application should be approved by an independent and impartial judiciary, as such laws may trespass upon human rights. [442]

The fourth principle is to arrange or organize regular, indepen-

---

439 United Nations (1966), International Covenant on Civil and Political Rights, URL: https://treaties.un.org/doc/Publication/UNTS/Volume%20999/volume-999-I-14668-English.pdf

440 https://www.humanrights.gov.au/news/speeches/incorporating-human-rights-principles-national-security-measures

441 Ibid.

442 Ibid.

dent, and impartial reviews of the operation and application of counter-terrorism laws. [443]

The fifth principle is to ensure the right of the people to question and challenge the validity of such legal reforms that can affect their fundamental rights. It implies that whenever a person's reputation is at stake or his/her fundamental rights are violated as a consequence of misuse or abuse of the new counter-terrorism laws and powers, the person should be given access to a judicial review and, therefore, an effective remedy. [444]

The sixth and the last principle is that governments should introduce a legitimate Charter of Human Rights. [445] The above-mentioned principles can be put into practice only by introducing this statutory Charter of Human Rights.

The Human Rights Act 1998 (United Kingdom) was reviewed in 2006 and the review committee reported that the introduction of a Charter of Human Rights had a significant effect on policy formation for three reasons:

1. It improves transparency and parliamentary accountability;

2. It removes the inconsistency that lies between human rights and counter-terrorism laws; and

3. Public authorities are more likely to behave in conformity with human rights. [446]

Thus, while on the one hand, people must compromise and sacrifice for their own safety and security, their government, on the other hand, must adopt a humanistic approach to counter-terrorism laws and all legal reforms. Governments should actively aspire to make human rights an integral part of law and policy. Kofi Annan rightly observed:

Compromising human rights... facilitates achievement

---

443 Ibid.

444 Ibid.

445 https://www.humanrights.gov.au/news/speeches/incorporating-human-rights-principles-national-security-measures

446 http://webarchive.nationalarchives.gov.uk/+/http:/www.dca.gov.uk/peoples-rights/human-rights/pdf/full_review.pdf

of the terrorist's objective - by ceding to [them] the moral high ground, and provoking tension, hatred and mistrust of government among precisely those parts of the population where he is most likely to find recruits. Upholding human rights is not merely compatible with successful counter-terrorism strategy. It is an essential element. [447]

Security and peace can never be maintained in a society which allows violation, contravention, and infringement of its citizens' human rights:

Development strategies that have as their key objectives the realization of core economic, social and cultural rights and civil and political rights have the best prospect of leading to tangible improvements in the lives of human beings: people-oriented development and human security... Respect for human rights is the requirement for efficiency and effectiveness in governance. One is all too familiar with societies which, in the past half-century of international cooperation, have squandered vast amounts of resources and aid basically because the government was unrepresentative and, as a direct consequence, inefficient and often corrupt. Put simply, development is illusory without freedom... The principle of non-discrimination, a bedrock principle of international human rights law, enables one to strive for more equitable societies even within the level of resources available. [448]

European Convention for the Protection of Human Rights

According to Article 8, the right to lead a private life without

447 http://www.un.org/apps/news/story.asp?NewsID=13599#.V6EaiLgrLDc

448 The Mutuality of Challenges Facing Human Rights and Human Security: A New Framework of Analysis Emmanuel Ome, Ani Casimir Department of Philosophy, University of Nigeria, Nsukka, Nigeria Email: dromemma@yahoo.com, cepperngo@gmail.com Received 14 January 2015; accepted 3 February 2015; published 5 February 2015

government interference is provided to individuals but with some restrictions. Everyone has the right to respect for his private and family life, his home, and his correspondence. Further:

There shall be no interference by a public authority with the exercise of this right except such as in accordance with the law and is necessary in a democratic society in the interest of national security, public safety, or the economic well-being of the country, for the deterrence of disorder or felony, for the protection of health or morals, or for the protection of the rights and freedoms of others. [449]

It becomes clear that the right to privacy, as in Article 8(1), is only not applicable when authority observes an incongruity and moves forward to protect nationwide security, public safety, the financial system, public health and morals, the rights and freedoms of other people, and to avert anarchy and crime.

U.K. Human Rights Act in 1998

The Human Rights Act is a United Kingdom law passed in 1998 that incorporates the Convention into English law. According to it, the courts should deduce the law in a way that is compatible with Convention right. It gives people the right to court proceedings if they think their Convention rights have been breached. The Human Rights Act orders authorities to act in a way that does not infringe Convention rights. Public establishments and authorities, like police, local councils, and government departments, should be aware of this law while determining whether a person or a body is a threat to public safety.

Major Legal Frameworks to Address Terrorism

Thirteen global conventions have been adopted under the aus-

---

449 http://www.echr.coe.int/Documents/Convention_ENG.pdf

pices of the United Nations, or its agencies, to combat specific aspects of terrorism. These have tended to be in response to a particular event or atrocity. They are:

1. Convention on Offences and Certain Other Acts Committed on Board Aircraft, 1963;

2. Convention for the Suppression of Unlawful Seizure of Aircraft, 1970;

3. Convention for the Suppression of Unlawful Acts against the Safety of Civil Aviation, 1971;

4. Convention on the Prevention and Punishment of Crimes against Internationally Protected Persons, including Diplomatic Agents, 1973;

5. International Convention against the Taking of Hostages, 1979;

6. Convention on the Physical Protection of Nuclear Material, 1980;

7. Protocol on the Suppression of Unlawful Acts of Violence at Airports Serving International Civil Aviation, supplementary to the Convention for the Suppression of Unlawful Acts against the Safety of Civil Aviation, 1988;

8. Convention for the Suppression of Unlawful Acts against the Safety of Maritime Navigation, 1988;

9. Protocol for the Suppression of Unlawful Acts against the Safety of Fixed Platforms Located on the Continental Shelf, 1988;

10. Convention on the Marking of Plastic Explosives for the Purpose of Detection, 1991;

11. International Convention for the Suppression of Terrorist Bombings, 1997;

12. International Convention for the Suppression of the Financing of Terrorism, 1999;

13. Convention on the Suppression of Acts of Nuclear Terrorism, 2005 [450]

---

450 United Nations (2016), International Legal Instruments, URL: http://www.un.org/en/terrorism/instruments.shtml.

The following are the key resolutions that form the basis of the United Nation's current approach of devising a counter-terror strategy. Among them, Resolution 1373 is of utmost importance. The main points of Resolution 1373 are:

1. States should prevent and suppress the financing of terrorism, as well as criminalize the wilful provision or collection of funds for such acts.

2. States should prohibit nationals or persons or entities in their territories from making funds, financial assets, economic resources, financial, or other related services available to persons who commit or attempt to commit, facilitate, or participate in the commission of terrorist acts.

3. States should prevent those who finance, plan, facilitate, or commit terrorist acts from using their respective territories for those purposes against other countries and their citizens. States should also ensure that anyone who has participated in the financing, planning, preparation, or perpetration of terrorist acts or in supporting terrorist acts is brought to justice. They should also ensure that terrorist acts are established as serious criminal offences in domestic laws and regulations and that the seriousness of such acts is duly reflected in sentences served.

4. States should take appropriate measures to ensure that the asylum seekers had not planned, facilitated or participated in terrorist acts. Further, States should ensure that refugee status was not abused by the perpetrators, organizers, or facilitators of terrorist acts, and that claims of political motivation were not recognized as grounds for refusing requests for the extradition of alleged terrorists. [451]

Apart from this, United Nations Security Council Resolution 1456 (2003), obliges states to ensure that any measures taken to combat terrorism comply with all their obligations under inter-

---

451 United Nations (2001), Security Council Unanimously Adopts Wide-Ranging Anti-Terrorism Resolution; Calls For Suppressing Financing, Improving International Cooperation, September 21, URL: http://www.un.org/press/en/2001/sc7158.doc.htm

national law. [452] Security Council Resolution 1624 (2005) calls on states "to prohibit by law incitement to commit a terrorist act or acts" as well as prevention of such acts and the denial of safe haven to perpetrators. It also calls upon states to "continue international efforts to enhance dialogue and broaden understanding between civilizations in an effort to prevent the indiscriminate targeting of different religions and cultures." [453] General Assembly Resolution 58/187 (2004) mentions that "States must ensure that any measure taken to combat terrorism complies with their obligations under international law." [454] In particular, international human rights, refugee, and humanitarian law raise awareness about the importance of these obligations among national authorities involved in combating terrorism. [455]

Measures taken by the UN Security Council

The United Nations Security Council, one of the principal branches of the UN, is tasked with the maintenance of international peace and security. It has the power to establish peace-keeping operations and international sanctions, authorize military action through Security Council resolutions. The Security Council is the only United Nations body authorized to issue binding resolution to member states.

Since the 1990s, the United Nations Security Council has consistently dealt with issues of terrorism by imposing sanctions on extremist actions across the world. It has urged nations to act in a cooperative way by adopting an integrated strategy, involving the agencies of each nation at all levels of functioning to counter the

---

452 UN Security Council, Security Council Resolution 1456 (2003) on combating terrorism, 20 January 2003, S/RES/1456 (2003), available at: http://www.refworld.org/docid/3f45dbdb0. html [accessed 13 April 2016]

453 UN Security Council, Security Council resolution 1624 (2005) [on threats to international peace and security], 14 September 2005, S/RES/1624 (2005), available at: http://www. refworld.org/docid/468372832.html [accessed 13 April 2016]

454 https://www.state.gov/t/isn/trty/81727.htm

455 United Nations (2004), Resolution adopted by the General Assembly on 22 December 2004 58/187. Protection of human rights and fundamental freedoms while countering terrorism, March 22, URL: https://issafrica.org/ctafrica/uploads/UNGA%20Res%2058:187.%20 Protection%20of%20human%20rights%20and%20fundamental%20freedoms%20while%20 countering%20terrorism%20.pdf

threat which terrorism poses. As a cardinal organ of the United Nations, the Security Council has taken it upon itself to act as a leader in the fight against terrorism.

The surge in terrorist activity over the past decade has been a cause of deep concern for the Security Council, which has been consistently engaged in working towards a terror-resistant global community. It is under the aegis of the United Nations Charter that the Council emphasises the necessity of, and supports, any efforts which foster as well as promulgate universal participation of nations in the measures for counter-terrorism. [456]

Chapter VII of the United Nations Charter deals with the matter of peace, and threats and breaches to peace. It also sets forth guidelines for the Security Council to undertake actions for the restoration of peace. [457] The Charter provides the Security Council with the authority to determine/acknowledge a threat to peace, suggest measures for restoration of peace (Article 39) and, if need be, call upon the concerned nations to conform to its recommendations (Article 40).

It remains the duty of the Security Council to decide upon the most appropriate measures to be taken without the use of armed forces to subvert terrorism-promoting activities and re-store/maintain international security and peace. Article 43 of the Charter mandates that member states provide, as and when possible, cooperation and assistance to the Council in its efforts of maintaining peace and to engage in mutual assistance with other nations to support the efforts of the Security Council.

The Charter also instructs the Security Council to absolutely refrain from infringement of human rights through any channel, in the occurrence of an armed attack involving terrorists. Thus, the Council possesses authority to undertake any requisite mea-sure, in line with respecting human rights and fundamental free-doms of individuals and groups, for countering terrorism.

Through revising its existing resolutions and forming new ones, the Council perpetually strives to adapt to modern ways

---

456 http://daccess-dds-ny.un.org/doc/UNDOC/GEN/N99/303/92/PDF/N9930392.pd-f?OpenElement - Resolution 1269 of the Security Council

457 http://www.un.org/en/sections/un-charter/chapter-vii/index.html - Chapter VII of UN Charter: Action with respect to Threats to the Peace, breaches of the Peace, and Acts of aggression

and techniques of countering the terror menace, and supports national efforts on the part of several nations in this regard. Identifying terrorism as a threat to international security and peace, the Security Council condemns any behaviour undertaken in this direction.

Paying no heed to the motivation behind terrorist acts, the Security Council defines all such activities as unjustifiable and extreme, and pushes member states to implement the anti-terrorist conventions. Considering the pervasive nature of terrorism today, the Council presses the need for adopting and adhering to multilateral agreements and treaties between nations as an extensive measure to contain terrorism.

Through various resolutions and conventions, the Council aims not only at the suppression of extremist activities but also the prevention of radical pursuits which have the potential to assume extremist dispositions. The Security Council ensures that no measure undertaken by it violates the provisions of the laws of respective nations or of the international covenants, and is in conformity with the fundamental freedoms and basic human rights enjoyed by everyone.

Article 41 of the United Nations Charter, under Chapter VII, provides for the Security Council to take any measure or sanction for the maintenance or restoration of international peace and security, and incorporates several options for the enforcement of these measures. [458] The aforementioned measures in Article 41 do not involve aid from the armed forces, but rather call for interruption, partial or complete, of sea, air, rail, postal or any other form of communication, of economic ties or diplomatic relations.

In pursuit of its objective to contain terrorism, the Security Council imposes various sanctions on belligerent nations and organizations ranging from broad economic sanctions to specific sanctions aimed at deterring commodity flow, restriction on travels, etc.[459] The sanctions are also put to use to espouse peace-

458 http://sc.iborn.net/en/sanctions - More about sanctions by the Security Council

459 http://www.securitycouncilreport.org/atf/cf/%7B65BFCF9B-6D27-4E9C-8CD3-CF6E4FF96FF9%7D/special_research_report_sanctions_2013.pdf - More about the objectives of UN Sanctions, their types and implementation

ful negotiations between nations, deter proliferation of ammunitions, and safeguard the fundamental rights of individuals.

The sanctions endorsed by the Security Council to curb terrorism and maintain international peace are not meant to be operated in isolation, but rather are effective when supplemented with comprehensive international policies for peace and cooperation. These sanctions are meant to augment non-proliferation of arms, conflict-resolution, and measures for counter-terrorism in a balanced and non-violent manner.

Apart from imposing sanctions, the Council also formed a Counter-Terrorism Committee after the 9/11 attacks in the United States of America. [460] The Committee has been constituted to undertake measures for the prevention of activities remotely connected with terrorism. It is also meant to foster cooperation among nations as well as advance their obedience to instruments meant to counter terrorism. This committee mandates regular submission of reports by each nation to present accounts of measures taken by them in this regard. It aids the nations in their expedition against terrorism by criminalizing the sponsoring of terrorist acts and restricting the flow of funds meant for any such activities. It also promotes information sharing among nations to aid in investigation and detection of terrorism.

The Security Council does not condone any act of terrorism, whatever the motivation, and invites all member states to adopt commitments on similar lines. Through various resolutions, the Council reminds governments of their unambiguous obligation towards countering terrorism and calls for firm actions in denying a safe haven to those involved in or supporting terrorism.

The Security Council undertakes its functions in consonance with the objectives of the United Nations Charter. [461] Taking a cue from the preamble of the Charter, the Council ensures that nations abide by their obligation to maintain security and peace, and encourages them to undertake unwavering endeavours in this direction. The Council also takes it upon itself to take decisive action in such case that a nation is rendered incapable of

460 http://www.un.org/en/terrorism/securitycouncil.shtml - Security Council actions to counter terrorism

461 http://www.un.org/en/charter-united-nations/ - Charter of the United Nations

protecting its citizens from terrorism.

Focusing on the fundamental principles of justice, peace, respect for human rights, and freedom of each individual, the Security Council aims at the establishment of measures for peace and counter-terrorism which are in the spirit of the United Nations Charter. The Council ensures that no effort taken by it violates the basic territorial integrity and sovereignty of a nation, thus undertaking effective counter-terrorism measures while sustaining the non-interference policy.

It remains at the core of policies of the Security Council to pursue such actions which eschew the use of violent means, force, or threat, to fulfil its objective of world peace. Additionally, the Council also ensures international cooperation through a system of multilateral agreements and summits to confront the challenges posed by terrorism.

The Security Council organized a World Summit in 2005 to solicit support from nations across the world in its fight against terrorism.[462] Reaffirming the significance of human rights in ensuring security and world peace, the summit witnessed member states acknowledging the necessity of human rights and multifaceted cooperation as well as committing to the furtherance of the Security Council's objectives.

The transnational threat presented by terrorism requires continuous enhancement of governments' policies so as to keep pace with the newer developments of terrorist groups. The Security Council has emerged as a frontrunner in this direction, introducing newer effective sanctions and implementing resolutions to strengthen its expedition against terrorism and helping member states to do the same.

Through such summits, the Security Council ensures that a nation's objectives for counter terrorism are translated into tangible security efforts. The mutual cooperation among nations and the Security Council's resolve at world security and peace guide the culmination of counter-terrorism efforts into concrete actions.

The determination of the Security Council to tackle and contain terrorism and uphold human rights, peace, and security re-

---

462 http://www.ifrc.org/docs/idrl/I520EN.pdf - 2005 World Summit Outcome

mains an indispensable aspect of its framework and influences the undertaking of each resolution and the imposition of every sanction by the United Nations body. Apart from this, the Council also acknowledges the importance of economic sanctions on dubious organizations as an effective means of curtailing terror funding activities across the world.

For the advancement of global development and security, the Security Council not only ensures cooperative dialogues among nations, but also engages various organs and bodies of the United Nations in a comprehensive policy of countering terrorism. The shared responsibility warrants a credible and efficient course against terrorism with the equal accountability of each nation.

The ultimate objective of the Security Council remains the protection of human rights and establishment of a just, peaceful, and secure world. Regarding terrorism as the gravest threat to international stability and peace, the Council censures any form or manifestation of terrorism and undertakes measures for resolving any issue which may impede its efforts to restrain terrorism.

In line with this concern, the Security Council has formed a Peace-building Commission, which is an advisory body encouraging and promulgating the efforts by various countries for establishing peace. [463] As an intergovernmental body, the commission forms an integral component of the international community's agenda for peace.

The commission is also instrumental in the integration of all institutions and organizations, the marshalling of resources, and the propagation of strategies for peace-building. Encouraging efforts for the maintenance of peace, the commission highlights the importance of peace for a just and stable international community, and aims to fill any gaps in peace through integrated efforts.

The measures adopted by the Security Council to deal with terrorism involve consistent and coordinated efforts for a comprehensive implementation in all member states. The Council believes that its counter-terrorism strategy can attain success only when the measures are implemented at international, national,

---

463 http://www.un.org/en/peacebuilding/ - The Peacebuilding Commission of the Security Council

and regional levels and address the circumstances and reasons which coerce an individual or group to pursue extremist actions. Acknowledging the need of conformity to international law and to human rights, and of cooperation among nations in the struggle against terrorism, the Security Council ensures that any action taken to restrain terrorist activities refrains from such violations which contradict its obligations to conform to provisions for a just and peaceful society. In keeping with these commitments, the Council also requires that member states follow suit.

Underscoring the need of multilateral cooperation, the Council urges nations to pursue coordinated efforts to ensure that their territories are not used for training new terrorist militants. It also pushes the nations to prevent the funding and organizing of terrorist events in any form.

In the process of its function to combat terrorism, the Security Council not only provides assistance to states to deal with the threat of terrorism, but also strives to assist victims of militant incursions by providing them support, and ensuring the provision of restitution to them, whenever possible. It also aims to enhance its surveillance and monitoring systems to solidify counter-terrorism measures.

To intercept the challenges posed by terrorism, the Security Council makes sure that an unwavering modus operandi is adopted for the implementation of its resolutions and sanctions. Reminding nations of their legal responsibilities to espouse measures for counter-terrorism well within the confines of human rights and international law remains of paramount concern to the Council.

Understanding that military might alone will not suffice to contain or prevent terrorism, the Security Council underscores the need to address factors conducive to the promulgation of terrorism among vulnerable populations. It is only through sustained efforts ranging from stringent actions and military strength to intelligence and cooperative dialogues that the advances of terrorists can be countered in an effective manner.

With an ever-increasing number of forces propelling populations towards extremism, the Security Council maintains the stance that any terrorist act stands unjustifiable without exception of any kind to the motivation or the situation. Regardless of the nationality or religion of the terrorists, the Council ensures that stringent action is taken against any person disrupting world peace or planning to undertake an action with such intentions.

Conclusion

Since the terrorist attacks in the United States on September 11, 2001, and with the rise of big data and integration of technology into society, matters of privacy have been surrendered to more pressing issues of security. While some have argued that privacy has taken a back seat to security concerns and that individual liberties can, at times, be sacrificed in order to apprehend possible terrorist attackers, there must be a balance. Proper checks and balances must be at work and legislation must have proper independent oversights in order to ensure that fundamental human rights of citizens are not abused. In less democratic countries, surveillance is indeed abusive and used for nefarious purposes

Throughout history, rulers have always monitored the activities of its people to maintain power and control, and also spied on their enemies to gain advantage in times of war. Today, with the rise of super computers and big data, electronic monitoring has taken on a new dimension. Long before 9/11, democratic and non-democratic governments were monitoring their citizens; after 9/11, with the introduction of new surveillance legislation in the United States of America, Canada, and Europe, monitoring of citizens became more expansive than ever before imagined possible.

The revelations of Edward Snowden were alarming to most civilians, with most reaching the conclusion that privacy is dead and we have entered the age of "Big Brother."

According to Derek Bambauer:

Security and privacy can, and should, be treated as distinct concerns. Privacy discourse involves difficult normative decisions about competing claims to legitimate access to, use of, and alteration of information. It is about selecting among different philosophies and choosing how various rights and entitlements ought to be ordered. Security implements those choices—it mediates between information and privacy selections. Important-ly, this approach argues that security failings should be penalized more readily, and more heavily, than privacy ones, because there are no competing moral claims to resolve and because security flaws make all parties worse off. [464]

Although reaching an acceptable balance between privacy and security has proven difficult, there is hope. If the developed countries of the world can unite and integrate their efforts in order to support both efficiency and accountability in the international community, it may be possible to create a peaceful, terror-free society, without unduly violating the rights of the citizens they seek to protect.

464 THE JOURNAL OF CRIMINAL LAW & CRIMINOLOGY Vol. 103, No. 3 Copyright © 2013 by Derek E. Bambauer Printed in U.S.A. 667 PRIVACY VERSUS SECURITY DEREK E. BAMBAUER pg 683

INDEX

D

E